Financing Roma Inclusion with European Structural Funds

This book provides an analysis of the highly politicized field of Roma inclusion and addresses the controversies surrounding the effectiveness of the funding initiatives derived from European Cohesion Policy. It confronts the widely held notion that European financial transfers (Structural Funds) are highly suitable instruments for addressing the systemic causes of poverty and for facilitating changes towards substantive equality for Europe's largest ethnic minority. Shedding critical light on the Structural Funds programme, it offers an innovative approach to thinking about the value of European funding schemes and the efficacy of national Roma inclusion strategies. Multidisciplinary in approach, it draws on rich interview material and literature from fields including policy implementation, new public governance, equality studies, and political representation. *Financing Roma Inclusion with European Structural Funds* examines the implementation of European funding in Spain and Slovakia, two countries with contrasting policy outputs, and offers a nuanced picture of the way European Cohesion Policy interacts with the intricacies of domestic policymaking. It thus sheds light on the key challenges facing Roma inclusion strategies in contemporary Europe and will be of interest to scholars interested in European studies, equality policy, new public governance, and minority studies.

Joanna Kostka is a Lecturer in Social Work at Lancaster University, UK.

Financing Roma Inclusion with European Structural Funds

Why Good Intentions Fail

Joanna Kostka

LONDON AND NEW YORK

First published 2019
by Routledge
2 Park Square, Milton Park, Abingdon, Oxon OX14 4RN

and by Routledge
52 Vanderbilt Avenue, New York, NY 10017

Routledge is an imprint of the Taylor & Francis Group, an informa business

British Library Cataloguing-in-Publication Data
A catalogue record for this book is available from the British Library

Library of Congress Cataloging-in-Publication Data
A catalog record has been requested for this book

ISBN: 978-1-138-74026-6 (hbk)
ISBN: 978-1-315-18364-0 (ebk)

Typeset in Times New Roman
by Deanta Global Publishing Services, Chennai, India

Contents

1 Introduction

In the last decade, the European Union (EU) has placed Roma inclusion on its political agenda, demonstrating its willingness to take a leadership role in addressing the marginalization of the largest European ethnic minority.[1] Interest in the Roma people as a 'policy problem' has accelerated dramatically since 2004 when the Central and Eastern European (CEE) countries, which house the majority of the Roma population, joined the EU.[2] The mass impoverishment and disenfranchisement of Roma people in the post-communist countries not only had dramatic implications for economic development in the region but also bluntly clashed with the wider EU values of equal opportunities and non-discrimination.[3] A growing concern with the deteriorating socio-economic standing of the Roma communities, combined with a growing fear of the accelerated East–West migration, heartened the calls for innovative policy responses and greater reliance on EU interventions. While some advocates put faith in EU conditionality, others demanded modification of the anti-discrimination frameworks and pressed for a pan-European Roma integration strategy. A common denominator in these discussions, however, was the assertion that fostering integration requires governments to set down their commitments in respect of Roma or disadvantaged people in general and to monitor and report on their progress. This meant that the EU's role should be one of supporting national governments to deliver on their commitments, but without the EU itself being responsible for the activities of initiated states (Kovats, 2012; Andor, 2018). The EU's 'added value' was thus to be anchored in the public commitments of governments, EU funding for projects and programmes, and linkage with the EU policy process (notably the EU's Europe 2020 growth strategy).

In line with this reasoning, the EU called upon all member states to create an institutional framework that would complement and reinforce the EU's equality legislation. The European Commission (EC) pressed member states to ensure that national, regional, and local integration policies focused on the Roma in a clear and specific way, and addressed the needs of Roma people with explicit measures to prevent and compensate for the disadvantages they face. To safeguard such developments, the EC has advised the member states to make full use of the EU's instruments, in particular, the system of financial transfers known as Structural Funds (SF). In 2010, the Progress Report on Economic and Social

Cohesion for the first time made an explicit reference to the Roma – 'deemed especially susceptible to social exclusion' (EC, 2010b), and denoted the SF as a key instrument for addressing Roma exclusion.[4] In effect, 'Roma ethnicity' has become an organizing principle for EU cohesion policy, with funds being targeted at Roma specific initiatives (through 'explicit but not exclusive' targeting[5]). Consequently, during the 2007–2013 SF programming period, the EU allocated close to €26.5 billion to Roma inclusion initiatives, an amount exceeding any previous financial support.[6]

In times of rapidly shrinking welfare provisions and the unravelling economic crisis, the multimillion-Euro investments in programmes and projects targeted at the Roma people have appeared to warrant a sliver of optimism for marginalized and impoverished minorities. However, today the actual impact of European funding schemes is difficult to account for. In fact, the question that haunts decision-makers, both in Brussels and in other EU capitals, is stark – what has the money invested in Roma inclusion achieved?

Paradoxically, the increase in expenditure and consolidation of the targeted approach has corresponded with the deteriorating socio-economic standing of the majority of Roma communities[7] and an escalation of violent anti-Gypsyism across Europe (McGarry, 2017). Indeed, the situation of Roma communities appears more precarious today than it has ever been with the ongoing economic crisis and the rise of the far right contributing to this predicament. The absorption of SF proved extremely low (particularly in countries and regions with a larger Roma population) while many of the implemented SF projects had problems demonstrating any real achievements. In 2010, the report prepared by the European Commission Roma Task Force, Roma Integration: First Findings of the Roma Task Force and Report on Social Inclusion,[8] asserted that strong and proportionate measures were not in place and SF were largely mismanaged at the national and sub-national level. The meritocracy-based and competitive funding mechanisms (similar to domestic grant schemes) were criticized for disadvantaging the most isolated and impoverished Roma communities. At the same time concerns were raised about funds being notoriously redirected towards other priorities (Hurrle et al., 2012). In 2010, the European Parliament (EP) called the use of SF a 'policy failure' in need of critical examination and immediate action by the national and regional polities (EP, 2010), a statement quickly backed by László Andor, the EU Commissioner for Social Affairs, Employment and Inclusion.

Three years after the 2007–2013 funding period came to an end, we still do not have much data which could fully explain this consistent policy failure. The long-awaited audit of the use of EU funding for Roma projects in 2007–2013 led by the European Court of Auditors (ECA, 2016a) generated surprisingly generic and disheartening conclusions. Henri Grethen, the Member of the European Court of Auditors responsible for the final report, admitted that a pervasive lack of data made the attempts to systematically evaluate the effectiveness of SF deficient:

> As things stand, we don't really know how well Roma are being integrated because we don't have robust data; we don't even know how many Roma

there are. Unless the data problem is resolved, policymaking will soon be hampered all the way to 2020.

(ECA, 2016b)

An increasing number of situational reports, toolkits, and ad-hoc SF evaluation schemes continue to recycle 'common truths' based on assumptions rather than far-reaching empirical research. The feeling of frustration seems omnipresent, fuelled by the sentiment among activists that all initiatives are failing and EU commitments to Roma inclusion are merely a decorative frame without substance or force (Nicolae, 2012). Such gloomy perceptions effectively mask instances where the utilization of SF has proven more effective, as well as scenarios where it generated and sustained suboptimal practices. Not surprisingly, those who want to understand the real 'added value' of European funding seem to be groping around in the dark for clues. The question of why generous funding schemes continue to fail remains unanswered.

This book fills this astounding knowledge gap and brings the use of SF out of the realm of presumptions and interest-driven anecdotes. In doing so, it revitalizes and reworks theories on policy implementation, creating a tenacious theoretical framework for analyzing the performance of EU funding in a specific policy domain. Empirically grounded, the book not only challenges standard arguments embedded in implementation research but also confronts the widely held notion that European financial transfers are highly suitable instruments for addressing the systemic causes of poverty and facilitating changes towards a substantive equality for European Roma communities. While this book focuses on a specific ethnic group, the analytical framework captures dynamics that are not unique to Roma policies but relate to how categories of deservingness are built and sustained within the European anti-poverty and anti-discrimination agenda.

Constructing Spanish success and Slovak failure

Over the last decade, European stakeholders have generated countless strategic documents, compendiums of 'good practices' and reports pointing out inconsistencies in funding management and implementation (Harvey, 2008; Ringold et al., 2005; EC, 2004, 2008, 2011, 2012; EP, 2011; EURoma, 2010, 2011; Brenner, 2012; Kóczé et al., 2014; Kullmann, 2015). The descriptive and technocratic nature of these reports has since been widely criticized by academics invested in Romani studies, who argue that the accumulated knowledge tends to complement or reinforce the dominant political discourses on the 'Roma problem', offering limited critical input (Surdu, 2016; Timmer, 2010). While the politicization of Roma issues has sharpened the criticism of strictly policy-driven research, and the calls for a conceptually rich analysis of established assumptions do echo across the academic community, knowledge of the socio-economic and cultural situation of the Roma is predominately presented through a policy-driven perspective. Similarly, in the area of cohesion policy, Roma issues are discussed inside snug expert circles, led by EC representatives, SF managers, and members of thematic networks (with headquarters in Brussels). Although, the scattered efforts at post-ante evaluations and monitoring have been able to demonstrate the heterogeneous performance of SF programming at the national level (i.e. through comparing the aggregated absorption rates, and the co-financing of various Operational Programmes), the picture of the actual exploitation of the funding in different policy areas and targeting of funds at delineated groups remains elusive. Even less is known about the way implemented projects have contributed to the overall strategic objectives, and how many quality projects reached Roma communities and individuals. Despite methodological catches, the policy discourse on Roma inclusion and SF continued to thrive during the 2007–2013 funding period. Amidst various high-level discussions, Spain emerged as a model to emulate while Slovakia established itself as an emblem for things going awry.

The EU has presented Spanish implementation of SF as a 'best practice' example and a model for other countries to follow (Tarnovschi, 2012). During the 2nd European Summit on Roma Inclusion held in Córdoba, Spain, in 2010, Viviane Reding, the EU Commission Vice President and Justice Commissioner, stated that: 'the Spanish model shows how to use EU funding most effectively and how to use it to promote social cohesion and combat poverty in the Roma communities'.[9] In the concluding session of the 2011 High-Level Event on the Structural Funds Contribution to Roma Integration in Bratislava, Nicholas Martyn, a Deputy Director General of the Directorate General for Regional Policy, once again highlighted Spain's achievements, affirming that: 'Spain has already developed good solutions, and the examples are worth following'.[10] Similar views were expressed by the representatives of the Decade of Roma Inclusion Secretariat Foundation, Open Society Foundation (OSF), and other major Roma stakeholders including the UNDP and FRA during the 2011 Conference, Improving Access to Housing for Roma: Good Local Practices, Funding and Legislation, held in Prague.[11] The fervent belief that there is finally a place where the funding is working has silenced the flow of valid concerns and criticisms raised by numerous Spanish scholars and activists.[12]

At the same time, testimonies coming out of Slovakia, disseminated by international stakeholders (e.g. the OSF, Roma Education Fund), pointed out the severe underuse of available funding and rampant mismanagement at the national and local level. The criticism of the 'Slovak approach' echoed across Europe, with Viviane Reding calling Slovak SF allocation to Roma inclusion a 'strictly tokenistic endeavour', and Rudolf Niessler, a Director of the Directorate General for Regional Policy, expressing his disappointment with the persistent reluctance to put political will behind Roma integration programmes. During the High-Level Event held in Bratislava in 2011, Nicholas Martyn, a Deputy Director General of the Directorate General for Regional Policy, stated that: 'Slovak authorities are unable to establish links between inputs and outcomes and even outputs', and stressed that: 'new approaches are indispensable if SF are to make any concrete impact'.[13] Criticisms were also intensifying at the local level, as non-governmental organizations (NGOs) and Roma representatives complained about the rampant practice of redirecting funding away from those who need it the most. Activists insisted that while EU-funded projects looked 'good on paper', the money has had little real effect in addressing the Roma circumstances (Grambličková, 2010).

The reasons for such divergence in performance have never been comprehensively analyzed, thus many of the explanations provided are backed up purely by anecdotal accounts, or grand assumptions about inadequate governance practices of the new member states. As Roma activists talk about the 'lack of political will' to channel money towards the most disadvantaged communities, policy experts point fingers at the limited administrative capacities and resources to exploit the complex funding schemes. Some voices continue to insist that the money made available is simply not enough for addressing the multidimensionality of Roma exclusion (Guy, 2011). Interestingly, there has been very limited critical discussion on the alleged success of Spain, with commentators pointing to abstract notions of a stronger civil society and less racial cleavages inside Spanish society (Daley and Minder, 2010; Cala, 2010; Smith, 2011). Overall, we know little about the factors driving SF performance, and even less about the contribution of the SF to the integration of Roma.

The conflicting and highly superficial accounts of Roma inclusion strategies within one of the most potent distributive policies developed by the EU inspired the research presented in this book. While *Financing Roma Inclusion with European Structural Funds* is primarily concerned with explaining the causes of the diverging performance in two member states, Spain and Slovakia, by doing so it also seeks to understand the wider power dynamics and legitimacy claims embedded in cohesion policy. Thus, the book develops a methodology that brings together structures and agency in an effort to unveil 'who-gets-what' out of inclusion policies, how integration is carried out and by whom, and most importantly who is deemed 'worthy of' or 'in need of' viable financial support.

Measuring success and failure

Before any analysis can begin, it is important to first operationalize the term 'success' and 'failure'. In fact, when analyzing political statements against the actual data, the picture of Spanish success and Slovak failure is not necessarily clear. The existing quantitative data on the implementation outputs of SF in different countries is often measured against an indigenous and highly diverse set of indicators. Comparing the amounts of money devoted to social inclusion across various Operational Programmes (OPs) is hardly possible given the structure of the priorities and types of measures are different. Similar measurement problems arise when comparing OPs from one programming period to the next. It is not unusual to come across enormous inconsistencies in data. For example, data collected in Slovakia via ITMS[14] shows that more than €132 million was allocated (contracted out) towards the horizontal priority, Marginalized Roma Communities (MRC). At the same time, data collected by the Centre for Strategy and Evaluation Services (2011a) points towards €183 million. In Spain, the amount of European Social Fund (ESF) funds assigned to the National OP Fight Against Discrimination (OP FAD) remains unclear even today, depending on whether one consults the national database or regional annals. Controlling for time and co-financing rates, the allocation is recorded either as €545 million or €381 million. Hence, it is fair to say that the continued absence of standardized monitoring mechanisms (at the EU level in particular) for the cross-country or even cross-priority comparison will generate different results.

Given the methodological difficulties, assessing any form of success or failure should be conducted with caution. More importantly, the very concept of success needs to be well operationalized if any conclusions can be made at all.

For the purpose of this book, two sets of indicators are inferred from the European Indicative Guidelines on Evaluation Methods: Monitoring and Evaluation Indicators (2006), against which success and failure of SF can be assessed in a more structured manner.

The first set of indicators pertains to inputs (the resources member states channel towards social inclusion goals). These are:

- Allocation of SF to social inclusion measures (budget for social inclusion measures);
- Absorption rate by final beneficiaries (selected projects, reimbursements, final Roma beneficiaries);
- Management of SF programming (streamlining, timely implementation).

The second set of indicators pertains to outputs (what is achieved with these resources):

- Sustainability of the SF initiatives (e.g. operation beyond the SF funding time-frame and scaling up);
- Legitimacy of introduced priorities/measures (e.g. addressing the identified needs, meeting expectations of the beneficiaries).

While the weight of these indicators appears to be relatively similar, the inputs are deemed most significant, given that earmarking and the exploitation of funds provide the clearest picture regarding commitments, priorities, and management. Nevertheless, the contention is that successful outputs are those that reflect all indicators.

In terms of allocation, the difference between these two countries is not as profound as politicians would like us to believe. Nevertheless, it does appear that Spain has been allocating more towards the social inclusion of ethnic minorities than Slovakia, and in fact all other relevant member states. Statistical data collected from 15 member states in 2011 (CSES, 2011a) indicated that Spain allocated the highest amount of ESF funds towards social inclusion and minority measures in the 2007–2013 funding period, reaching close to €1.2 billion.[15] This constitutes just over 10% of the entire ESF budget (over €11.5 billion). In turn, Slovakia was ranked last in the sample, with an ESF allocation of only €500,000, less than 1% of the total ESF funding (€1.7 billion). This difference is unexpected particularly because the Spanish Roma account for only 1.8% of the total population, while in Slovakia they account for 10%. However, the CSES study did not take into consideration that Slovakia aggregated social inclusion funding from both the European Regional Development Fund (ERDF) and the ESF. When this is accounted for the allocation stands at €200 million. Moreover, the CSES focused only on OP Employment and Social Inclusion (OP E&SI) and ignored OP Education (about 30% of all Slovak ESF funds are marked for this OP, and two education priorities are targeted at Roma communities). Nonetheless, even when these factors are taken into consideration, Slovakia still allocated less funding than Spain (taking into consideration the size of the ESF and population), falling behind all other countries in the sample. The study commissioned by the EP (2011), Measures to Promote the Situation of Roma EU Citizens in the EU, confirms this trend (even though the data is even less precise). The evaluation of 12 member states showed that Spain allocated more ESF budget per capita, directly targeting the social inclusion of Roma citizens than any other member state.[16] Slovakia appeared at the other end of the continuum allocating the least amount in the evaluated sample.

A look at the absorption rates of funds earmarked for the social inclusion of ethnic minorities (and other vulnerable groups) provides a clearer picture. Here Spain once again emerged ahead of Slovakia, although it has been surpassed by Ireland, Portugal, and Sweden. According to the EC's (2013) Strategic Report on Implementation, in Spain, the selection of social exclusion projects reached just over 70% while the percentage of paid expenditures stood at around 52% (above the EU average). Although in Slovakia the selection of projects was also quite high, standing at 65%, the paid expenditures reached only 20% (the only two countries with a lower score were Bulgaria and Romania). Moreover, Slovakia has experienced excessive delays in launching proposals under ESF priorities (the social inclusion proposals were announced in 2010 and set in motion only at the end of 2012). In reaction to errors made when drawing EU funds and running the OP for which those funds were intended, the EC suspended Slovakia's ability to draw these funds for various OPs (payments have been completely suspended for the Regional OP and OP Education, and partially for three other programmes) (EPRC, 2015). The low rate of contracting and withdrawal in the initial years for all ESF OPs was marked as an urgent issue resulting in residual absorption of funding (KPMG, 2016). Finally, through the modification of the ERDF regulation in 2010, an aggregate amount of €80 million was allocated by eight member states (Bulgaria, Czech Republic, France, Greece, Hungary, Italy, Romania, and Slovakia) to integrated housing programmes targeted at marginalized groups residing in substandard conditions and segregated areas (the majority of which were recognized as Roma communities). Seven years later, the Slovak government is unable to provide any proof that the allocated funds have been channelled towards any type of housing initiatives in Roma settlements or communities with a large proportion of Roma population.

Comparing data on the final beneficiaries of SF projects constitutes perhaps the most difficult task given the lack of data disaggregated by ethnicity. Valid and reliable ethnic data is a fundamental building block for identifying the differences in treatment and for developing targeted interventions for improving the quality of the public services delivered to specific population groups. However, the collection of such data is problematic. Its usefulness is often limited in terms of representativeness and comparability as a result of methodological choices and because research is often only conducted once. Whereas self-identification often leads to the under-representation of Roma in data collection efforts, external identification on the basis of visual observation risks over-representing individuals who correspond to the observer's stereotypical view of who a Roma person is (Van Caeneghem, 2017). Moreover, the heterogeneity of Roma communities and the subjective, multifaceted, and fluid nature of ethnic identification necessitates a consideration of the different characteristics and problems, an aspect difficult to control in standardized evaluation projects. These methodological catches are further aggravated by the ambiguous feelings many Roma have towards ethnic data collection.[17] In the 2007–2013 funding period, data collection on participation according to whether participants have an ethnic minority background has improved as a result of the new reporting requirements introduced by the Commission (Annex XXIII of the Implementing Regulations). Nevertheless, numerous problems remain, and existing estimates should once again be viewed with caution.

Nevertheless, once again Spain has demonstrated a much higher number of Roma beneficiaries than Slovakia. By the end of 2013, the Spanish initiatives benefited approximately 57,000 individuals with Romani backgrounds (FSG, 2016). In Slovakia, the number has been estimated at 8,000 (CSES, 2011b).[18] Taking into account the population in both countries, the number of beneficiaries is extremely low, if not insignificant. However, it must be highlighted that Spain under its OP FAD committed 95% of funding towards measures directly targeted at the discrimination of minority groups (with Roma communities being prioritized). Close to 75% of this funding was directed at institutional changes, including awareness campaigns, thematic networks, and institutional assistance, which plausibly benefited the Roma indirectly. Similarly, the regional ESF OPs have outlined measures within the general approaches for targeting the most vulnerable people at risk of exclusion. OP ESF Andalusia channelled €489 million directly at measures promoting the social inclusion of the most disenfranchised group (under Priority 2). The Andalusian region (which has the highest concentration of Roma communities in Spain) introduced the Integrated Territorial Plans for Employment in the most excluded localities, where the Roma population was often concentrated. Thus it could be expected that the number of Roma beneficiaries was much higher.[19] In Slovakia, the picture appears much grimmer. According to a UNDP study, Uncertain Impact: Have the Roma in Slovakia Benefited from ESF? (Hurrle et al., 2012), people and communities at risk of social exclusion were not included in the mainstream measures. Only one fifth of the implemented projects were located in the most segregated and underdeveloped localities. Despite efforts made by the Slovak Government Plenipotentiary for Roma Communities to collect data on final Roma beneficiaries, in 2017 such data is still missing.

Spain also performed better in regard to the sustainability of SF projects. Evaluation of the OP FAD (2013) showed that close to 80% of the projects continued beyond the stipulated funding period. The national social inclusion project, Acceder, entered the 3rd SF funding period, while regional Integrated Territorial Plans for Employment continued beyond 2013. Even in the midst of the economic crisis, projects operating under OP FAD continued being co-financed by national and regional governments. Slovak country reports and a UNDP study (Hurrle et al., 2012) clearly identified the lack of sustainability. While explicit data is not available, the interviews with the Managing Authorities (MAs) confirmed that less than 5% of the introduced projects were sustained beyond the time-frame of grant payments. It is important to highlight that the co-financing of social inclusion projects was set at the minimum of 15%, with no extra public funding made available for sustaining the operation of the initiatives.

The legitimacy of SF outputs extends to the way SF projects account for the needs and expectations of the final beneficiaries. While quantifying legitimacy is difficult given the lack of surveys and opinion polls undertaken among the Roma population, existing evaluation reports provide basic insights into the legitimacy issue. Thus once again the UNDP study in Slovakia comprehensively illustrated the lack of legitimate responses to the Roma issue (see UNDP, 2012, p. 8),[20] pointing out that they neither addressed the most pressing needs of the communities (particularly high unemployment rate) nor were they considered useful or needed by the participants. In turn, the evaluation of OP FAD in Spain demonstrated that the majority of the European funding was concentrated on issues identified as the greatest impediment to meaningful social inclusion (EURoma, 2010; CSES, 2011b). The interviewed NGOs were largely in agreement that the available financial support was indeed useful and needed. The Decade Watch Survey (OSI, 2010), which developed a methodology to measure the impact of government policies (as perceived by the final beneficiaries), also placed Spain at the top of the ranking list while giving Slovakia the lowest score. The survey revealed that the 'Spanish model' has been effectively promoting high-quality inclusion projects, most pronounced in the area of employment (supported mainly through the ESF). Questions regarding the legitimacy of SF outputs will be further scrutinized in the empirical section of this book.

Methodology and data collection

In a policy area characterized by a dearth of data, capturing the exact performance of member states is difficult. Nevertheless, as shown above, the accounts of Spanish success and Slovak failure are not simply a figment of the political imagination, and divergence in outputs can indeed be observed. Statistical evidence could be an important step in furthering research on the relation between European financial incentives and Roma inclusion processes. However, in many respects, Roma issues are placed in the backwaters of cohesion policy research and wider Europeanization scholarship, which have so far failed to account for the complexity of inclusion initiatives. The 'added value' of SF in the social inclusion domain remains both undertheorized and under-researched empirically. The scientific literature on cohesion policy rarely takes account of questions of legitimacy, falling silent on issues regarding minority representation and power asymmetries. It tends to consider the 'objects' or targets of policy in isolation from wider governance and cognitive and moral maps orienting the actions and routines of policymakers. In this manner, it obscures a vexing dispute between those who see Roma exclusion as a product of discriminatory practices, norms, and behaviours within public institutions and those who attribute it to an inadaptability of certain groups or individuals.

Cohesion policy involves a complex system of financial transfers, realized through an array of institutions, multifarious partnership arrangements, and layered administrative protocol. It is driven as much by rational compromises as it is by ideological stances and normative assumptions. The inherent complexity escapes parsimonious analytical categories and cannot be easily applied to the quantitative analysis dominating research on cohesion policy (Piattoni and Polverari, 2016). In effect, there are few social inquiries into the intricacies of the implementation process. The Europeanization literature focuses on macro-level developments related to the ongoing redefinition of power relations between regions and central governments (Marks and Hooghe, 2004; Ferry and McMaster, 2005) and wider institutional restructuring (Bafoil and Hibou, 2003; Adams et al., 2011). Consequently, there are relatively few empirically 'thick' accounts of how cohesion policy actually works in practice. At the same time, qualitative case studies are excessively immersed in the micro-level performance of individual SF projects, and rarely problematize the content of overarching strategies and consolidated institutional norms. As such, they tend to exaggerate the rationality of the policymaking processes and the power local actors have in shaping policy outputs, placing SF programming outside of the ideological and discursive dynamics.

Given the urgency of the Roma predicament and volatile performance of European cohesion policy, it is important to analyze the dynamics, which unravel across the entire implementation process. To understand the reasons encumbering or facilitating the effective use of the funding, public policy inquiry must construct an analytical bridge between the micro and macro developments and open them up to rigorous empirical scrutiny. In short, it is necessary to explore the difference between policy and practice.

This book builds on a qualitative method of data collection, which includes the content analysis of strategic policy documents and statutes, semi-structured interviews conducted with major SF and Roma inclusion stakeholders, and the case studies of six implemented projects. Leech and Onwuegbuzie (2007) contend that there are two major goals when using multiple sources for collecting data, namely representation and legitimation. Representation refers to the ability to extract adequate meaning from the information at hand. In terms of legitimation, using multiple source types allows the researchers to combine the information from various sources in order to understand the phenomenon better. In other words, using multiple source types allows the researcher to get more out of the data, thereby (potentially) generating more meaning and, in turn, enhancing the quality of syntheses. This method is suitable for extracting information about severely under-researched topics, where reliable data is scattered and hard to come by.

The comparison of member states that differ substantially in terms of institutional and political conditions poses a methodological challenge. Yet, Chapter 2 will demonstrate that these differences do not necessarily influence the variation in the implementation outputs. To account for the differences in the institutional set-up of the two countries (i.e. decentralization in Spain and centralization in Slovakia), the scope of the investigation is narrowed to specific regions: Andalusia (Spain) and Eastern Slovakia (Slovakia). Both of these regions fall under the NUTS 1[21] convergence priority stipulated by European cohesion policy regulations and thus are the main beneficiaries of SF (from both the ERDF and the ESF). Additionally, the majority of Roma communities and settlements are concentrated in these two regions (approximately 43% of the Roma in Spain live in Andalusia while almost 80% of the Roma in Slovakia reside in Eastern Slovakia), which also exhibit the highest levels of social exclusion and unemployment (EURoma, 2010). Finally, both of these regions have implemented the highest number of SF projects aimed at Roma inclusion (CSES, 2011b).

The analytical focus falls on the 2007–2013 programming period. The reason for this limited time-frame is twofold. First, Roma issues only came onto the European political agenda in full force in 2004 and in the context of cohesion policy Roma inclusion priorities crystallized and expanded only in the 2007–2013 funding period. Second, Slovakia entered the EU in 2004, thus participating in the first programming period for only two years. While Roma inclusion priorities were already articulated by then, their expansion and in particular the adoption of horizontal priority MRC only took place in 2007. As such, it is more viable for comparative purposes to focus on the objectives, priorities, and measures developed and implemented in the 2007–2013 period.

European cohesion policy is made up of the ERDF and the ESF. This book focuses explicitly on the implementation of the ESF. This choice is dictated by the fact that Roma integration goals have been largely confined to the ESF, both in terms of stipulated objectives and the actual amount of funds earmarked and spent (EC, 2004; ECRTF, 2010; EURoma, 2010). The ESF focuses on four key areas: increasing the adaptability of workers and enterprises, enhancing access to employment and participation in the labour market, reinforcing social inclusion by combating discrimination and facilitating access to the labour market for disadvantaged people, and promoting partnership for reform in the fields of employment and inclusion. The data outlining Spanish success and pointing out Slovak underperformance is predominately focused on ESF activities, with only limited references made to other funds. Nevertheless, in an effort to avoid biases (e.g. Slovakia's inclusion efforts could rely more on ERDF) the book also takes a look at the relevant goals and activities stipulated by ERDF programming.[22]

In the realm of social science, content analysis is 'codified common sense, a refinement of ways that might be used by laypersons to describe and explain aspects of the world about them' (Robson, 1993, p. 352). In public policy research, it is a method used for deconstructing policy texts (legislation, procedures, reports, evaluation, etc.) according to pre-established analytical categories (often based on theoretical assumptions) and a set of standardized questions. This work analyzes the content of SF programming in two dimensions: a) instrumentality – identifying objectives, priorities, tools, and regulatory provisions, and b) the discursive elements – policy framing, i.e. an 'organizing principle that transforms fragmentary or incidental information into a structured and meaningful problem, in which a solution is implicitly or explicitly included' (Verloo, 2005, p. 20). Strategic documents identified for the analysis include the National Strategic Reference Frameworks (NSRF) (which establish the main priorities for spending EU SF between 2007 and 2013) and OPs (which set out a region's priorities for delivering the fund). The OPs were selected on the basis of their visible commitment to social inclusion and Roma integration. These are:

- Spain – OP Fight Against Discrimination, OP Employment and Adaptability, and OP ESF Andalusia;
- Slovakia – OP Employment and Social Inclusion, OP Regional Development, and OP Education.

The analytical focus on programmatic synergies (see Chapter 3) necessitates an exploration of the domestic policies addressing issues of poverty, exclusion, and discrimination. While it is helpful to map the scope and nature of such texts, it is rarely possible to examine them all in similar depth. Thus, a feasible number of key texts were selected which represents the policy assemblage. These include:

- National Action Plans against Poverty and Social Inclusion 2004–2006 and 2008–2010;
- National and regional Roma inclusion strategies;
- Regional development plans;
- Anti-discrimination legislation.

Given that in Spain the responsibility for social policies and education policies rests mainly in the jurisdiction of the Autonomous Communities (AC), the statutory provision as outlined by the regional authorities in Andalusia is also analyzed. An effort is made to cross-examine the collected data within each country, in order to determine the level of congruity among the objectives, tools, and commitments and to infer any possible discrepancies and contradictions. The analysis of these documents follows a methodology developed by equality research in the framework of the Quing research project (2012). While the coding method was not employed here, the content of strategic documents was examined along questions proposed by the Quing methodology, which account for the diagnostic and prescriptive aspects of the policies.

Diagnostic

1   What is defined as a problem? (*behaviour of actors – institutions, individuals, groups*)
2   What causes or reproduces the problem? (*socio-economic processes, individual or institutional behaviour*)

3 Is there a specific Roma dimension articulated inside the problem? (*direct reference to collectives or communities*)
4 Have specific policy sectors been identified?
5 Is the problem definition supported by scientific research?

Prescriptive

1 What are the proposed objectives and measures? (*what will be done and how*)
2 What is the target group? (*institutions, individuals, communities*)
3 What are the main priorities? (*innovation, continuation, specific activities*)
4 Is there a specific Roma dimension articulated in the objectives and measures?
5 Have equality and anti-discrimination been incorporated into objectives and measures?

However, it should be noted that it is critical to not simply 'read off' a policy text and assume what will happen: as researchers we need to see how they are taken up, where, by whom, and to what ends. For that reason, the content analysis is triangulated with interview-based investigations and case studies.

The use of interviews as a data collection method is based on the assumption that the participants' perspectives are meaningful, knowable, and can be made explicit, and that their perspectives affect the success of the project. As such they are well suited not only for gathering 'descriptive' data but also for exploration of attitudes, values, beliefs, and motives (Richardson, 1965; Smith, 1975). The questions used in the semi-structured interviews were developed using the suggestions of Patton (1990) and the pre-assessment of SF programmes using secondary data. The questions sought to generate factual knowledge about the existing administrative procedures, departmental responsibilities, and institutional interactions. Efforts were also made to inquire about stakeholders' perceptions of the effectiveness and legitimacy of SF approaches. The interviewees were also asked to describe their role and experiences in the specific projects and when possible provide expert comments about the general workings of SF programming and other domestic social inclusion strategies. In total 86 semi-structured interviews were conducted with major SF stakeholders over a span of six years (from 2009 to 2015).

Additional data was collected during thematic conferences, High-Level Events, and workshops. The information received during thematic discussion groups and focus groups was recorded and transcribed with the full knowledge and consent of the participants. When relevant, information was gathered through minutes from the meetings and post-ante publications. In this way, it was possible to verify if the opinions gathered through the semi-structured interviews were reflective of the official statements.

In addition, case study research was conducted. All case study research starts from the same compelling feature: the desire to derive an up-close or otherwise in-depth understanding of a single or small number of cases set in their real-world contexts (Bromley, 1986, p. 1). The closeness aims to produce an invaluable and deep understanding – that is, an insightful appreciation of the case(s) – hopefully resulting in new learning about real-world behaviour and its meaning. For the purpose of this research, this method was employed to gain an in-depth understanding of the implementation at its final stage – individual SF projects.

The culling of the cases was preceded by a review of over 30 social inclusion projects implemented in both countries in the 2007–2013 funding period. Data was accumulated through the examination of national databases, projects' fiches, monitoring accounts, and external evaluation reports. Given the lack of uniform evaluation schemes, the information regarding projects' performance was also obtained through the examination of secondary data (EURoma reports, UNDP, and EC situational and evaluation reports) and interviews with stakeholders and project managers. To maintain analytical rigour and provide some grounds for comparison, the selection relied on descriptive indicators: territorial reach (national, regional, local); project size (aggregated funding); duration; and target group/area. Attention was also paid to whether the project accounted for the Roma population – either through explicit or indirect targeting.

The outline of *Financing Roma Inclusion with European Structural Funds*

The book's main focus starts with the question: *What are the causes of diverging outputs in the utilization of SF for Roma inclusion in Spain and Slovakia?* It focuses on policy process rather than outcomes (a policy's societal consequences after the policy has been implemented). Hence, the analysis cannot serve as a tool for determining which country generates the optimal socio-economic conditions for the Roma population. Such normative judgement is difficult to make given a lack of ontological agreement on the optimal way to address the exclusion dilemma against which ongoing practices could be adequately measured. In addition, the absence of longitudinal, comparative studies on the socio-economic aspects of Roma inclusion, and a lack of reliable data disaggregated by ethnicity, dramatically limits apposite assessment of any long-term impacts. This is not to say that this research is not relevant or its integrity has been compromised. Returning to the classical questions of public policy research (Dye, 1976), implementation output is a policy at its most operational level, thus it lends itself to an insightful analysis. The book offers conceptual tools to interrogate the ideas, structures, and agency entangled in implementation processes in the hope of unveiling their direct influence on funding dynamics. While empirical data is drawn from only two countries, the findings have much wider implications for scholarship in social inclusion policymaking.

The book starts with a review of academic literature on European public policy, clearly demonstrating that existing models and theoretical arguments fail to explain the diverging performance of SF in the two countries under study. Upon identifying the major explanatory lacunas in the research on cohesion policy, Chapter 2 introduces the rationale for an expansive theoretical framework, able to scrutinize the entire implementation process, without losing sight of both structure and agency.

Chapter 3 argues that in order to understand the complexity of multi-level programming the analysis must venture beyond traditional top-down/bottom-up approaches characterizing the study of implementation and adopt a more synthesized analytical focus. Building on a review of the concept and theory of implementation and governance, it offers a revised theorization of the interrelated role of normative ideas, participatory dynamics, and administrative practices in structuring policy outputs. In this way, it shows that – against frequent assumptions – local capacities to elaborate and implement public policies are often limited.

Chapter 4, 5, 6, and 7 comprise the empirical content, presenting the analysis of SF programming implemented in Spain and Slovakia during the 2007–2013 funding period. The chapters draw upon six years of in-depth empirical research, which includes 86 semi-structured interviews with senior policymakers, project managers, and Roma rights activists, triangulated with an in-depth textual analysis of strategic policy documents, and case studies of six implemented SF projects.

Chapter 4 analyzes the design of overarching strategies, interrogating the representations of 'social exclusion' embedded in SF programming. It identifies and exposes a pivotal difference in the way Spanish and Slovak policymakers understand and frame Roma exclusion, and how this ideational aspect effectively structures the shape and aims of interventions and their subsequent outputs. The chapter shows that framing Roma exclusion as a phenomenon driven by institutionalized discrimination (Spain) prompts the adoption of 'ethnically neutral' strategies more conducive to successful implementation outputs. At the same time, a strategic focus on individual adaptability and the ethnic dimension of exclusion (Slovakia) legitimizes the targeted approaches that isolate Roma issues from mainstream socio-economic objectives, facilitating implementation failure. The counterintuitive findings challenge the legitimacy of the ethnic targeting championed by the EU and the majority of international Roma advocacy groups, adding critical insights to the debates on equality mainstreaming.

Chapter 5 examines the institutional design of partnership, a core governing principle of cohesion policy, sensitive to the normative debates surrounding the legitimate representation of Roma voices in policymaking. The chapter explores the role of agency in structuring implementation outputs, by analyzing who participates, in what capacity, and how decisions are linked with policy or public action. The findings show that the institutionalization of a *corporatist partnership model* based on substantive representation with a clear designation of decision-making responsibility and technical assistance greatly contributes to successful outputs. On the other hand, the *all-inclusive model*, based on descriptive representation but not reinforced with technical assistance and clearly designated decision-making responsibilities, leads to dramatic policy failure. The findings largely contest the normative assumption about the relationship between descriptive representation and legitimate policy interventions.

Chapter 6 is concerned with the effect of administrative coordination and programmatic synergies on SF outputs. It analyzes the way domestic elites comprehend and coordinate the 'added value' of SF programming with domestic initiatives. It argues that successful implementation outputs are largely dependent on programmatic synergies (connecting SF objectives with domestic action plans). The analysis of the Spanish case shows that aligning SF strategies and procedures with domestic practices was pivotal in securing effective and sustainable SF outputs. In the case of Slovakia, implementation of SF took place in isolation, without any linkages to domestic services or programmes, thus leading to implementation failure. A paramount finding of this chapter is a trade-off between effective outputs and innovative approaches. The analysis shows that SF generate more effective outputs when they add value to the already existing and well-functioning programmes. As such their potential to induce institutional change is extremely limited, and there is a risk of reinforcing suboptimal practices.

Chapter 7 draws on the in-depth case study research of six funded initiatives (three in each country) to demonstrate the combined effect of policy design, partnership, and administrative coordination on policy success and failure. It demonstrates that effective SF outputs in the area of Roma inclusion are contingent on: a) a clear policy design that recognizes the structural dimensions of social exclusion, b) a partnership design that relies on co-productive interactions that include experts and community stakeholders, and c) the synchronization of SF interventions with domestic policies and exploitation of the 'added value' of SF. The examined projects include: PROMOCIONA, Granada Employment, and Transition to Employment (EDEM) in Spain and National Project Field Social Work, From Benefits to Paid Work, and Integrated Education in Slovakia.

Chapter 8 summarizes the empirical findings and major arguments. It also articulates the implications of the analysis for the current funding period, not only in Spain and Slovakia but also in other member states committed to addressing Roma inclusion with SF.

Notes

1 'Roma' is a political term used as an umbrella name for all members of the Romani ethnic community. Its usage in political and academic discourse demonstrates a strong tendency towards treating the extremely ethnographically diverse Roma communities as a largely homogenous group, overshadowing the various appellations preferred by the individual groups and subgroups (i.e. Sinti, Kale, Rudari, Boyash, and Travellers). This book recognizes that from an ethnographic point of view, the Romani community is extremely diverse and all Romani groups, subgroups, and metagroups have their own ethnic and cultural features (Mayall, 2004). Nonetheless, this book considers the use of 'Roma' as an umbrella term practical and justifiable in the context of European cohesion policy, which deals above all with issues of exclusion and discrimination, not with cultural identity. In no way should this choice of terminology be taken as an endorsement of approaches aimed at homogenizing Roma and other groups perceived as 'Gypsies'.

2 While Roma are widely dispersed across the world, they are a European minority, found in every country on the continent, though located principally in CEE. It is estimated that the population of Roma in Europe is between 10–12 million. Following the consecutive enlargements (2004, 2007, and 2011) the population that identifies itself as Roma has increased in the EU by 75%.

3 The problem of Roma marginalization while more acutely felt in CEE is by no means confined to this region. Discrimination is widely spread in Italy, France, Germany, and

the UK. The recent migration of the Roma from Eastern European countries to Western European countries resulted in great hostilities in all member states allegedly committed to diversity and equal opportunity (Yıldız and De Genova, 2017).

4 It is important to note that the EU did not immediately make Roma integration a specific political priority. No reference was made to Roma integration in the initial versions of the 2007–2013 regulations. Nor was there any requirement to include it as a specific priority in ERDF or ESF OPs. The first specific reference to Roma integration appeared in 2010, when the eligibility conditions in the ERDF regulation governing housing measures were amended.

5 Explicit but not exclusive targeting implies focusing on Roma people as a target group but not to the exclusion of other people who share similar socio-economic circumstances (EC, 2011).

6 For the ESF, €9.6 billion were allocated for measures targeting socio-economic inclusion. In the case of the ERDF, more than €16.8 billion were planned for social infrastructure. The assessment of the 2000–2006 funding period shows that only €2.92 billion were spent on measures targeted at Roma inclusion (CSES, 2011a). Data on the exact expenditure is imprecise given the problems with accounting for the beneficiaries with a Romani background, and thus should be treated with caution. Nevertheless, the earmarking of EU funds has increased.

7 According to the statistical indicators presented by the EU Agency for Fundamental Rights (FRA) the situation on the ground has hardly improved.

8 The Commission Roma Task Force was created on 7 September 2010 to streamline, assess, and benchmark the use (including the effectiveness) of EU funds by all member states for Roma integration.

9 Transcript from the conference (Córdoba, Spain, 2010).

10 Transcript from the conference (Bratislava, Slovakia, 2011).

11 Transcript from the conference (Prague, the Czech Republic, 2011).

12 A report prepared by The Federation of Roma Associations in Catalonia and The EMIGR Group (Bereményi and Mirga, 2012) has challenged the success of the 'Spanish model'. Although the report presented valid concerns, it was criticized by the EU-sponsored networks for presenting inconsistent data. The analysis of one strategic plan presented by the researchers, the Comprehensive Plan for the Gitano Population in Catalonia, was deemed not reflective of nation-wide inclusion initiatives.

13 Transcript from the conference (Bratislava, Slovakia 2011).

14 ITMS is an information system that is used to provide a uniform method of recording, processing, exporting, and monitoring data on programming, project, and financial management, control, and audit of interventions financed by the SF and Cohesion Fund.

15 The allocation data is based on planned rather than actual expenditure (the same applies for Slovakia).

16 The per capita measurement took into consideration the size of the Roma population in each country.

17 Numerous Roma representatives express legal and moral concerns about the rationale being a preservation of individual privacy against potential abuses, which have historically occurred in both totalitarian and democratic countries.

18 This low number can be attributed to the delay in launching measures targeted at the Roma people. According to my follow up interview with a Social Development Fund employee conducted in 2014, the number of direct Roma beneficiaries was still estimated at 15,000 to 20,000.

19 In an interview with Fundación Secretariado Gitano and Caritas both organizations claimed that close to 50% of Roma living in Spain had a chance to benefit (directly or indirectly) from programmes introduced in the framework of SF.

20 The lack of legitimate responses to Roma issues was also addressed during the 2011 EC High-Level Event held in Bratislava and Košice, where stakeholders agreed that

not enough funds were being invested in programmes tackling rampant unemployment among Roma, and that available financial assistance had not addressed the prevailing structural barriers to inclusion. Moreover, the CSES report (2011b) identified instances where SF actually reinforced the segregation of Roma people in schools (for example SF were used to build schools in segregated settlements, often without providing operational funds for developing quality education).

21 The Nomenclature of Territorial Units for Statistics (NUTS) was drawn up by Eurostat more than 30 years ago in order to provide a single uniform breakdown of territorial units for the production of regional statistics for the EU. The NUTS classification has been used in EU legislation since 1988, but it was only in 2003, after three years of preparation, that a EP and Council Regulation on NUTS was adopted.

22 The ERDF supports programmes addressing regional development, economic change, enhanced competitiveness, and territorial cooperation throughout the EU. In May 2010, the ERDF was amended to limit the segregation of marginalized communities living in poor housing conditions. Also, new amendments allow for the so-called integration approach whereby individual OPs can provide for interventions financed from both the ESF and the ERDF.

2 Theorizing cohesion policy

About a third of the EU's budget is devoted to cohesion policy, the primary instrument for supporting regional economic and social development, especially in the poorer states of the Union. With €347 billion at its disposal in the 2007–2013 funding period, it represented the second largest item in the EU budget after the Common Agricultural Policy. This makes its effectiveness a subject of great interest due to the potentially high opportunity costs these funds might have. Traditionally, cohesion policy was based on the logic of inter-governmental redistributive bargaining organized around aggregated measurements of disparity, mostly GDP per capita and unemployment rates. However, the escalation of intertwined socio-economic problems across the European Community (youth poverty, an increasingly strained welfare state, and escalating discrimination aimed at ethnic and racial minorities) prompted the EU to rethink and reshape its business-as-usual approach. Consequently, the articulation of the thematic tailoring of SF, less contingent on spatial dimensions, has penetrated the regional development agenda of the EU (EC, 2003). In particular, the European Social Fund (ESF) was designated as the main mechanism for channelling money directly at human resources, with special attention given to 'groups at risk of exclusion' (EC, 2010a). These strategic alterations meant that the Roma became one of the beneficiaries, and the only ethnic group singled-out in the strategic documents (EC, 2010).

Already in 2004, the ESF were presented as highly suitable instruments for addressing the systemic causes of inequality and facilitating changes towards a substantive equality for Roma people (EC, 2004). The EC openly stated that: 'SF could make a very significant difference to the situation of Roma, Gypsies and Travellers in Europe' and that: 'member states should place a priority on this issue and commit adequate counterpart funds' (EC, 2004, p. 14). In the 2007–2013 funding period, the social inclusion theme was placed under both the *convergence objective* and the *regional competitiveness and employment objective*, espoused in the Community Support Framework (CSF), supported with both the ESF and the ERDF.[1] However, it was up to each member state to define inclusion priorities and suggest the key elements of implementation within their NSRF and Operation Programmes (OP). The cohesion regulations gave the member states more room for manoeuvre in implementing specific measures, as long as they adhered to the principles of additionality and partnership. As a result, the social inclusion strategies were open to interpretation and left in the domain of national, regional, and local decision-making.

The EU made efforts, albeit feeble ones, to *secure* member state's commitments to Roma minorities, stubbornly calling for targeting SF at specific inclusion themes. The EU Commissioner for Employment, Social Affairs and Inclusion has been a leading figure in advocating for the use of SF to address the 'multidimensional aspect of Roma exclusion', and invest in projects in four key areas: education, employment, healthcare, and housing.[2] Issues concerning discrimination were to be addressed through the transposition of relevant equality directives[3] and a stronger commitment to awareness raising activities. In 2009, the 10 Common Basic Principles on Roma Inclusion were accepted in the form of a Council Conclusion and provided guidelines for the design and implementation of actions to support Roma minorities (including SF programming). The most often cited section of this document is the explicit, but not exclusive, targeting principle. The principle supports social inclusion actions, from which the Roma benefit, which do not exclude people who share similar socio-economic circumstances. The idea was to avoid creating new inequalities or injustices by leaving behind similarly unprivileged groups (Kóczé et al., 2014). While calls for the mainstreaming of inclusions policies was also articulated, it became apparent that 'Roma ethnicity' has become an organizing principle for the implementation of Roma inclusion objectives, scattered across various national NSRF and regional OPs.

The rising profile of the European cohesion policy has brought about a greater level of scrutiny. From an academic perspective, scholars have increasingly sought to explain the impact of strategic funding on economic convergence, regionalization processes, and new forms of power-sharing in policymaking (Piattoni and Polverari, 2016; Dąbrowski and Graziano, 2016; Charron, 2016). However, the robust focus on macro-level developments tends to overshadow a more in-depth inquiry of this boundary-spanning policy, which impresses its own intricate metagovernance. The analytical attention to high-level political negotiations and institutional restructuring does not fully account for the more nuanced dynamics related to policy framing, the participation of marginalized actors, and multifaceted administrative management. Moreover, much of the language of European cohesion policy eschews the idea of trade-offs between efficiency and equity, suggesting it is possible to maximize overall growth while also achieving continuous convergence in outcomes and productivity across Europe's regions. Yet, even though there seems to be an agreement that cohesion policy has at least partly altered the pathways of development, its effectiveness in reducing social exclusion continues to be heavily disputed (Bachtler and Mendez, 2007). As noted in the introduction, academic attention to the effect of SF programming on Roma inclusion, remains in the domain of report literature, with few cohesion scholars taking an analytical interest in the impact of EU funding on social justice and equality.

Hence, there is a need for a fresh examination of cohesion policy which is more attentive to factors structuring implementation outputs in a highly complex and contested area of social inclusion. This chapter first reviews relevant literature for thinking about cohesion policy with the goal of identifying the varied analytical approaches and their implications for the study of SF outputs. The focus falls on scholarship which theorizes compliance as well as theoretical models accounting for domestic implementation capacities, multi-level governance, and return on investment. The larger goal is to clarify why the performance of Spain and Slovakia defies widely adopted theoretical propositions, and why theories on policy implementation are better suited for capturing and explaining factors driving policy outputs.

Europeanization lens

The study of cohesion policy tends to be nested within a larger field of Europeanization research. This vast body of work has been instrumental in conceptualizing and problematizing the interwoven relationship between the EU and its member states. A key question posed by Europeanization scholars is why governments comply with the rules of a supranational regime, even when these rules appear in conflict with domestic interests or values (Keohane, 1984; Börzel, 2005; Börzel and Knoll, 2012). This question is pertinent given that the European financial transfers mandate makes radical changes to the architecture of domestic institutions, governance practices, and administrative arrangements, which often exceed the expected return of investments (Bachtler et al., 2013; Bachtler et al., 2016). A wide variety of qualitative and quantitative research designs have been deployed to analyze and better understand the transposition and implementation of hard and soft EU laws. Although there is little theoretical agreement on key variables driving acquiescence to EU regulations, the analytical attention of the majority of Europeanization scholars tends to focus on the impact of external pressure (conceptualized in form of incentives and coercive mechanisms).

International pressure

The rationalist accounts of EU integration argue that strong supranational pressure, supported with incentives and coercive mechanisms, will trigger member states' compliance with EU law, especially if the expected conformity lowers the transaction costs of domestic policymaking (Moravcsik, 1998; Majone, 2000; Pollack, 2003; Tallberg, 2003; Börzel, 2005; Börzel et al., 2007; Majone, 2000). The EC has extensive powers to issue warnings to member state governments with a questionable implementation record using informal and formal letters and to pursue formal infringement proceedings before the European Court of Justice (ECJ) in the case of persistent non-compliance. The Commission even has the power to propose, before the ECJ, punitive fines to be issued against member states that violate EU law (Pollack, 2003, p. 86). As such supranational pressure is viewed as a 'management-enforcement ladder' where both amicable and coercive mechanisms employed by the EC can largely resolve implementation problems (Tallberg, 2003; Jönsson and Tallberg, 1998).

In the context of Roma inclusion, policy experts and politicians have often argued that the EU's pressure constituted the most important motivational factor behind the changes in countries' policies towards the Roma minority (see Barany, 2002; Vermeersch, 2006; O'Nions, 2007; Andor, 2018). While these claims are now widely disputed, with arguments that the EU's promotion of, and support for, the improved treatment of Roma has left member states with an inconsistent mix of policies, practices, and norms that support both inclusion and exclusion (Ram, 2014), the European pressure should not be underestimated. Throughout her post, the Roma Decade Facilitator, Tunde Buzetzky maintained that EU pressure played a central role in initiating the Decade of Roma Inclusion,[4] the creation of national Roma inclusion strategies (under the EU framework), and the establishment of various Roma representative bodies. Even the direst critics of 'overly bureaucratized Europe' maintain that without a supranational warden, the treatment of Roma would be even worse (see Guy, 2013, pp. 172–176).

Nevertheless, the EU's specifications to allocate funding towards specific inclusion goals, and use it to improve the governance of equality policies, have in fact delivered rather ambiguous results. When looking at the performance of Spain and Slovakia, a complex and largely counterintuitive picture emerges, showing that spending decisions are often driven more by what national and regional administrations are prepared to co-finance than what the EU insists they should do.

Since the accession talks with the CEE countries, EU pressure to address the situation of national/ethnic minorities has been particularly acute in Slovakia, at one point threatening Slovakia's aspiration to enter the EU.[5] In 1993, the European Council in Copenhagen made minority rights one of the four criteria that candidate countries had to meet in order to become legitimate members of the club. Conditionality was supported by pre-accession funding (PHARE), regular monitoring, and, of course, the perceived benefits deriving from EU membership. The available subsidies generated considerable attention for Roma exclusion, at least at the highest political level, and while the assessment reports of Slovakia (1994–2004) clearly indicated a continuous implementation gap,[6] the government professed its ongoing commitment to improving the integration of its marginalized minorities (Kahanec and Sedláková, 2016). Between 1999 and 2003 close to €26 million was allocated and spent, even though the results of the delivered programmes appeared negligible (Heil et al., 2012). The period also saw the founding of the Office of Governmental Plenipotentiary for Roma Communities, with the direct financial assistance of the EU (through pre-accession funding assistance, PHARE) and World Bank.

Following accession to the EU, funding for Roma inclusion in Slovakia increased substantially, particularly in the eastern region (under convergence regulation) where the majority of the most impoverished Roma communities reside.[7] In 2004, the Social Development Fund (SDF) was established to secure a more targeted use of SF for the population living in the most disadvantaged regions and to involve regional and local stakeholders in dealing with poverty and social inclusion issues. For the 2007–2013 funding period, Slovak NSRF introduced a

horizontal priority, MRC, to strengthen the impact of SF funding While the available funding instigated high-level discussions about Roma issues and spawned
various ad-hoc initiatives, the overall performance of SF programming once again
remained highly ineffective. The 2012 report, Uncertain Impact: Have the Roma
in Slovakia Benefited from the European Social Fund?, demonstrated that the
socio-economic standing of the majority of Slovak Roma continued to deterio-
rate; while equality policies remained underdeveloped and SF were continuously
diverted from the most impoverished areas. It appeared that while EU pressure has
prompted Slovak authorities to formulate official inclusion objectives (largely in
line with EU recommendations), their enforcement remained weak. The ad-hoc
measures that were indeed realized proved of little 'added value', and were neither
sustained nor scaled up. As noted by a manager from a Regional Development
Agency in Prešov: 'from here Brussels and even Bratislava seem far away, and I
am not sure they really care what we do or where we are'.[8]

The Spanish case confirms the abstruse impact of EU pressure on the way
member states exploit SF. At the outset, it is imperative to note that during the
accession talks with Spain and Portugal, minority issues were not addressed or
elaborated on. In fact, the silent treatment of minority rights characterized the
EU's relations with the Iberian Peninsula for the next two decades (O'Nions,
2007). Even after 2000, the EC has refrained from pressuring the Spanish authorities to accelerate their anti-discrimination and integration efforts.[9] Nevertheless,
the absence of supranational conditionality to address the exclusion of minorities
has not prevented Spain from taking advantage of the EU funds during the development of public initiatives targeted at groups at risk of social exclusion (Powell,
2001). Although some scholars argue that the Spanish legislative policies on
equality have been inspired by the EU and international law (Benítez, 2016), the
majority of post-Franco reforms were driven by internal dynamics linked to the
processes of democratization, not related to supranational pressure or financial
incentives (Arriba and Moreno, 2005). Democratic transition reinforced social
demands for progressive and redistributive policies, especially for public infrastructure, and education, health, and social programmes. It also set forth an array
of social reforms, which in a relatively short span of time helped Spain to develop
progressive gender equality and anti-discrimination legislation.[10] Eventually, the
system of equality governance stimulated policy diffusion, innovation, and experimentation with different approaches across all regions (Alonso and Verge, 2014).
While the focus was predominately placed on gender equality, the legislation and
programmes often served as an umbrella for claims by other discriminated groups,
including the Roma. As noted by a local Roma activist:

> We really benefited from all this gender equality talk, if not our men at least
> us women, every project that focused on women wanted us on board, a lot of
> reaching out they did and it worked.[11]

Even more indicative of the fact that the EU pressure has not been the leading
factor in prompting Spain to address Roma issues, was the formulation of the

National Programme for the Development of Roma and its regional counterparts (i.e. The Andalusian Plan for the Roma Community). Already introduced in 1989, it constituted an antidote to the state-sponsored discrimination of the Roma during Franco's dictatorship. According to the 2000 annual report of the Service Unit of the National Programme (Villarreal, 2001), an average of 100 projects (co-financed with SF) had been implemented annually since 1995, directly benefiting an estimated 50,000 people. The National Programme functioned uninterruptedly until 2014 when it was replaced with the newly adopted National Roma Integration Strategy. It is important to note, that the adoption of the EU-led strategy was presented as a continuation of the previous policies, with little concessions made to include the main EU recommendations. Although the impact of national and regional inclusion projects and initiatives should not be exaggerated, their substance went far beyond the symbolic commitments so apparent in Slovakia. The formulation of inclusion objectives within the Spanish NSRF and national and regional OPs (particularly OP ESF Andalusia[12]) appear more reflective of domestic needs and priorities than of the burgeoning commitment to Roma inclusion endorsed by the EU.

Compliance with EU recommendations

While it is widely acknowledged that national governments should play a leading role in addressing the socio-economic exclusion of Roma, experts invested in Roma issues continue to caution that without strong supranational pressure and continuous oversight the inclusion policies will not be prioritized inside SF programming (Guy, 2011; Mirga-Kruszelnicka, 2017; McGarry, 2017). The main assumption is that the ineffective performance of Slovakia (and other member states in the CEE region) stems from a 'lack of political will' to enforce and monitor the use of funding on the ground. This, in turn, is blamed on the residual and inconsistent pressure exerted on the member states by the supranational polity. There appears to be an unshaken belief that a more coercive stance will address any instances of insubordination, particularly in policy areas deemed 'unpopular' among the electorate. Not surprisingly, recommendations flowing out of numerous shadow reports and policy toolkits highlight the need for stronger ex-ante conditionality, monitoring, and the stricter application of infringement proceedings (Nicolae, 2012; Kóczé et al., 2014; Mirga-Kruszelnicka, 2017). The prescriptions to anchor EU presence in all matters related to Roma continue to be driven by fears that following the accession new member states will lower their commitments to minority treatment, and the EU itself will become less alert to ongoing violations (Sasse, 2005).

However, evidence shows the political salience of Roma exclusion at the supranational level has hardly subsided after the accession. The EU has continued its advocacy for Roma issues by exerting pressure and more importantly by continuing its targeted financial support (EC 2011, 2014).[13] The situation in Slovakia, in particular, received unprecedented attention from the EC, EP, and other international stakeholders, with the Open Society Institute (OSI) often leading the way. High-Level Events and regional workshops were organized with the specific purpose of improving the use of SF and facilitating more effective implementation. The appalling treatment of the Slovak Roma remained in the public eye. Infringement proceedings against the state were put in motion in 2015 and the EU Justice Commissioner has called on the Slovak government to fight the discrimination of the Roma more actively and focus on the elimination of hate crime and harmful stereotypes (Romea.cz, 2015).

What is particularly striking in the case of Slovakia is that the failure to deliver effective SF outputs corresponds with a fairly strong record of compliance with EU law and recommendations. In the context of SF programming, Slovakia was the first member state that included a specific horizontal priority, MRC, in its SF programming, which required each OP to designate a section describing how general measures will contribute to Roma integration. Adhering to the EU recommendations, an integrated approach to Roma exclusion was developed based on combining resources from different OPs and allocating them to Roma inclusion projects. Efforts were also made to earmark SF for local demand-driven projects targeted at Roma communities, and housing development in the most impoverished communities in Slovakia. Finally, efforts were made to engage Roma representation in funding programming under the auspice of the Slovak Government Plenipotentiary for Roma Communities and SDF. Leaving the actual impact of these efforts aside, they fully reflect EU recommendations and conditionality.

At the same time, Spanish compliance with EU law and recommendations has been quite selective and at times apprehensive. The Spanish authorities appeared to be 'handpicking' principles and ideas proposed by the EU, opting for those that suited the ongoing domestic approaches to social inclusion and equality (i.e. placing Roma issues under endogenous equality approaches). Specific references to the Roma as a target group in the SF programming were scarce, confined to the multi-regional OPs, Fight Against Discrimination (OP FAD), and Technical Assistance (OP TA) (even inside these strategic documents reference to ethnicity as a target of SF interventions was articulated with caution). The regional OPs and project-calls refrained from targeting funds at ethnic groups altogether, preferring to adhere to territorial and sectorial indicators. Moreover, the Spanish SF programming has not adhered to the integrated approach, so strongly promoted by the EC. Instead, individual OPs addressed a single and clearly defined public issue (i.e. unemployment, secondary education, vocational training). The engagement of Roma representation under the partnership principle was limited to large NGOs, with limited input from local representative bodies. In short, there is little evidence that the championed Spanish model of inclusion has been strongly aligned with the EU vision.

Looking at these two cases it is difficult, if not misleading, to explain the diverging patterns of SF implementation with the EU pressure and scrutiny argument. The weak explanatory power of this line of reasoning lies in the conceptualization of compliance in terms of the sole transposition of EU regulations into national legislation (Falkner et al., 2008; Schimmelfennig and Sedelmeier, 2005; Börzel, 2005; Börzel et al., 2007). The concept of SF implementation is not a straightforward one. The EU strategic framework must first be transposed into national ones, unless they are directly binding and readily applicable, after which they are applied and enforced. Most rationalist approaches in cohesion policy literature are not clear on the implementation concept. In effect, an inquiry into what happens after the enactment of the EU rules and the relationship between a statute and its subsequent implementation is largely glossed over. While it is possible to identify the 'presence of Europe' in national legislation (i.e. Roma inclusion strategy), it is difficult to see to what extent and purpose this presence has been exploited on the ground. Hence, the sequel of the correct application of SF in the national, regional, and local context is fully obscured and undertheorized. More importantly, few scholars critically scrutinize the content of the overarching inclusion strategies and the structuring effect the discursive elements of policy can have on implementation outputs. This gives the impression that the implementation gap is driven by a combination of non-compliance, with value-free strategies and inadequate institutional capacities to absorb and allocate funding. The thought that inclusion strategies might in themselves be faulty, or based on an inadequate causal theory of inclusion, remains on the fringes of mainstream cohesion scholarship.

Administrative capacity

The discourse on the role of administrative capacities in the utilization of SF has taken the spotlight in evaluation reports and policy recommendation toolkits. The latest ex-post evaluation studies stubbornly argue that what cohesion policy achieved (or not) in 2007–2013, depended strongly on the administrative capability of individual member states (ECA, 2016a). Policy experts point out that some of the major recipients of Structural and Cohesion (now Investment) Funds (usually the new member states) have had serious deficiencies in administrative capacity, rooted in the incomplete reforms of public administration and weaknesses in governance (Dotti, 2016). Hence, the strengthening of administrative capacity is now a critical thematic objective for 2014–2020. Both the Directorate General for Employment, Social Affairs and Inclusion and Directorate General for Regional and Urban Policy have established administrative capacity units, in line with a recommendation in the report by Barca (2009), in the hope they can help to improve the administration of cohesion policy, particularly in the member states with low absorption rates.

The need for an efficient administrative apparatus and political wilfulness to optimally exploit available resources is often presented as axiomatic. Few theorists argue against this seemingly common sense logic. Political economy scholars have effectively demonstrated that administratively weak regions are unlikely to receive shares of public transfers in accordance with equity considerations (Oates, 1999). Their main observation is that regions with expansive indigenous resources (financial and administrative) and greater political authority can not only influence the allocation of funds in their favour (Marks and McAdam, 1996; Oates, 1999; Brock and Owings, 2003; Farole et al., 2011; Bodenstein and

Kemmerling, 2011), but also implement them more effectively. This leads to a paradox whereby the regions and localities with the greatest problems and the weakest resources may need the EU funds most of all, but are not able to handle the bureaucratic complexity and political pressure and thus lose out the most (De Rynck and McAleavey, 2001). While these are all valid claims, this line of argumentation generally accounts for macro-level distribution processes (parcelling out SF among member states and regions), with a relatively scant analysis of the actual delivery processes. Moreover, there is an assumption that administrative efficiency is essential for improving overall public governance, including approaches to equal treatment and social inclusion. What is understated is that a drive towards efficiency and speedy absorption rates can actually push aside equality interests in favour of higher productivity and convergence rates (Bailey and De Propris, 2002; De Rynck and McAleavey, 2001).

The capacity argument is fortified by an omnipresent perception that countries with longer EU membership status are likely to use SF more effectively. Most pronounced in sociological debates about integration, the experience argument assumes that with time member states acquire knowledge about European rules and procedures and internalize EU values and norms (Dąbrowski, 2010; Rodríguez-Pose and Novak, 2013). Regular interactions between the EU and domestic actors are thought to set in motion a policy-learning process, which with time reduces integration costs, administrative discrepancies, and resistance. It is assumed that with time domestic actors become familiarized with the procedures and supranational expectations, which helps them navigate the system more effectively and optimize all its potential benefits (Ezcurra, et al., 2007). This argument, however, fails to explain why countries with similar membership duration are not equally effective in their utilization of SF,[14] or why, despite proven effectiveness, they do not channel SF towards social inclusion issues (i.e. France and Italy). Moreover, once again the supranational expectations and overarching inclusion strategies are not problematized in terms of legitimacy and the appropriateness of their aims and adopted policy tools. At best, scholars call for simplification of the allocation and co-financing procedures, so the funds could be more accessible to less resourced actors, but without paying attention to the normative underlining of inclusion objectives (Sabau-Popa and Mara 2015).

Capacity-building arguments have dominated virtually all discussions on Roma inclusion and SF programming. Improving administrative efficiency has been presented as a cure for all evils, and 'gaining experience' was often articulated as a driving factor of success (EURoma 2011). As the EC urged member states (particularly the new joiners) to invest in administrative reforms, local stakeholders called for a simplification and streamlining of the overly complex procedures and higher investments in local administration. These demands resulted in a proliferation of workshops and seminars aimed at teaching the bureaucratic cadre, NGOs, and local authorities how to manage Roma inclusion projects 'better'. It also induced an array of administrative reforms, most pronounced in CEE member states.[15] Yet the capacity argument proves to be weak when directly applied to the case of Spain and Slovakia. Here the causal link between administrative capacity and effective, let alone sustainable and legitimate, policy outputs is not as obvious as insisted by the EC and a growing number of Roma inclusion stakeholders.

First, the widely held perception that Slovakia, with its limited administrative capacities and no experience with equality policies, is unable to access and utilize SF needs to be challenged. Under accession conditionality, Slovakia underwent unprecedented institutional and administrative reconstruction (including the creation of the EU NUTS regions) which outpaced the administrative reforms introduced in Spain, both in terms of scope and budgetary investments. With EU support, the Slovak government earmarked close to €34 million from the PHARE programme for the development of administrative capacities in the area of social inclusion and minority integration. In contrast, it is important to note that external financial support was not provided to Spain during its accession process.[16] In Slovakia, the money was channelled towards an array of Roma inclusion pilot projects as a way to prepare the ground for wider equality programmes (Heil et al., 2012). The government also invested in specialized units to foster inclusion strategies (i.e. the SDF) and ran an impressive number of training programmes for public bureaucrats, including MAs and Intermediate Bodies (IBs). The OSF played a leading role in developing and facilitating these training endeavours via its programme, Making the Most of EU Funds for Roma Inclusion.[17] Given these far-reaching developments, and obvious capacity to induce administrative changes, the poor performance of SF in the context of Roma inclusion does not appear excessively link to weak administration. What is especially interesting is that in Slovakia the rate of absorption and allocation of SF has varied dramatically across policy sectors and policy issues. However, interventions in the area of Roma inclusion have consistently demonstrated the poorest results (Frank, 2011).

In turn, the effective use of SF in Spain has been almost automatically equated with longer membership status and stronger administrative capacity (Leonardi and Nanetti, 2011). According to thematic EC reports, experience with the EU procedures made Spain more adept at optimizing the available opportunities for addressing a wide range of issues including the social exclusion of the Roma (EC, 2016). However, Spain started to use SF for Roma integration a decade after its accession, meaning it had approximately the same amount of time as Slovakia to develop Roma inclusion strategies within its SF programming. Hence, the experience variable does not really explain why Spain would learn 'faster and better' than Slovakia, especially if one takes into consideration the impressive institution building process undertaken by Slovakia following the transition period. More importantly, Spanish bureaucracy has often been criticized for its 'sluggish' response to external initiatives, delays in financial transfers, and tensions between central and regional administrations (Dudek, 2003, 2014). While in terms of absorption (a key indicator used to measure administrative efficiency) Spain performs better than Slovakia, it is by no means a leader among all the other member states (Piattoni and Polverari, 2016). Studies have shown that at the local level the capacity to interact with SF in an innovative and sustainable manner is still low and vary across the regions. At the same time, the management and public procurement of EU funds are not free of political patronage and clientelism (Hagemann, 2017).

The main weakness of the capacity argument is the assumption that the basic character of the SF processes is largely technocratic, based on a top-down procedural system with important vertical coordination between administrative levels (Olsson, 2003). Bache and Chapman (2008) found elite policy experts to be pivotal actors in allocation processes, insisting that their action adhered to rational choice perspectives. For years, the most cited work on cohesion policy asserted that the distribution of regional transfers follows a set of transparent principles that narrow the scope for autonomous and strategic politics (Bache and Olsson, 2001; Olsson, 2003; Scott, 1998). These rationalist accounts see value decisions as originating elsewhere and as extraneous to the process of implementation. They explicitly accept a view that cohesion policy is based on some consensus about social relations, specifically endorsing the model of a market economy. Crucially, these theorists stress *expertise* rather than *political participation* in their analyses, disregarding the normative arguments made by implementation theorists that policymaking responsibility should be shared by a plurality of interacting policymakers, analysts, and community representatives (Lindblom, 1980; Geddes, 2006).

Agency and decision-making

The strand of literature that challenged this strictly technical approach emerged from discussions on multi-level governance (MLG). This term was coined by Gary Marks to describe the way in which cohesion policy operates through a 'system of continuous negotiation among nested governments at several territorial tiers' in which 'supranational, national, regional, and local governments are enmeshed in territorially overarching policy networks' (Marks, 1993, p. 402). The analytical focus was placed on the ongoing redefinition of relations between various policy actors, a perspective ideally suited for examining partnership, a core governing principle of the SF which informed successive waves of reforms aiming to involve an increasingly wide range of stakeholders in the planning and implementation of cohesion policy (Marks and Hooghe, 2004; Ferry and McMaster, 2005; Bache, 2010). The MLG approach has now become a 'palatable, easily digestible paradigm for grasping how the EU works in practice' (Stephenson, 2013, p. 817) and for describing a policymaking system based on vertical and horizontal interactions and interdependencies across levels of government and sectors.

While the MLG approach offers important insights into power relations, the studies conducted to date do not provide a clear-cut picture of the impacts and effects of MLG on policy outputs. Part of the problem is the lack of normative conception of what an 'effective' and 'legitimate' partnership should look like and what it should strive to achieve. The assumption that the restructuring of power relations allows for drawing on the knowledge of sub-national actors and NGOs to tailor strategies and programmes to the territorial specificities (Bache, 2010) is yet to be verified empirically. Moreover, few studies can demonstrate that a stronger regionalization and empowerment of sub-national actors correlates with more effective and equitable policy outputs. When such correlations are identified, they account for efficiency outputs only – showing how stronger interaction among various actors ensures the rapid distribution of the SF (Begg, 2009; Dall'Erba et al., 2009; Eckey and Türck, 2006). The relationship between regionalization and legitimate or sustainable outputs appears more complex, with little empirical data gathered so far. Hence, the common argument that regionalization in Spain contributes to 'better inclusion strategies' whereas centralization in Slovak leads to inefficiencies needs to be treated with caution and submit to a more in-depth empirical analysis.

In recent years there has been an increasing number of contributions on the political determinants of SF (Bodenstein and Kemmerling, 2011; Bouvet and Dall'Erba, 2010; Dellmuth, 2011). The role of political parties and 'pork-barrel' politics has been put forward as a determining factor in final allocation decisions (often going against official eligibility criteria). While more sensitive to the politicization of cohesion goals and strategies, these studies remain concerned with macro-level distribution criteria in a quest to prove empirically that regions do not always receive shares of EU transfers in accordance with equity or efficiency considerations. The role of political parties is put forward as a determining factor in an effort to challenge the picture of SF programming as an expert-driven, rational process. However, once again the dynamics unravelling throughout the sub-national implementation process remains invisible. The latest research by Surubaru (2016) goes deeper in its investigation of political influences, convincingly arguing that domestic levels of politicization can mediate the outcome-driven performance of the policy. Nevertheless, the analysis of localized imbroglios loses sight of wider structural frameworks and their structuring impact on actors' behaviour. None of these studies gives a substantial role to the civil society or engages in normative discussions on legitimate representation (an important dimension when minority issues are concerned).

The insights into the widening participation in cohesion policymaking have been used to strengthen the arguments about the need to develop and implement Roma inclusion policy initiatives in close cooperation with regional and local authorities (EC, 2011). At the same time the rhetoric, if not the substance of Roma participation has become a mantra for all national and international, governmental, and inter-governmental institutions in a way that was formerly inconceivable (Jovanović, 2013). Given that Roma representation is still largely confined to civil society organizations, the EC has pressed member states to expand the dialogue with and participation of non-governmental interests in SF programming.[18] According to the 10 Common Basic Principles of Roma Inclusion, member states need to design and implement Roma inclusion policy initiatives in close cooperation with civil society actors such as NGOs, social partners, and academics/researchers (Principle 9). The involvement of civil society has been recognized as vital both for the mobilization of expertise and the dissemination of the knowledge required to develop public debate and accountability throughout the policy process.

In line with this rhetoric, the Spanish model has often been attributed to the well-established Spanish civil society and the consolidation of the horizontal dimension of the partnership principle, which is argued as being more open to consultations and interactions with the third-sector organizations. It has also been argued that the Roma community is more organized (and recognized), particularly in regions such as Andalusia. In contrast, Slovakia's apparently frail NGO sector, weak civil society, and the reluctance of authorities to engage in meaningful social dialogue were put forward as key factors accounting for policy failure (Petrova, 2007; Potluka et al., 2017). The deep-cutting racial cleavages and tensions between Roma and non-Roma citizens have also been put forward as the main reason for the failure of Roma inclusion policies and programmes. However, a closer look at these two countries undermines the plausibility of these explanations.

Although in the last 20 years Spanish civil society has grown substantially, the autonomy of NGOs and their ability to shape policies has been highly contested (see Fernandes, 2012). In the context of European cohesion policy, public consultations with civil society have increased, but the opportunities to implement and manage European funding continue to be restricted to 'expert' organizations and designated authorities (see Chapter 5). The actual Roma involvement in the management of SF projects has been confined to a few well-established NGOs with a nationwide reach and other interests to represent. The State Council for the Roma People, serving as a consultative body attached to the Ministry of Labour and Social Affairs, has played a rather residual role in SF programming (both in terms of design and implementation). Moreover, critics have argued that no efforts were made to use SF as an empowering tool for the more localized representation of Romani interests (Bereményi and Mirga, 2012). And yet, Roma inclusion objectives have emerged on both national and regional political agendas (albeit not as a main priority) and, more importantly, were sustained with concrete measures and financial allocations, even as governments changed and financial crises cascaded through society.

A slightly different dynamic can be observed in Slovakia. Following the separation from the Czech Republic, the Slovak state has also witnessed an unprecedented growth and activism of civil society, including a growing number of Roma-led associations and local NGOs (Zielonka, 2001). The political disenfranchisement of the Roma has pushed numerous advocates and local leaders into the third sector. Consequently, local NGOs became the most pronounced form of representation for Roma collective interests, a dynamic recognized by the national authorities. Roma-led NGOs received substantial support from international donors advocating for Roma rights and often acting as the sole providers of services to the marginalized communities (Mušinka and Kolesárová, 2012; Trehan, 2001). The Plenipotentiary Office acted as a state agent for maintaining the social dialogue with the local Roma representation, with a pronounced focus on SF. It is important to mention that Roma-led organizations operating in Spain rarely enjoyed access to international donations, and were more dependent on state/ regional support. Nevertheless, the new 'representation' has been unable to influence SF programming. Although, like in Spain, consultations with NGOs have been increasing, the local voice has rarely been translated into actual objectives and measures. Investment in Roma-led NGOs has neither translated into greater influence over policymaking nor secured a greater allocation of SF towards the Roma. Moreover, the dramatic increase in Roma-led organizations has, in fact, led to the fragmentation and diffusion of collective interests (perhaps more so in Slovakia than in Spain). As noted by Trehan (2009), cooperation efforts were seriously hindered by the competitive nature of grant seeking and a high level of mistrust between Roma and non-Roma communities.

In view of these developments, the civil society argument on its own only partially explains the empirical puzzle. The feebleness of this explanation lies in its preoccupation with who participates, rather than how and to what effect. The literature on cohesion policy rarely focuses upon the most marginalized actors under the assumption that the ongoing devolution of power and the expansion of the partnership principle will automatically empower even the most disen-franchised groups. The conceptualization of interaction between policymakers and third-sector actors remains weak, curtailing the understanding of the range of institutional possibilities for public participation. The MLG framework main-tains an artificial division between policy formulation (the influence sub-national and third-party actors have in generating strategic objectives) and policy delivery (participation in project management), which muddles the understanding of how participants communicate with one another and make decisions together. At the same time, the burgeoning scholarship on Roma representation focuses on the benefits of so-called descriptive representation under the strong presumption that only the representatives of Romani origin can best represent the interests of Roma communities (see Guy, 2013). While such representatives bring in important and largely overdue insights on the importance of ethnic identities within public policymaking, they fail to critically examine what a legitimate Roma representa-tion should look like and how it should be executed. Given the controversy and contestations surrounding issues of cultural, ethnic, and social identities, this is a rather surprising oversight (Klímová-Alexander, 2004; Caluser, 2008; Surdu 2016; Gheorghe, 1997; Guy, 2013).

The gravity of the problem

Finally, in the context of cohesion policy (as well as in other distributive and regu-latory policies) European theorists contend that member states are more likely to channel EU resources to the areas where the social costs of reform are high, the so-called 'blame avoidance' phenomena (Weaver, 1986). However, in both countries, the on-the-ground situation challenges these theoretical arguments. The Roma in Slovakia makes up almost 10% of the entire population,[19] while in Spain the Roma represent only 1.8% (not including the recent Roma migrants from CEE). Having a large Roma population should be a strong incentive for Slovakia to use the available funds to alleviate exclusion, especially given that the deteriorating situation of the Roma population entails social instability and represents a predicament in economic terms (Marcinčin and Marcinčinová, 2009).

Although Spanish Roma face many similar problems to their Eastern counter parts, particularly in accessing opportunities in the labour market, education, housing, and living conditions (Ringold et al., 2005, p. 155), the small size of their population makes it 'easier' to overlook their exclusion, especially given the lack of strong political representation of the Roma at all levels of government, and an absence of social mobilization and lobbying leverage. More importantly, the recent economic crisis that instigated an array of austerity-driven cuts to social spending should have severely impacted Roma inclusion strategies. And yet, this has not taken place, with national governments and autonomous regions actually strengthening their financial support of inclusion (albeit predominately in the field of employment). In this light, the gravity of the problem does not provide a viable explanation of why there are diverging outputs in the utilization of SFs for Roma inclusion in Slovakia and Spain.

What is proposed?

The above analysis shows that the common approaches to studying cohesion policy cannot fully account for the diverging policy outputs in the area of Roma inclusion (and social exclusion more generally). The case of Spain and Slovakia seem to defy widely held notions about the factors which drive implementation success or failure. The rationalist approaches embedded in the main theoretical models duly inform us that implementation failures are largely driven by either inadequate compliance with EU frameworks, or weak administrative capacities to gain access to funding. In this light, cohesion policy is presented as a technocratic process where value decisions are relatively straightforward, and where policymakers come up with the best solutions given cultural, political, and economic constraints. While sociological approaches are more sensitive to normative 'misfits' between international and domestic contexts, they docilely argue that with time policymakers will learn to use the SF not only more efficiently, but also according to a greater European vision. In light of the ongoing infringements and non-compliance apparent even in countries with long-standing membership, the policy-learning arguments fall short on capturing the main reason for the progression of 'backsliding'.

Similarly, the strong determination of MLG scholars to link the devolution of power to more effective policy outputs continues to dwell in a sophisticated theoretical realm, that clings to a rational choice perspective. Writers in this group (Marks, 1993; Hooghe and Marks, 2001; Bulmer, 2005; Bache, 2008) argue that a system of negotiations and compromises works well in democracies which, ideally at least, give voice to a number of groups. Their chief goal is to find ways to keep the system transparent through concerted attempts to ensure that the process of decision-making is as open as possible, and through measures to increase the access to influence for less powerful groups. Again, the assumption is that a wide range of participants, together with the appropriate use of technical knowledge, will result in a satisfactory policy solution. The empirical evidence supporting such claims is scarce, often confined to isolated and overly contextualized case studies. The focus on transparency and 'strength in numbers' fails to identify factors which might structure or constrain partnership relations and their actual voice in SF programming. More importantly, in exposing new forms of network governance (Rhodes, 1996, 1997; Kohler-Koch, 2002; Maggetti and Gilardi, 2014), the literature seems oblivious to the strong role of the national tier in making, maintaining, and empowering policymaking partnerships.

However, the main weakness of cohesion literature is that the analysis rarely ventures beyond legislative commitments and macro-level decision-making processes. This means it fails to shed light on the extremely complex implementation processes, laden with conflicting norms, values, and legitimacy claims. The intricacies remain obscure, and more often than not the outputs and even wider outcomes are attributed to the weakly theorized and largely assumed behaviour of the implementers. More importantly, cohesion scholars fully disconnect implementation from the process of policy formulation under the mistaken assumption that a policy is a straightforward matter of finding technical answers to readily identified problems and generally agreed on solutions.

The main thesis of this book is that in order to fully explain policy outputs the analysis must focus on the implementation process in its entirety. This means that the analysis must be formed before any statutory articulation. In brief, it must start with the very definition of the problem and finish with the articulation of overarching strategies on the ground. As convincingly argued by Bacchi (1996), every policy contains within it an explicit or implicit diagnosis of the 'problem' and such diagnosis effectively structures the implementation process. At the same time, the analysis cannot lose sight of the actors and administrative procedures, which not only interact with such diagnoses but are also constrained by normative claims. Hence by shedding light on the nuances of implementation and building on constructionist approaches to policymaking, this book draws attention to the very questions cohesion scholars consider unessential.

Notes

1 It is important to note that the majority (over 85%) of the 'soft' inclusion projects implemented in convergence regions were supported with the ESF. The ESF focuses on four key areas: increasing the adaptability of workers and enterprises, enhancing access to employment and participation in the labour market, reinforcing social inclusion by combating discrimination and facilitating access to the labour market for disadvantaged people, and promoting partnership for reform in the fields of employment and inclusion.

2 These four areas were eventually incorporated into the EU Framework for National Roma Integration Strategies, to serve as a priority template for the National Roma Integration Strategies to be submitted to the EC by all relevant member states. It is important to note that while the CSF mainly prioritized intervention linked to employment, in the case of Roma inclusion the EC pushed for the development of housing and health initiatives, a conditionality not presented in the supranational framework. In 2010, Regulation No 1080/2006 (Article 7) on the ERDF was modified to permit ERDF financial support for housing interventions in favour of marginalized communities living in the member states that acceded to the EU on or after 1 May 2004. Effectively, €80 million were allocated for housing action in six new member states,

with a strong expectation that funds would be targeted at segregated Roma settlements facing extreme deprivation and marginalization (COM(2009) 382 final).

3 Mainly Council Directive 2000/43/EC of 29 June 2000, implementing the principle of equal treatment between persons irrespective of racial or ethnic origin.

4 The Decade of Roma Inclusion was an initiative of 12 European countries (Albania, Bosnia and Herzegovina, Bulgaria, Croatia, Czech Republic, Hungary, M acedonia, Montenegro, Romania, Serbia, Slovakia, and Spain) to improve the socio-economic status and social inclusion of the Roma minority across the region. The initiative was launched in 2005, with the Decade of Roma Inclusion running from 2005 to 2015, and was the first multinational project in Europe to actively enhance the lives of Roma. The activities introduced under this project, were often fully supported with SF.

5 Although the EU appeared more concerned about the treatment of the Hungarian minority, the situation of the Roma minority was pointed out as an obstacle to Slovak accession (EC, 1998).

6 The 2003, Comprehensive Country Monitoring Report for Slovakia, stated: 'despite continuous efforts across all sectors, the situation of the Roma minority remains very difficult. The majority of the persons belonging to the Roma community are still exposed to social inequalities, social exclusion and widespread discrimination in education, employment, the criminal justice system and access to public services' (EC, 2003a, p. 34).

7 At least two thirds of Slovak Roma live in Central and Eastern Slovakia. The highest concentration of Roma communities is in the Košice and Prešov regions, where Roma represent 26.5% (Košice) and 32.8% (Prešov) of all inhabitants (Kusá, 2011). Districts with a higher proportion of Roma people have above average unemployment, lack of vacancies, less developed transport infrastructure, and less developed public services.

8 Interview #55, 26 July 2011 (Prešov).

9 While with time, the EU began to be more critical of minority treatment in older member states (especially following illegal eviction and deportations of Roma people taking place in France, Italy, and Greece) the new members with substantial Roma populations continue to receive greater scrutiny (O'Nions, 2007; Yıldız and De Genova, 2017).

10 Gender-equality was made a priority under the government of Prime Minister José Luis Rodríguez Zapatero, supported by the Partido Socialista Obrero Español (PSOE) party, and the Autonomous Regions. The Law on Gender Equality passed in 2007 and was supported by all parties in parliament except the conservative Partido Popular (PP). The creation of a Ministry for Equality in 2008 was perhaps the most dramatic move. In addition, new laws and specialist courts on gender violence were developed and the legalization of same sex marriage, a more liberal abortion law, gender mainstreaming in all public organizations, and a new powerful dependency law, were introduced.

11 Interview #74, 1 October 2014 (Granada).

12 The majority of Spanish Roma communities and settlements are concentrated in the southern region of Andalusia (approximately 43% of Spanish Roma). While the living conditions and social status exceeds that experienced by the Roma from Eastern Slovakia, Andalusian Roma continue to be at risk of social exclusion, facing daily discrimination in all vital areas including employment, education, health, and housing.

13 A paramount factor responsible for the acceleration of the EU's attention to the 'Roma question' was the accession of Bulgaria and Romania in 2007. With a large and severely impoverished Roma population, these two countries began to be perceived as a threat to economic and social stability by Western member states. A surge of immigrants from Bulgaria and Romania to Germany, France, the UK, and Spain met with political hostility and an escalating anti-Gypsyism. In face of these developments and the inability of existing policy frameworks to contain, let alone resolve, the issue, the EU was in no position to relinquish its role in facilitating inclusion and anti-discrimination.

14 For absorption and allocation data see: http://insideurope.eu/taxonomy/term/35.

15 It has been demonstrated that the Europeanization of regional development policy triggered several changes in the planning process and led to the partial inclusion of new actors. However, rather unexpectedly the main effect of this was a growing centralization of development policymaking (visible in Slovakia but also Hungary, Poland, and Bulgaria).

16 Spain did not receive pre-accession funds. Although substantial sums were spent on administrative restructuring after the accession, Roma integration entered the Spanish SF agenda only after the 2000 Lisbon Treaty.

17 The programme was designed to encourage dialogue at the local level on equality and inclusion, supporting municipalities and civil society organizations in their efforts to access EU funds, providing technical assistance, and administering cash-flow loans to bridge the gap between expenditure and reimbursement, Making the Most has helped to channel over €50 million of EU funds into more than 700 projects addressing Roma exclusion in CEE countries. The programme was fully operational until 2015.

18 The expansion of the so-called horizontal dimension of the partnership principle should not be seen as a process started or demanded by Roma stakeholders, a perception maintained by some Roma advocates. The changes in cohesion regulations were a result of the unified lobbying efforts of a wide network of civil society organizations, often working in the area of environment sustainability and gender equality. The 1999 reform reinforced the horizontal dimension by expanding the range of partner organizations to 'other competent bodies' as well, primarily equal opportunities and environmental groups (Article 8, Council Regulation 1260/1999). In 2006, the regulation explicitly recognized the role of civil society organizations in partnership arrangements (Article 9, Council Regulation 183/2006).

19 Although official data indicates that the Roma minority constitutes only 2% of the Slovak population, the reality appears very different. So, for instance, the London-based Minority Rights Group NGO estimated the total number of the Roma in Slovakia to be between 480,000 and 520,000 or 9–10% of the entire Slovak population (Liegeois and Gheorghe, 1995). A similar estimate has been provided by the Centre for Strategy and Evaluation Services (CSES, 2011a,b).

3 Theorizing implementation

Cohesion policy is an example of extremely complex decision-making procedures, operating in a multifaceted institutional landscape and adhering to a range of principles, regulations, and interests. The level of complexity has been increasing over successive programme periods, with layers of regulatory requirements and conditions added in each reform phase. While positivist scholars equate SF programming with technocratic decision-making that narrows the scope of political choices (Bache and Olsson, 2001; Olson, 2003; Scott, 1998), constructionist approaches see SF programming as a product of conflicting norms, aims, and power asymmetries (see Hoerner and Stephenson, 2012). Indeed, for Peterson and Bomberg (1999, p. 146) cohesion policy is 'one of the most ambitious, complex and misunderstood areas of EU decision-making'. Despite this complexity, scholarship on cohesion policy remains committed to the parsimonious analysis of macro-level dynamics with the consequence that there are relatively few empirically 'thick' accounts of how cohesion policy is implemented in practice. There is an implicit assumption that once the technocrats agree on and finalize SF programming, the implementation process will follow automatically with the desired results, being close to those expected by the initial decision-makers. This postulation, in large part, accounts for the neglect of the policy implementation process in the models constructed to explain the nature and workings of cohesion policy. Case study analyses aim to fill this gap by stressing the role of 'sufficing' interests and management of European funding on the ground. However, the attention to micro-level managerial dynamics tends to lose sight of wider institutional contexts and normative assertions underpinning strategic design (Linder and Peters, 1987).

The central thesis of this book is that to understand the causes of diverging SF outputs, the analytical inquiry must venture beyond legislative provisions and idiosyncratic managerial tactics. It needs to shed light on the interactions and tensions embedded in implementation processes. Implementation inevitably takes different shapes and forms in different cultures and institutional settings (Hill and Hupe, 2014). In the specific context of cohesion policy, successful implementation is contingent on the compounded effects of strategic planning, the participation of a wide number of stakeholders (both public and private), as well as the ability of the 'centre' to orchestrate a dispersed system of public administration. As such, during the process of policy implementation, tensions tend to be generated between and within three key components: the ideational aspects of policy proposals, the participatory arrangements, and the administrative workings of public bureaucracy. Building on the implementation and governance literature, this chapter explores and amalgamates these three components into an analytical framework, which is then used to examine the role of structure and agency in interpreting, shaping, and importantly contesting the strategic vision of cohesion policy. By clarifying the way discursive elements of policy (the representation of social exclusion) interact with a broad range of agencies nested in various administrative and political constellations, the analysis captures implicit incongruities and conflicting interests, which shape implementation processes. By unpacking the intricacies of SF programming, this chapter illustrates that the political devil is very much in the detail of normative perceptions about the policy aims and administrative handling of ambiguous interests and values. The scrutiny of these 'details' allows for the conceptualizing of ways in which policymakers can minimize tensions and prevent the failure of policy outputs to match policy expectations.

The chapter commences with a review of policy implementation literature, in an effort to analyze key factors, which might affect implementation processes. By merging rational choice and constructivist perspectives, the chapter arrives at a concept of *policy design*, placing it at the centre of the proposed analytical framework. The following section explores theoretical arguments upheld by governance and metagovernance literature about the modern processes of participatory policymaking and the resulting coordinative challenges. It analyzes the relationships that form and unravel in a decentralized and polycentric government. Two additional concepts are introduced, that of *partnership design* and *programmatic synergies*. The last section unveils the tri-dimensional framework arguing for the compounded effect of these three factors on the implementation processes and successful outputs.

Revitalizing implementation theory

Over the last 40 years, the implementation of public policy mandates has been analyzed from different perspectives, representing different research strategies, evaluation standards, concepts, focal areas, and methodologies. As a result, the implementation literature commands little general agreement on a common theoretical perspective (see O'Toole and Mountjoy, 1984). In order to circumvent, at times, a chaotic quest for a grand theory of implementation, scholars argue for the acceptance of theoretical diversity (Robichau and Lynn, 2009). Winter (2005) notes that conceptual clarification and the application of comparative research design (rather than the reliance on single case studies) could be instrumental in sorting out the influence of different implementation variables. Some scholars have argued for synthesizing diverse variables into one expandable model (Matland, 1995; Sabatier, 1988), while others called for incorporating them inside multi-level governance perspective (Robichau and Lynn, 2009). The intellectual pursuit of simplicity has clashed with an increasingly complex nature of public policy. The inductive work by implementation pioneers, Pressman and Wildafsky (1973), demonstrates that implementation processes are affected by a multitude of contextual and shifting factors. Their focus on the 'complexity of joint action' as the key implementation problem, neither relies on a central theoretical framework nor offers a normative perspective on implementation. As such, despite important findings, the methodology is not well suited for comparative research. In the late 1990s, a forerunner of implementation research (Hill, 1997) went as far as to ask whether implementation was 'yesterday's issue'. More than a decade later the answer given to that rhetorical question is a definitive 'no'. The analytical focus on policy implementation can still effectively guide us through the maze of post-legislative processes providing that it loosens up its instrumentalist corset and recognizes that the design of policies is a product of conflicting representations of public problems, as well as contests over basic structures of social organization.

Official templates for action: top-down approaches

Public policy scholars interested in studying the relationship between legislation and administrative behaviour place implementation processes at the centre of their analytical inquiry. Their main assertion is that the legal frameworks bind the behaviour of implementers (Linder and Peters, 1987) and non-compliance results from abstruse instructions rather than the autonomous decisions of the imple-menters (Mazmanian and Sabatier, 1989). Labelled as the 'top-down approach', this strand of research argues that a comprehensive analysis of implementation needs to commence with a specific political decision, usually a statute that is likely to be manipulated by decision-makers at the central level. The atten-tion given to the importance of 'adequate causal theory', a concept coined by Pressman and Wildavsky (1973), prompted scholars to agree on the premise that the analysis of implementation should not be divorced from policy and should not be regarded as a process which takes place after and independently of the policy design (Pressman and Wildavsky, 1973; May, 2003; Winter, 2005). This gave rise to a long line of research, predominately focused on scrutinizing the content and components of official statutes, searching for causal relationships between statu-tory design and its consequences.

The classical top-down analytical model was developed by Mazmanian and Sabatier (1989) who insisted that the analytical focus on statutes is important since 'many of the case studies which form the bulk of the implementation litera-ture become so immersed in the details of programme implementation that they lose sight of the macro-level and political variables, which structure the entire process' (1989, p. 538). In their model, arrival at a desirable policy output is deemed to be influenced by factors such as unambiguous objectives, a clear des-ignation of authority, and the allocation of adequate resources. Mazmanian and Sabatier (1989) also account for a wider context considering the role of the trac-tability of the problems addressed by legislation and social and political relations in determining the course of the implementation process. With time, the design of statutes have become a core variable explored by public policy research, which assumed a control perspective on implementation and refuted the assumption that the realization of stated goals is strongly contingent on the skills and capacities of the implementing bodies (Mazmanian and Sabatier, 1989; Winter, 2005; May, 2003). However, the causal relationship between well-designed and unequivocal statutes and optimal outputs was strongly criticized for providing an overly mechanical and optimistic picture of policymaking. Scholars invested in administrative behaviour began to contest a notion that a clear template for action on its own can orchestrate and restrain a host of interactions involved in realizing official decisions.

Contesting formal decisions: a bottom-up approach

The harshest criticism of the top-down model comes from scholars who argue that an analysis must take a special interest in 'the bottom' of the implementation process, the place where public policies are delivered to citizens or firms (Berman 1978, 1980; Hjern and Hull, 1982, 1987; Bogason, 2000; Lipsky, 1978). The forerunner of the bottom-up implementation perspective, Michael Lipsky, maintains that a more realistic understanding of implementation can be gained by looking at a policy from the view of the public service deliverers. Following his reasoning, Berman (1978) asserts that policy implementation occurs on two levels, at the macro-implementation level, where centrally located actors develop a government programme and at the micro-implementation level, where local administrations react to the central plans by devising their own programmes. Leaning on insights from the principal-agent theory (March and Simon, 1958), Berman avows that politicians and administrative managers have extremely limited control over front-line staff, a situation driven by different interests and asymmetrical information. Other bottom-uppers point out that the contextual factors within the implementing environment can completely dominate rules created at the top of the implementation pyramid, thus undermining policy designers' control of the entire process (Palumbo et al., 1984).

The bottom-up perspective turns the policy process upside-down, arguing that the goals, strategies, and activities of the actors involved in the micro-implementation process must be carefully analyzed in order to understand implementation and predict its outputs (Weatherley and Lipsky, 1977; Bogason, 2000). The findings of extensive empirical work conducted by Benny Hjern (1982) and his colleagues (Hjern and Hull, 1985, 1987) show that central initiatives are often poorly adapted to the local conditions. They argued that the success of a programme largely depends on the ability of local actors and implementation bodies to adapt policy design to local conditions. Bogason (2000) adds that local-level implementers need a certain degree of autonomy in order to adapt the programme to local conditions, as without such a leeway for action the programme is likely to fail. Such a stance contradicts the assumptions and arguments of top-down researchers, reinforcing scepticism about the possibility of developing a single theory of implementation that is context-free (Maynard-Moody et al., 1990; Bogason, 2000).

While we should not discount the concerns offered by advocates of the bottom-up approach, as they bring forward local perspectives so often neglected in macro-level analyses, their conceptualization of local autonomy tends to be exaggerated. Bottom-up scholars, busy tracing local decisions and behavioural patterns, pay limited attention to the strength of control mechanisms wielded by the central governments, an issue particularly pertinent when analyzed against democratic accountability. In a democratic system, policy control is exercised by actors whose power derives from their accountability to sovereign voters. Hence, while service providers may receive discretion over official objectives, it still occurs within a context of central control. Linder and Peters (1987) point out that the existence of flexibility and autonomy at the local level is often incorporated into the statutory design, thus it should not be considered an 'uncontrollable factor' beyond the reach and understanding of central officials. They further argue that while central actors do not act in detail or intervene in specific cases, they do structure the goals and strategies of implementing bodies and front-line agencies. As such, the institutional setting, the available resources and access to implementing arenas are determined centrally. Moreover, the incentives (positive and negative) provided by central policymakers can effectively restrain local goals and interests, especially if they differ substantially from those stipulated by the legislative provisions (Weaver, 2009). Thus, even when implementation bodies and service deliverers are prone to 'suffice' and act upon their own interests (and capacities), their behaviours remains strongly bounded by protocols and incentives embedded in the policy design.

Synthesizing implementation models

Most scholars now agree that some convergence of these two perspectives is necessary for the field to develop. While the top-down analysis provides a framework for exploring the structuring effects of overarching strategies, the bottom-up model brings attention to the role of autonomy implementers enjoy. In the context of SF programming, these dynamics unravel simultaneously. While implementation appears to rest in the hands of sub-national actors (in line with the subsidiarity principle), the strategic provisions and official regulations do severely curtail local flexibility (a situation criticized by the cohesion stakeholders themselves). Hence, it is not uncanny to assume that the design of SF programming (especially if equipped with clear aims, adequate policy tools, and the designation of authority) will indeed bind the behaviour of implementers, while at the same time being contested by interests nested in various organizational settings. The challenge thus lies in capturing where (in the process of implementation) the contestations are more likely to take place, and who has the power to significantly defy or alter the official plan for action. Simultaneously, it is important to locate and understand spaces where cooperation and compromise form and persist. Governance literature provides useful analytical insights for scrutinizing these dynamics, which this chapter discusses below.

First, however, it is important to point out that both the top-down and bottom-up models continue to take the statutory language as their starting point, thus failing to consider the significance of actions taken earlier in the policymaking process (Nakamura and Smallwood, 1980). The centrality of legislation in the analysis arguably stems from the fundamental assumption that there is a best collective decision over public interests that can be rationally and analytically determined and implemented if the correct, neutral procedures are stipulated and followed (Dudley and Vidovich, 1995). This assumption is based on a positivist epistemology, endorsing the view that there is a real world, which is accessible to objective description and analysis. Intrinsically, value decisions appear to be relatively straightforward as normative differences of opinion are assumed to be sorted out through processes of negotiations, bargaining, and compromise (Dimock, 1958). However, the view that policymaking is a technical process (corrupted only by self-serving local interests) fails to account for the conflicting values pervading important social problems, which instrumental action cannot always resolve (Drysek, 1990).

A constructionist approach to implementation

Implementation scholars critical of the rational choice approach to policymaking have expanded the analytical focus from rational instrumentality to political interests and values underpinning policy design (among others, Kingdon, 1984; Béland, 2005; Bleich, 2002; Campbell, 2002; Hall, 1993; Lascoumes and Le Gale, 2007). The pioneer of policy formulation studies, John Kingdon, compellingly argues that the formulation of strategies does not always follow a rational comprehensive model, whereby policymakers define their goals clearly and canvass many (ideally all) alternatives that might achieve these goals. Instead, he asserts that policy formulation is often driven by political ideologies, institutional values, or external pressures that dictate what needs to be done and how (1984, p. 93). In that sense, normative convictions about 'what needs to be done' are likely to inform the selection of policy action plans, even with the absence of the thorough empirical assessment of their efficacy and impacts. This, in turn, may result in policy proposals that overlook or in fact purposely omit local experiences and needs, as decision-makers far removed from the local context endorse ideological courses of action. Hence, it is crucial to start the analysis of implementation processes by unpacking the ideational aspect of policies, turning the lens towards different representations of public problems articulated in official documents.

This line of inquiry, which calls for scrutiny of public problems, lies at the core of the social constructionist approach which challenges the presumed objective status of scientific knowledge (Backhouse, 1996). When applied to public policy, social constructionism negates the assumptions held by public choice implementation literature that societal problems are readily identifiable and can be studied and addressed objectively (Holstein and Miller, 1993). Instead, the emphasis is placed on the role of subjective ideas and active learning in shaping (or constructing) policy information about real-world problems (Bacchi, 1999; Edelman, 1985; Goodwin, 1996; Kooiman, 2003; Fischer, 1990). The assumption put forward is that the articulation of public problems rarely stems from clearly identified situations or explicit public demands. Instead, the identification process is strongly contingent on perceptions (Kooiman, 2003) or political biases (Edelman, 1985). Goffman (1974) refers to this phenomenon as 'framing', a concept implying that articulated problems are not simple descriptions of reality but specific representations that give meaning to reality. The basic premise refutes the notion that different individuals can observe the same social and natural phenomena and necessarily arrive at similar conclusions. Bacchi's (1999) 'what's the problem' approach teases out the presupposition in competing interpretations of social conditions, arguing that: 'every postulated solution has built into it a particular representation of what the problem is, and it is these representations and their implications that need to be discussed' (1999, p. 21). In Ness Goodwin's (1996, p. 67) words, policies are framed 'not as a response to existing conditions and problems, but more as a discourse in which both problems and solutions are created'. It is not to say that disturbing social conditions do not exist, rather that they are *constructed* by policy actors, themselves driven by cognitive and moral maps dominating a given policy sphere (Bacchi, 1999). A scrutiny of these processes unveil the implications which flow from the shape of claims made about identified situations or public demands.

While the analysis of problem representations allows for a greater reflection upon the way in which attention to 'social problems' generates particular courses of action, on its own, it provides little insight into the actual interworking of the implementation processes. In many ways, the analysis condenses once problem representations have been located and scrutinized inside the postulated solutions. The questions left unexplored are why some policies are easier to implement than others, and why implementation gaps persist in particular policy fields. To overcome this lapse, *Financing Roma Inclusion with European Structural Funds* proposes a concept of *policy design* that captures both the discursive and instrumental aspect of policy implementation. Policy design is understood as a fundamental policy decision being put in motion, which indicates the articulation of problem(s), stipulated objectives, and priorities to be pursued, and allocated tools for their realization. The assumption here is that policy implementation is a strategic and instrumental process. However, the main conflicts are not confined to who favours or resists a particular policy initiative, but how initiatives are shaped by problem representations. Hence, the analysis of implementation outputs commences with the deconstruction of established frames, which policymakers mobilize in discussions about social and Roma exclusion. Since the very concept of social exclusion is vague and prone to politicization, there is a need to review theoretical debates about its various forms and interpretations (provided in Chapter 4). As argued by Gusfield (1989), the very use of terms like 'social problems' or 'social exclusion' portrays its subjects as 'sick' or as 'troublesome', thus individualizing causal factors and precluding any understanding of social problems as systemic. Such rhetoric can have a detrimental effect on the legitimacy, as well as sustainability, of SF interventions.

At the same time, the framework emphasizes the role of clear-cut policy design (in this case SF programming) in structuring implementation outputs. The assumption is that a realization of policies (no matter how they frame public problems) is dependent on a detailed action plan, which specifies objectives, allocates budget, designates responsibility, and so on. Moreover, without proper implementation tools (i.e. budgetary allocations) even the best intentions are likely to fail – or remain at the strictly symbolic level. The same logic can be applied in reverse; even the most detailed action plan is unlikely to deliver effective and legitimate programmes if the interests of those unwilling to challenge the status quo are used to frame public problems. Hence, the concept of policy design, as used in this book, merges the contentions put forward by rational choice and constructivist scholars to reveal the assumptions made about the nature of the problem in a postulated solution and the technicalities of the implementation processes.

As explained in Chapter 2, few studies place policy design at the centre of the analysis of cohesion policy and look at how overarching actions plans structure the implementation processes. Somewhat surprisingly, the inquiries neither problematize the way cohesion stakeholders define Roma exclusion[1] nor deconstruct the adopted solutions.[2] The preserved impression is that once adopted the SF programming reflects the 'real' needs and interests of target groups and communities (under the assumption that these groups provide extensive input during the formulation stage). There is a widely held notion among international and domestic stakeholders (including the EC) that problems facing Roma communities have been clearly mapped-out and plausible solutions have been coherently discussed and to some degree agreed upon (e.g. in the EU Framework for National Roma Integration Strategies up to 2020). While new voices criticize this stance, (Surdu, 2016; McGarry, 2017; Law and Kovats, 2018) it is common for policy analysts to view policy design as an 'objective' analysis of public concerns and ascribe implementation failure to local mismanagement or the incapacity of excluded groups to improve their living conditions. Policy design challenges these perceptions by showing that policymakers often construct public problems to suit a specific political agenda and propose solutions based on the prevailing norms and value systems. This book argues that ineffective policy outputs might, in fact, be driven by the articulation of the situation of Roma people as an individualized 'social problem', which in turn legitimizes a set of interventions not conducive to systemic change.

Agency within a decentralized system of governance

While policy design highlights the role of ideas and norms in shaping implementation processes, it glosses over agency and the way various actors contest or champion proposed action plans. Much of the implementation literature remains anchored in a set of public administration theories that portray government agencies as tightly structured hierarchies insulated from market forces and from effective citizen pressure. Even bottom-up theorists, more interested in the role of front-line workers, have not fully unpacked the hermetic chain of command, implicitly accepting the vertical dimension of policymaking. Such methodology renders inherent power asymmetries and the disenfranchisement of certain voices in the political arena invisible. Not surprisingly, this oversight undermined the validity of implementation theory in explaining complexities inherent to a decentralized system of governance (Russell, 2015). Today a coherent analysis of policy outputs cannot succumb to the luxury of treating implementation as a hermetic process, sealed from 'outside' influences and diverse interests. The input of new partners and delivery agencies raises new questions about effective governance (informed policies) as well as the legitimacy of new forms of representation and delivery methods. Hence, any thorough analysis of policy implementation must shed light on these participatory dynamics now embedded in a complex and multi-level system of modern governance. Power dispersion and the growing influence of third-party actors sit at the core of governance scholarship. A review of the main arguments posed by governance literature is vital for conceptualizing agency and placing it in the analytical framework proposed by this book.

Breaking down the hierarchy

The majority of public policy commentators have agreed that traditional forms of top-down government are undergoing a dramatic change, especially in advanced economies, but also in many parts of the developing world. Globalization and the pluralization of service provision are the driving forces behind these changes. Policy problems faced by governments are increasingly complex, disjointed, and global, rather than simple, linear, and national in focus. In the context of the progressive fragmentation of socio-economic interests, it ceased to be possible for the state to govern without the cooperation and input of other actors. New spaces have therefore opened-up for mobilizing the knowledge, skills, and resources of a variety of actors. Salamon (2000, p. 1613) called this new policymaking landscape 'a system of third-party governance, in which crucial elements of public authority are shared with a host of non-governmental and administrative actors, frequently in complex collaborative systems'. In a way, the administration of public problems has leapt beyond the borders of public agencies and embraced a wide assortment of parties that have become intimately involved in the public's business. This shift required a fundamental rethinking of government roles in coping with and addressing public problems.

The analysis of new forms of governance has been conducted by scholars with radically different normative stances on the role of government, which resulted in a disparate scholarly discourse (Rhodes, 1997; Stoker, 1998; Osborne, 2001; Salamon, 2000; Newman, 2001; Kooiman, 2003; Swyngedouw, 2005; Geddes, 2006; Pierre and Peters, 2000). While some scholars contend that the governments should maintain some level of control over decentralization through steering the complex networks of interactions (Osborne and Gaebler, 1992), others theorize on the possibility of governing without government (Rhodes, 1996). The new-found faith in liberal economic theories argues for the application of private-sector managerial techniques to public bureaucracies, a vision that nourished the rise of New Public Management (McLaughlin et al., 2002). Despite disagreements about 'the best way of governing public affairs', at its core governance scholarship nurtured an all-pervading view that the devolution of power is a miracle cure for all ills generated by sluggish, centralized bureaucracies and their hierarchical chain of command. Normative inquiries of this type constrain a more critical inquiry into the actual effects devolution has on policy outputs. Hence, questions regarding the effectiveness and legitimacy of the new forms of governance remained driven by ideologically charged interpretations, which are rarely empirically tested on the ground.

New public governance: implementation within a pluralist framework

The emergence of new public governance (NPG) literature marks a shift in the way the devolution of power arrangements is now analyzed. Posed as a response to 'disillusion with excessively disembodied neoliberal market forces' (Jessop, 2004), the NPG paradigm proposes a 'third way' approach for understanding contemporary policymaking (Osborne, 2010). The attention given to issues of legitimacy and the instrumentality of new cooperative arrangements has moved the analysis closer to implementation scholarship. The analytical lens is placed on the manner in which the congestion of various interests and norms affects the implementation process (Peters and Pierre, 2004; Olsson, 2003). Methodologically, NPG prioritizes the exploration of both the efficacy, as well as the limitations, of the decentralized regime. It aims to identify specific models the dispersion of power should take in order to enhance implementation processes – both in terms of their effectiveness and legitimacy.

Governance scholarship establishes various normative modes of 'good governance', including joined-up governance, network governance, co-production, and cooperation, all considered as suitable alternatives to the privatization of public service provision, particularly in the realm of social policy. The focus on the active participation of citizens and local communities is put forward as an 'optimal tool' for addressing the accountability deficit and delivering legitimate public interventions reflective of local needs and expectations (Michels and De Graaf, 2010). The NPG scholars appear in agreement that in all its forms partnership with social actors fosters policy learning (through knowledge exchange), generates innovation and allows for the amalgamation of resources needed to deliver comprehensive and well-informed programmes (Taylor, 2007; McQuaid, 2010). Additionally, partnership with social actors is presented as having the capacity to address concerns about the democratic deficit by re-engaging citizens with the institutions of government and contributing to a higher degree of legitimacy of decisions taken at the centre (Bekkers et al., 2007).

NPG theorists also pay extensive attention to the way new modes of governance can tackle social exclusion and promote empowerment of marginalized groups. Finn (2000) asserts that by engaging local stakeholders with expertise providing a social inclusion service and experience working with particularly disadvantaged client groups, governments can expand the reach, diversity, and quality of social interventions. Others add, that by sharing decision-making, budgets, and responsibilities at the planning stage, public authorities could engender a sense of shared ownership of the delivered services, and legitimize official goals among hard to reach groups and communities (McQuaid, 1999; Blunkett, 2003). The promotion of societal knowledge and resource inputs lays at the core of these assumptions, which share a vision of empowered and active communities, where people increasingly do things for themselves and the state supports and enables citizens to invest their grassroots expertise in policymaking. In the realm of theoretical debates, partnership is, in fact, constructed as a key variable for 'empowering' local constituencies and excluded groups, with that adding to the quality of pluralist democracy and maximizing the appropriateness, quality, and legitimacy of policies. It could be argued that the analytical shift towards 'people' and normative reflection on the value of public input aims to remedy the failure of austerity policies in addressing financial meltdown, which hit the world economy in 2007–2008. Based on a flawed theory of the role of budget deficits, which neglects their relation to private-sector debt, austerity created a system characterized by unequally shared sacrifice and growing discontent (Kelton, 2015). As such, the analysis of 'good governance' began to conceptualize ways in which governments could move away from debt-reduction strategies and put more emphasis on deep reforms, more informed by public demands and perspectives (Krugman, 2013).

Critiquing the ideals of participatory governance

Nevertheless, not all governance theorists support what they call the 'idealized normative model' of participatory governance. Alberta Sbragia (1992) has long argued that MLG with its non-hierarchical networks continues to be highly constrained by territorial affinities and legislative mandates. Empirical studies confirm these concerns, showing that sub-national activities in all phases of the policy-cycle remain tightly structured by a carefully choreographed inter-tier play directed by the centre (or region, in a federalist context) (Stevens et al., 1998: Geddes, 2006; Taylor, 2007). Shirlow and Murtagh (2004, p. 60) show that policies and programmes formulated with the input of community organizations are more tied to the priorities of the state than to the primacies of the local people. The work by Geddes (2006) and Taylor (2007) demonstrates that local involvement in new governance spaces is most often confined to 'micro-politics', while strategic issues (i.e. social inclusion, urban planning) remain outside their control. Swyngedouw (2005, p. 1994), in turn, argues that the predisposition of governance literature to imply a common purpose and framework of shared values ignores the contradictory tensions in which most forms of governance are embedded, often imposed against a background of widespread mistrust and without accountability. Similarly, Newman and Gittell (2001) criticize governance discourse for neglecting to address issues of power, agency, and the fundamental inequalities in bargaining positions. They argue that consolidated 'interest boundaries' are not conducive to the creation of partnership with groups far removed from the sphere of influence. Their research identifies instances where the dispersion of power and responsibility actually reinforced hierarchies and masked underlying power relations.

Peters and Pierre (2004) further challenge the assumption that collaboration offers the most effective response to public policy dilemmas by highlighting the intrinsic trade-off between efficiency and democratic decision-making. They raise questions regarding the extent to which public bureaucracies and politicians are in fact interested in utilizing local knowledge and resources. Geddes (2006) argues that the willingness of the ruling elites to cede power or foster empowerment continues to be extremely weak. Empirical research stubbornly evidences resistance to community participation and the propensity to rely on standard operating procedures and consolidated bureaucratic norms (Stevens et al., 1998; Taylor, 2007; Coaffee and Healey, 2003). Researchers working on community empowerment often argue that where communities are given entitlement and status, it is often only a minority of acceptable voices that get heard – and often these are not the ones most accountable to the public they supposedly represent (Trehan, 2001; Kröger, 2008; Geddes, 2006). This dynamic often stems from the confinement of interactive processes to a dominant value system (i.e. active employment policies). In this understanding, new voices that hold a radically different perception of public problems and offer unprecedented solutions are likely to be barred from decision-making processes. Geddes (2006) further asserts that partnership is often used to off-load responsibilities over service delivery and policy performance onto the local agents without actually allowing for the creation of a high-quality pluralist system of governance. In this way empowerment becomes a simple co-option of local agents, placing them at the service of the ruling elites.

Governing implementation

While there is little agreement on the relationship between the devolution of power and effective policies, few scholars contest the ongoing decentralization and dismantling of hierarchical systems of governance. Hence, any analysis of implementation processes needs to be placed in a context of an ever-increasing number of actors partaking in policymaking, in different configurations and at different stages. The focus on the way agency interacts with official statutes is particularly important in the domain of cohesion policy, which explicitly mandates a wider participation in policymaking through the partnership principle (Bachtler and Mendez, 2007). However, rather than succumbing to the normative view of partnership as a driving force of legitimate and well-informed policies, a more critical approach needs to be undertaken. The analysis must recognize that partnership in SF settings (but also in other policy areas) is not a straightforward mechanism for capturing local knowledge and expertise, but a highly politicized process, which is often enacted to manipulate perceptions about the aim of devolution and competency of the actors involved.

Research has shown that in the context of cohesion policy the centre continues to play a decisive role in legitimizing and facilitating access to partnership (Harlow and Rawlings, 2014). This book takes a similar stand, arguing that central governments develop, dispense, and legitimize mechanisms, which foster, exploit, or maintain partnership relations with local and non-state actors. Who is 'allowed' to participate is not only contingent on the lobbying power and capacity of those making demands, but also on the way governments frame public issues and enable participation of less powerful interests. As such, partnerships are likely to reflect domestic political interests and power asymmetries (with all their inherent tensions). In order to see the impact, these partnerships have on the implementation outputs we first need to scrutinize how the authorities interact with actors traditionally excluded from policymaking processes and public debates (e.g. socially excluded Roma communities). The proposed analytical framework puts forward a concept of *partnership design*, which captures the way central policymakers envision and realize participatory arrangements. The focus rests on mechanisms of participation, which vary along three important dimensions: who participates, through what means, and how different voices are linked with public action (Fung, 2006). Different areas of this institutional design space are more and less suited to influence implementation processes and contribute to legitimate, sustainable, and effective outputs. Chapter 5 will explore these influences empirically, with the aim of identifying arrangements, which are most likely to deliver successful outputs.

While the EC has deemed participatory processes crucial for transforming community voices into policy action (EC, 2013b), it provides little pragmatic guidance on how member states should include excluded voices. The incessant disenfranchisement of Roma minorities from policymaking challenges theoretical contentions that the dispersion of power automatically facilitates the empowerment of marginalized communities. Far more often, community participation takes place in the 'shadow of hierarchy', being nested on the fringes of the governance infrastructure. Yet, discussions regarding Roma inclusion in the context of cohesion policy have rarely critically analyzed the role of central government in facilitating quality partnerships with disenfranchised communities. The majority of scholars invested in Romani studies tend to focus either on the impact the 'Europeanization' of Roma issues has on a state's actions or on the role of ethnic mobilization and Roma agency at the local level (i.e. the way NGOs interact with local authorities to implement policies and funding schemes). While commentators often point out that 'political will' is a leading factor in either promoting or hindering effective Roma inclusion policies, the concept itself has rarely been operationalized and juxtaposed against the growing Roma activism. Thus, the shape and impact of mechanisms used by national governments to engage (or disengage) minority groups in policymaking remain undertheorized. At the same time, the organizational capacity of Roma communities and the legitimacy of Roma representation continues to generate polarized responses with few scholars examining the actual relationship between the presence of Roma people in partnership arrangements and policy outputs (legitimate representation of Roma people in policymaking will be discussed in detail in Chapter 5). A common argument that ethnic mobilization is a necessary component of legitimate policies targeted at marginalized communities (Jovanović, 2013) often disregards the complexity of modern governance and the need to conflate policy expertise with community-based knowledge. The concept of *partnership design* is more attentive to the gatekeeping strategies developed by the centre to manage the shape and purpose of partnership, and the way these are challenged or exploited by Roma communities and their representatives.

Coordinating complexity

Progressive decentralization of public governance is based on a normative idea that solving public problems is a combined responsibility of the different tiers of government (including the supranational level), the market, and civil society – be it in different and shifting combinations of interactions between actors and institutions within and between them (Kooiman, 2003). The very complexity of these interactions implies that new forms of public management and bureaucratic oversight are necessary to assure the effective implementation of policies. Not surprisingly, in a highly bureaucratized system of cohesion policy, calls for streamlining, administrative modernization, and long-term planning are lodged within supranational and national regulatory frameworks. The assertion is that member states need to provide direction to the administrative system; a direction that would at once maintain the virtues that have been produced by delegated and devolved forms of governing and secure central direction and control. In this setting, it is acceptable to assume that the type of managerial strategy member states adopt will influence and structure the implementation processes. Yet, the concepts of *policy design* and *partnership design* do not fully account for the specific relation between implementation outputs and administrative coordination. In fact, the implementation literature often implies that coordination of a decentralized public sector takes place almost automatically as long as policy design is clear and partnerships work in a framework of shared values and common purposes (Rhodes, 1996; Mazmanian and Sabatier, 1989). The self-coordination hypothesis appears exaggerated especially when juxtaposed against empirical research showing that policymaking is prone to departmentalization and working in silos, which in themselves are often linked to policy failure (Froy and Giguère, 2010; OECD, 2009; Dingeldey et al., 2017). To address these dynamics and their impact on implementation outputs the analytical framework proposed in this book accounts for coordinative strategies adopted by member states to harmonize SF programming with the wider workings of public administration. The literature on metagovernance provides relevant insights on the governability and effective oversight of complex institutional inter-workings.

Metagovernance: the need for oversight

An overarching argument of metagovernance scholars is that some form of 'steering' is indispensable for effective policymaking and programme delivery (Mueleman, 2008; Bell and Park, 2006; Sorenson, 2006). This stands in contrast to Rhodes' (1996) 'governance without government' conception, which rejects the need for the overt involvement of public bureaucracies in service delivery. The metagovernance approach takes the involvement of government not only as given (and unavoidable) but also as necessary for securing the stability and long-term strategic focus of public interventions. McGinis contends that despite the consolidation of 'polycentric governance' (1999, p. 6) the state is still the most central and omnipresent governance actor that steers and controls public activities from local to international levels. Müller and Wright (1994, p. 1) assert: 'while the state may be in retreat in some respects, its activity may be increasing in others. And nowhere has its key decision-making role been seriously undermined'. What the metagovernance literature brings forward is the idea that to maintain its influence the state must master a host of different technologies for public intervention, each with its own decision rules, rhythms, agents, and challenges. Public administrators must weigh a far more elaborate set of considerations in deciding not just whether, but also how to act, and then how to achieve some accountability for the results.

Moreover, the literature stretches the rationale for steering beyond a rather intuitive supposition that some degree of leadership is required to orchestrate a complex system of interactions. It accounts for the complexity of modern problems and the need for addressing their different aspects and causes (Lindsay et al., 2008). Kooiman notes that:

> No single actor, public or private has all knowledge and information required to solve complex, dynamic and diversified problems; no actor has sufficient overview to make the application of needed instruments effective; no single actor has sufficient action potential to dominate unilaterally in a particular governing model.
>
> (1993, p. 4)

Due to this limitation, there is an intrinsic need to unite administrative efforts and 'normalize' cross-sector coordination. Such efforts facilitate the delivery of multipurpose and complementary services, limit inefficient overlaps, and streamline multifarious bureaucratic protocols. What is central to such arguments is that effective policy outputs are conditioned upon the ability of central authorities to set common direction and provide tools for cementing inter-sectorial, inter-departmental synergies. This is particularly important in the context of cohesion policy, characterized by a multi-level *modus operandi*, which merge domestic policymaking cultures with (imposed) EU regulations.

The metagovernance perspective also draws attention to the ongoing internationalization of national policymaking, whereby supranational organizations exert concrete influence over national and sub-national policymaking. Surprisingly, top-down implementation scholars have paid scarce attention to the 'presence' of supranational imperatives inside the national statutes or to the reality that nationally provided public goods such as human rights or labour standards have essentially become globalized (Kaul et al., 2003; Kaul, 2005).[3] An increasingly transnational character of public problems has, according to Stone (2004, p. 38), provided the rationale for 'research collaboration, information sharing, and cooperation', which accelerated the diffusion of ideas and policy transfer. Interaction processes among various actors in international politics are now more frequent and intense, giving rise to what Ladeur (2004, p. 5) refers to as 'flexible institutions' taking place beyond the state. In the case of the EU and the member states' relations, the opportunities to lead the policy process are provided for both domestic actors and international agencies. As such, the transfer does not simply occur in a unilateral hierarchical process from supranational to national to sub-national, but is ongoing and multidirectional, characterized by 'overlapping areas of policy, norms, values, power relations, and social interaction, where actors are not confined to a single scale' (Macrae, 2006, p. 528). Hence, the comprehensive orchestration of such an environment is vital for assuring that EU policies fit with and reinforce domestic legislation.

Examining a coordinative toolkit

Much of the traditional management within the public sector has been conducted within individual programmes and organizations, and even when successful in improving individual performance, it has rarely managed to add value to the overall functioning of an entire governing apparatus (Scharpf, 1994). This arguably takes place because each individual organization and programme tends to pursue its own goals, often at the expense of broader systemic objectives. Scharpf (1994) convincingly argues that enhanced performance within a single organization actually reduces the overall performance of a system. Metagovernance scholars are optimistic that the pathology of organizational self-interests can be eliminated through strategic management, which can coordinate organizations around principal goals, set for the political system and the society as a whole (Torfing and Triantafillou, 2011; Peters, 2010). They caution, however, that strategic management should refrain from specifying the exact means for achieving those goals. Peters (2010) observes that establishing goals and then permitting choices about attaining them provides substantial controls over policy directions, and the style of implementation, while at the same time preserving some aspects of the autonomy of organizations and networks. In his argumentation, this at once strengthens compliance with central initiatives and allows for the tailoring of public intervention to local needs.

Nevertheless, devising a means to realize common objectives requires strong organizational capacities, expertise, and discretion. Hence, allotting managerial control to individual agencies and organizations is constructed as another important element of coordination, in particular, the control and management of public budgets. Bell and Park (2006) argue that public budgeting has been reformed to provide managers with a greater latitude in making decisions about the use of money. What is now known as 'bulk budgeting' provides managers with a global budget, which they can use freely to make their programmes perform well, within the bounds of the law. According to Scott (1998), this curtails an 'offloading' dynamic, whereby implementation bodies are asked (or are expected) to deliver complex programmes, working with heavily constrained budgets and rigid bureaucratic protocols. In this manner, managerial control reinforces compliance with an overarching action plan and secures the flexibility needed to realize it according to local needs. Managerial control also extends to other basic inputs in the policymaking system. For example, controlling personnel allocations can be viewed as a simple source of control over individual organizations albeit perhaps not as direct as it might have been when a greater share of the public sector's activity was provided directly by career public servants (Salamon, 2000).

While strategic management that facilitates substantial control over day-to-day administration can indeed compel (or simply ease) organizational complicity with grander policy objectives, it is unlikely to dramatically streamline organizational values and norms. In a complex governing system where the acceptance and legitimacy of formal rule have decreased, reliance on 'softer' tools is deemed necessary. A concept of 'soft law' championed by Europeanization scholars highlights the role of shared norms and values in generating effective governance (Mörth, 2004). Smismans (2008) argues that soft law is one of the cheapest and most effective incentives in coordinating policymaking in an environment marked by the absence of formal authority. According to him, when the overseers can shape the values and the incentives to which the individuals making decisions respond, then the desired outcomes can be reached with little investment of resources, and with a continuing effect. Undeniably, public values shared within the public sector itself, are not easily extendable to other structures involved in policymaking and service delivery (i.e. supranational organizations, civil society, markets). However, Moore (1995) insists that precisely this extension of 'public' values to devolved structures may strengthen the alignment of programmatic purposes, increase the exchange of information, and produce approaches that are more comprehensive. Discussions regarding soft law strongly reflect ideas of constructivist scholars, who argue that a shared understanding of programmes and their purpose among different actors can shape and secure effective and legitimate policy outputs.

Concerted effort

In the context of cohesion policy, strategic coordination is particularly important given the manifold administrative environment. While it is the member states who design SF programming they do so by following procedures and regulations derived from the EU. To accommodate supranational programmes, member states establish a specific managerial infrastructure (e.g. MAs, Monitoring Committees (MCs)) that specializes in European administration and operates according to a specific set of rules not always reflective of domestic administrative apparatus. As such, there are often inherent incongruities between national/local and supranational 'ways of doing things'. To avoid conflicts of interests, overlaps, and the duplication of procedures, administrative synergies between SF programming, and domestic policies are deemed necessary.

As shown above, coordination is not a self-organizing process, but one that requires a strong input from the central authorities (i.e. the allocation of managerial tools) and the creation of a shared system of values or norms. The latter might be difficult, considering the pervasive path-dependencies characterizing modern bureaucracies and continuing predisposition of working within an organizational value system.[4] Thus, it is important to scrutinize the efforts undertaken by the centre to coordinate and synergize SF programming with domestic action plans. The central authorities develop an overarching strategy for action while making sure that the subordinate bodies have no reasons to resist it and are capable of realizing the posed objectives in an efficient and effective manner. How this is achieved and to what degree can have far-reaching effects, not only on the quality of delivered SF projects but also on policy convergence and social cohesion. An analytical focus on *programmatic synergy* captures the institutionalization of coordination, including its purpose and structuring effect.

Programmatic synergy is the last dimension of the proposed analytical framework. It is conceptualized as the coordinative efforts undertaken by central authorities to orchestrate a multi-level bureaucratic apparatus, with the goal of linking SF programming design (norms and instruments, including partnerships) with the domestic bureaucratic *modus operandi*. Although attention is paid to the type of instruments used for synergizing SF programming with domestic policies, the analytical focus rests on the way domestic stakeholders interpret the purpose and aim of SF programming in order to disclose how they exploit the 'added value' of cohesion policy. The aim is to unveil whether domestic decision-makers use SF to reinforce domestic policies and approaches, or whether they are more prone to exploit exogenous funding for purposes not necessarily reflective of domestic policies (i.e. fully innovative initiatives). The main argument is that political reluctance to see the auxiliary character of EU funding and proclivity to craft novel programmes not linked to domestic initiatives, hinders coordinative schemes, resulting in bureaucratic congestion or departmentalization. While innovative approaches in themselves could promote needed changes to the status quo, in the context of SF programming the probability of such a dynamic is relatively low. What needs acknowledging is that the coordinative mechanisms are highly diverse and political elites have different traditions of 'steering' complex administrative environments. Thus, it is important to engage in normative debates on joined-up governance and explore the trade-off between synergy and innovation (these are explored in Chapter 6).

The shape and impact of administrative coordination in a multi-level system of governance have not been thoroughly analyzed in the context of SF programming. While cohesion policy scholarship and Europeanization research pay extensive attention to domestic factors, the focus falls predominately on the transposition of directives, domestic political interests, and resource dependencies (Beyers, 2004; Beyers and Kerremans, 2007). In general, implementation problems have been ascribed to non-compliance or non-capacity, while factors such as weak coordinative traditions or administrative imbroglios have been largely glossed over. Researchers working on Roma integration pay even less attention to administrative coordination, instead focusing on issues pertaining to local capacities and micro-level political factors. In these accounts, the ineffectiveness of SF outputs is often presented as a product of political hostility towards the Roma people or an inability of the localities to absorb available funding. The focus on programmatic synergy challenges the above claims, by demonstrating that diverging implementation outputs are often driven by administrative factors, largely disconnected from political variables, such as compliance or political will.

Applying the framework

Financing Roma Inclusion with European Structural Funds contends that to gain a germane understanding of the workings of cohesion policy the implementation process needs to be thoroughly scrutinized. Only by dissecting the complexity of policy implementation, which takes place in a decentralized and congested system of modern governance, can we gain insight into what drives policy success or contributes to policy failure. For that purpose, the book offers a three-pillar analytical framework, which incorporates key factors that structure implementation processes and determine their outputs. Inferred from discussions and arguments presented by the implementation and governance literature, these factors are conceptualized as *policy design*, *partnership design*, and *programmatic synergies*. The decision to settle on these three features (or pillars) stems from the complex character of cohesion policy, the ambiguity of goals it aims to achieve (social inclusion), the institutionalization of participatory arrangements, and the tailoring of supranational procedures to domestic standards. It is difficult to fathom that a parsimonious model can thoroughly address these dynamics. It is also implausible that the ideational dimension will have a greater impact on policy outputs than participatory or coordinative arrangements. Therefore, this book brings the role of ideas, agency, and procedures together and researches them empirically.

The framework leans towards a top-down approach under an assumption that overarching strategies are tangible blueprints for policy action, able to shape the behaviour of implementers and policy stakeholders. However, rather than focusing strictly on the 'instrumental' aspect of the design (clear objectives and the availability of tools) it also examines the structuring potential of normative ideas and the framing of public problems (social exclusion). This book argues that the central decision-makers, who ascribe to certain ideological convictions, are actively involved in constructing policy knowledge about Roma exclusion. Resulting problem representations not only determine which policy tools will be used and by whom, but from the very start can hinder (or ease) successful outputs. Nevertheless, as argued before, the central policymakers are now expected to work in partnership with a wide variety of actors. While the centre continues to act as a potent gatekeeper, the input of third-party actors must not be belittled. Who is able to participate and how is likely to have a considerable impact on implementation processes as actors will either promote or contest overarching policy designs. A focus on agency and the way representation is stipulated in policy design is particularly important when looking at Roma representation. The historical disenfranchisement of this ethnic group from policymaking means that their active participation in SF programming will be limited and the government will need to make efforts to bring their voice to the table. Again, how this is achieved and to what extent is likely to influence successful outputs. Finally, policy design and partnership on their own do not address the extensive coordinative efforts needed to 'domesticate' EU administrative procedures and regulations. Member states erect specialized institutions to manage and distribute European funding according to the additionality principle. While policy design accounts for coordinative tools, their potency for orchestrating a complex bureaucratic setting might be limited by persistent path-dependencies but also by the way decision-makers commit to exploiting the 'added value' of SF. How synergies are formed and managed are likely to influence implementation outputs. It is viable to foresee that even when policy design and partnership are geared towards successful outputs, weak coordination and administrative disorder will prevent the effective use of SF on the ground.

Notes

1 While debates on the complex situation of Roma communities generate increasingly polarized responses, in the domain of cohesion policy contestations remain subdued with few scholarly inquiries challenging the official discourse driven by policy experts and EU agencies.

2 As argued in Chapter 2, the focus falls on administrative capacities, with only limited inquiry into the actual legitimacy of the provided measures. Growing demands for active monitoring and comprehensive evaluations do show that there is a rising consensus that SF interventions do not address the disenfranchisement of Roma communities. However, without theoretical understanding of the available mechanisms, monitoring and evaluation will offer only a partial solution to what appears to be a larger systemic problem.

3 Over the years, issues regarding the Roma minority have also become progressively internationalized (see Marushiakova and Popov, 2015).

4 Professionalization of policy areas where highly technical knowledge and expertise is necessary can effectively dwarf the potential for inter-departmental collaboration.

4 Policy design

Constructing problems and solutions

Previous chapters have demonstrated that the performance of the EU's investment in social inclusion cannot be understood outside of governing norms, discursive frames, and administrative practices. This chapter explores the ideational aspect of policymaking and examines how the cognitive maps orienting actors working in the domain of cohesion policy are expressed and used to develop strategic policy plans. It pays heed to the effect of framing in order to capture the implicit (and sometimes explicit) characterization of public problems and reflects upon the implications of those characterizations for the articulation of funding goals, targets, and measures. Attention to the discursive aspect of policy design is combined with a critical analysis of implementation tools. This is imperative since too often policies and projects are set into action without proper delivery planning, which can lead to a good policy idea failing to achieve the desired outcomes.

This chapter starts by offering reflections upon the central concept of this book – *social exclusion*. While the concept has come to occupy a central position in the EU discourse on socio-economic cohesion, its exact meaning remains elusive. In regard to the circumstances of the Roma population, the concept has been largely diluted by fractious theoretical positions on the ethnic dimensions of poverty and marginalization (Kovats, 2002; Vermeersch, 2006, 2012, O'Nions, 2007; Ram, 2014). The competing representations of Roma exclusion are grounded in the different views of both Roma identity and structural inequalities more generally. Even when there is agreement about either of these issues, disagreement surfaces on the possible causes and meanings of the unequal socio-economic standing of Roma minorities and over desirable solutions. Inside the European funding schemes, there have been two constants in the representation of the Roma 'predicament': a) Roma minorities are disproportionately affected by a dynamic and multidimensional process of exclusion, stretching across different policy fields, and b) Roma people face a set of problems which differ considerably from those faced by the majority of the population. These frames have strongly informed EC's recommendations issued to member states, calling for cross-cutting policy responses based on the targeting of SF at Roma communities *to help them realize their full potential* (EC, 2013b). The central claim of this chapter is that successful SF outputs are contingent on policy plans that go beyond the ethnic conception of exclusion and recognize the structural dimension of inequalities, which can only be addressed through a long-term policy commitment to transformative change.

The empirical section of this chapter explores how the EU framing of Roma exclusion was mobilized inside Spanish and Slovak SF programming. It first analyzes how these two countries constructed the problem and their associated strategies. It then demonstrates the way in which these factors shaped the implementation process and its outputs. The analysis shows that in Spain the articulation of Roma exclusion as a systemic issue resulted in the consolidation of a long-term strategic approach based on earmarking EU funding for the institutionalization of anti-discrimination principles, albeit almost exclusively in the area of employment. While criticisms were raised about the narrow understanding of exclusion (i.e. discrimination in the labour market) and ethnically neutral policy responses to specific Roma 'quandaries', the implementation outputs were deemed effective and legitimate by the majority of interviewed stakeholders, including civil society representatives. At the same time, in Slovakia, the framing of Roma exclusion in terms of individual adaptability resulted in the creation of short-term projects targeted at a 'problematic population' – labelled as MRC. While targeting measures were underpinned by a consensus that scarce resources needed to be directed to those who needed or 'deserved' them most, they generated an array of unsuccessful initiatives, which by and large contributed to the further stigmatization of Roma communities. Overall, the findings confirm that without structural adjustments, the targeting of funds at ethnic communities constitutes a gross policy failure.

Social exclusion: an elusive concept

The concept of *social exclusion* has become a lynchpin of EU social policy and a foundational idea for the reform of many national welfare states in Europe. Yet while the notion acquired strategic connotations, by stressing structural and cultural/societal processes, it remains subject to fractious interpretations (Atkinson and Davoudi, 2000). Not surprisingly, Walker, (1995, p. 102) observes that: 'inside political discussions social exclusion means different things to different people', a dynamic that prevents the formulation of normative claims. The conceptual ambiguity has forestalled numerous theoretical efforts to delineate the essential features and patterns of social exclusion. While some scholars describe exclusion in terms of 'not belonging' or lacking social connection (Spicker, 1997; McGarry, 2010), others conceive exclusion in terms of the denial – or non-realization – of citizenship rights, directing attention to institutionalized discrimination and political disenfranchisement (Robbins, 1994; Berghman, 1995). Still, others contend that it is dependent on 'distance' whereby people become removed from the benefits of participating in a modern society (Woodward and Kohli, 2011). Although defining the concept has become an intellectual challenge for academics from various disciplines, it is the EU where the most thinking on social exclusion has arguably taken place. As such, the term resides (often uncomfortably) in the borderland between academia and policy (Daly, 2006).

Drawing on available theoretical frames, the EC has adopted an expansive definition of social exclusion, calling it 'a dynamic and multidimensional process, stretching across different policy fields [...] causing individuals and groups to become excluded from taking part in social exchanges, from the component practices and rights of social integration and identity' (EC, 1992, p. 8, 1993, p. 20). While this framing prompted debates about the need for greater coordination between economic and social policy, it generated little common agreement on the underlying causes of exclusionary dynamics. The pivotal instability concerns the question of whether exclusion is a characteristic feature of contemporary societies or a living condition visited on particular individuals and/or minority groups. The former notion relates the incidence of poverty and disadvantage to the wider processes of restructuring economies and welfare states (Révauger, 1997). It sheds critical light on the existing patterns and privileges perpetuated by institutional arrangements, persistent socio-economic disparities, and discrimination. As such, it problematizes the system as a whole and argues for the reconsideration of the hierarchy of goals and the set of instruments employed to guide socio-economic progress (Fraser, 1997). The latter tends to discuss disadvantaged groups (i.e. Roma people) in relatively isolated terms. It takes the moral fabric (or cultural characteristic) of groups and not the social and economic structures of society to be the root of the problem (Wilson, 2000). As argued by Silver (1994), there is a tendency to exaggerate the portrayal of risk categories under a new label (excluded groups) and publicize the more spectacular forms of cumulative disadvantage, distracting attention from the general rise in inequality, unemployment, and family dissolution affecting all classes. In short, exclusion is presented as a product of adaptability, whereby people's interests, skills, or motivations function outside the core of society, which consists of people who are integrated into sets of relationships that are considered 'normal'.

Framing social exclusion inside cohesion policy

Traditionally, cohesion policy was based on the logic of inter-governmental redistributive bargaining, lodged inside the framework of market liberalization (Hooghe, 1998). The bulk of cohesion policy was organized around aggregated measurements of disparity, mostly GDP per capita and area unemployment rates, which neither guaranteed benefits for the most disadvantaged groups, nor targeted other policy areas linked to poverty and exclusion (including health, housing, and discrimination). Strong political pressure to spend 'on time' gave natural advantage to strongly organized political groups, which tend to be better informed and linked to the relevant networks – typically those elites whom policymakers needed to reconcile with the idea of creating a Single Market and lifting national protective mechanisms (De Rynck and McAleavey, 2001). Thus, somewhat paradoxically in order to benefit from the European financial mechanisms earmarked for deprivation, the poorest regions were expected to amass resources beyond their capacity.

In the late 1990s, the EU redirected the focus of cohesion agenda towards an enhanced recognition of sub-regional deprivation, micro-level underdevelopment, and individual deprivation. The refocusing of the priorities were ascribed to the new EU's ambitions of becoming the most competitive knowledge-based economy by 2020, wholesomely committed to maintaining solidarity and equity (EC, 2000). Consequently, the articulation of the thematic tailoring of policies, less contingent on spatial dimensions, has penetrated the regional development agenda (EC, 2003). Although a number of critics argue that territorially-grounded economic development continues to enjoy a privileged role,[1] the Commission's preoccupation with the better targeting of deprivation as experienced by individuals and disadvantaged groups became increasingly pronounced. The seven consecutive Progress Reports on Economic and Social Cohesion (2001–2007), as well as the Strategic Report 2010 on the Implementation of the Programmes 2007–2013, proclaimed the need to ring-fence expenditure for specific target groups and local development. The reports also endorsed the multidimensional conception of social exclusion by expounding imperatives to raise employment, improve education and skills, and deliver anti-poverty actions across the entire policy spectrum. A thematic focus was further elaborated by recommending the use of SF for policies that promote gender equality; support people with special-needs and integrate migrants and minorities into the labour market and broader social-economic activities (EC 2010b). The European Platform Against Poverty and Social Exclusion made an explicit reference to targeting the specific needs of minority groups – like the Roma people – deemed especially susceptible to social exclusion (EC, 2010).

However, the exacerbated focus on the human dimension of inequality has been weakly integrated into the EU's broader economic governance and macro-economic development objective.[2] It could be argued that this disconnection was driven by the individualization of exclusion inside key priorities adopted inside the ESF (2007–2013). Attention was paid to the presumed 'incapacity [of persons at risk of exclusion] to take part in the normal relations and activities at hand to most people within the society, no matter if these belong to the economic, social, cultural or political domain' (EC, 2010, p. 1). Terms such as 'citizenship rights', 'equality rights', and 'social solidarity' gave way to labour activation, training, and participation.[3] In general terms, social exclusion became equated with 'a lack of basic competencies and lifelong learning opportunities' (EC, 2010) and in the case of ethnic minorities with discriminatory attitudes, which in themselves were vaguely defined. To be fair, issues concerning the lack of or denial of certain resources, rights, goods, or services received considerable attention. However, the implicit assumption was that access would dramatically improve the moment marginalized groups gained the necessary skills (i.e. education, vocational training) (EC, 2010, p. 4). As argued by Cameron (2006, p. 397), social exclusion 'appears in [the] invocations of *normal* social expectation/participation or more commonly 'mainstream' applied to various things that people are understood to be excluded from: the labour market, economy, society, culture, citizenship, etc. The meaning and location of the mainstream is routinely taken to be self-evident.

Framing Roma exclusion

The framing of the Roma 'quandary' did not escape the individualizing undertones pervading discussions about the causes of social exclusion. On the surface, it did appear that the discourse on Roma poverty embedded in economic liberalism and social conservatism (Bancroft, 2005) gave way to a more structural and multifaceted notion of Roma exclusion, more attentive to the all-pervading discrimination (anti-Gypsyism) and barriers preventing access to social services. As stated by the EC (2010c):

> [Roma] face limited access to high quality education, difficulties in integration into the labour market, correspondingly low-income levels, and poor health which in turn results in higher mortality rates and lower life expectancy compared with non-Roma.

However, while the multidimensionality of Roma exclusion achieved the status of a gospel truth, the focus continued to be placed predominately on the (in)adaptability of Roma communities (i.e. low education attainment, problems accessing available services, and long-term unemployment). Attention to systemic factors (i.e. structural racism, lack of multicultural education, austerity measures, etc.) was overshadowed by concerns about existing 'gaps' between Roma and non-Roma people, conceptualized strictly in terms of 'access to education, employment, healthcare and housing' (EC, 2011). The reluctance to recognize the structural nature of these 'gaps' has perpetuated (and strengthened) the pervasive trend of seeking the cause of failures and justification for funds invested in vain, in the community itself and its specific culture (Marushiakova and Popov, 2015). Forlornly, despite concrete empirical evidence attesting to the systemic nature of Roma exclusion – including increasingly unequal economic distribution, restrictive access to public services of high quality, and institutionalized racism (Marcinčin and Marcinčinová, 2009; FRA and UNDP, 2012; Trehan, 2009), there was still a predisposition, particularly in neoliberal political circles, to blame the problem on the behaviour of Roma minorities – their incapacity or unwillingness to integrate or benefit from available resources (see Drál, 2008). While the blaming discourse was often ascribed to far-right political groupings active at national and local levels, it was also echoed at the supranational level. In 2014, Viviane Reding, the European Commissioner for Justice and Fundamental Rights, told *Euronews* that Roma communities need 'to be willing to integrate and to be willing to have a normal way of living'. The human rights activist Bernard Rorke (2014) commented that the EU has been placing the onus on the minorities to make the adjustments and accommodations deemed necessary for social cohesion.

The 'adjustment' rhetoric means that few policy analysts and surprisingly few social theorists[4] consider Roma issues within a wider landscape of the rising levels of social inequality and erosion of worker's rights, civil liberties, and human rights. Rather than focusing on structures and power asymmetries, the research probes disadvantaged communities and individuals, discussing the Roma in isolated terms, as a 'category' of its own (Surdu and Kovats, 2015). Such a narrow approach not only precludes the possibility for a comparative analysis (going beyond the comparison of various Roma communities), but also tends to naturalize the criteria used 'to evaluate Roma's human capital as one of poverty, exclusion, and marginalization' (Magazzini, 2016, p. 58). The focus on deprivation anchors Roma identity in a narrative of deficiency, which is entwined within and across the different sites of representation, policy, and expression, and is active both within and outside Roma communities. Hence, inside the policy literature, Roma are often portrayed as a unique cultural group that faces a set of problems which differs considerably from those faced by the majority of the population (Ringold et al., 2005; Kendea et al., 2017).

While it has been argued that the focus on specific aspects of exclusion can help to devise a policy more aligned with peoples' needs, there is a risk that a differentiating discourse may, in fact, reinforce alienations and orientalize basic human conditions. Levitas (1996) convincingly argues that placing an exaggerated emphasis on the specificity of exclusion can essentialize group characteristics and link economic deprivation to cultural dynamics or individual failure. A long-time critic of Roma identity discourse, Martin Kovats (2012) warns that ethnicization of exclusion acts merely as a tool for inserting the Roma into mainstream society and fails to unleash structural reforms and address the general decline in the inclusivity of the modern welfare state. Michael Surdu (2016), in turn, insists that presenting the Roma as essentially different from everyone else affects social solidarity by disconnecting and distancing Roma from their fellow citizens.

In the policy expert circles, the need to focus explicitly on the 'ethnic aspect' of Roma exclusion appears unshaken (EC, 2011, 2017). And while policymakers shy away from endorsing fully-fledged positive action schemes they fullheartedly argue for targeted approaches, particularly when financial allocation is concerned. There is a strong perception that without explicit targeting, the money will be redirected towards other priorities. As argued by an EC official from the Directorate-General of Regional Policy region:

> We need to make sure that the money goes to the most hard-to-reach groups, this can be achieved only through conditionality, member states must earmark a chunk of SF for specific groups such as the Roma [...] money becomes 'lost' when it's not clear who should be benefiting from SF project.[5]

The EU Framework for National Roma Integration Strategies up to 2020 and resulting national strategies all promised to tackle exclusion through targeted interventions, tailored to Roma-specific circumstances. To justify this approach, the EC maintains that a targeted approach for the Roma does not undermine the broader strategy to fight against poverty and exclusion or exclude other vulnerable and deprived group from support and is compatible with the principle of non-discrimination both at EU and national level (EC, 2011).

Targeting or mainstreaming?

Targeted approaches have long been a staple of cohesion policy. Initially, SF were administered according to territorial criteria. However, the eligibility for financial allocations was incrementally expanded to cover specific policy sectors and delineated social categories (unemployed, minorities, and people at risk of exclusion). Proponents of targeting insist that it is more efficient to direct resources to precisely defined target groups or areas (Ravallion, 2003). Such a strategy allegedly prevents the dilution of assistance and strengthens the impact of the policy. This rationale has been strongly conditioned by fiscal deficits, the rise of neoliberal ideology, and the shifting priorities for social assistance. However, it also stems from the expectation that focused action is able to induce immediate and suitable responses.[6]

While thematic targeting reflects economic and organizational concerns (cost benefits and efficiency), the tailoring of policies to social categories is often based on a conviction that circumstances and patterns of exclusion of some groups differ from disadvantages experienced by mainstream society. The difference is conceived either as a result of discrimination and negative stereotypes, usually related to the particular characteristics of a group or an individual (i.e. gender, race, and ethnicity) (Bowring, 2000; Bleich, 2002), or as an unequal socio-economic position, which is pinned on group inadaptability or pathological behaviours (Abrahamson, 1996). Whitehead (2000) argues that by definition, targeting inscribes differences in class, gender, and other characteristics in official policy. This not only makes social differences seem natural and permanent but also divides societies into 'givers' and 'receivers'. These divisions can lead to stigmatization and the reluctance to use valued EU financial resources for the advancement of the 'deviant' sector of the population. Moreover, focusing on target groups rather than institutional shortcomings can be superfluous as the acquisition of new skills or resources is unlikely to prompt institutional changes (see Bacchi, 2004).

Not oblivious to these concerns, the EU cohesion agenda has loosely endorsed a mainstreaming approach as a means to combat existing inequalities particularly in relation to gender (see European Standard, 2013). Developed by equality scholars, the concept of *mainstreaming* at its core calls for public interventions to place critical focus on structural power arrangements and strive to remodel the institutional order, which is plagued by biases that disenfranchise certain groups and individuals who for a variety of reasons do not 'fit' accepted standards (Reese, 1998; Verloo, 2001; Woodward, 2003). Jacquot (2010) argues that to be effective mainstreaming needs to consider inequalities as trans-sectorial – resulting from actions in various policy domains and address it through transversal policy instruments. The critical expectation of equality scholars is that the incorporation of the equality dimension, in all envisioned objectives and measures, will alter decision-making structures and processes, tackle deeply rooted organizational cultures, and retune policy priorities (Lombardo, 2005). As argued by Squires (2005), the main task of mainstreaming would be to recognize the complexities of social exclusion and inequality and to build organizations, policies, and projects informed by a desire to accommodate and benefit from the strengths of diversity.

However, there is little evidence that the EU cohesion agenda has endorsed a far-reaching transformative course of action, opting instead for non-binding instruments and soft policy tools, developed predominately in the gender equality domain.[7] In relation to ethnic or racial minorities, the discussions about main-streaming equality in SF programming has been excessively vague and often conflated with anti-discrimination or equal opportunity measures.[8] In reference to the Roma minorities, the EU insisted that inclusion funding schemes are best approached from the perspective of both targeted and mainstreamed policy provision. The 10 Common Basic Principles for Roma Inclusion recognized this, calling for both: *aiming for the mainstream* (Principle 4) and *explicit but not exclusive targeting* (Principle 2).[9] However, neither the EU's recommendations nor the national commitments specify or elaborate how these principles should be (or will be) realized in practice. The normative conviction simply calls for 'some level of explicit targeting within mainstream policies, supported by disaggregated data collection to allow for monitoring and evaluation of outcomes' (Guy et al., 2010). The implementation of these measures, however, rests in the hands of domestic policymakers, who are driven by their own normative understanding of exclusion and dominating political interests.

Mobilizing social exclusion in Spanish and Slovak SF programming

The content analysis of the Spanish and Slovak SF programming demonstrates that the diagnosis of social exclusion in the documents differs substantially, both in terms of defining the underlying basic features and causes of exclusion and specifying the circumstances of the Roma population. In Spain, the situational analysis of exclusion directed attention to macro-economic factors, ranging from low productivity and dependence on imports to inflation and unfavourable labour conditions (NSRF, 2007, p. 28–32; OP E&A, 2007, p. 31–35). The concept of *exclusion* itself was discussed mainly in terms of the persistent institutional barriers to socio-economic activity. The Spanish NSRF defined social exclusion as 'a condition generated by institutional barriers, which prevent groups or individuals from participating in socio-economic life' (NSRF, 2007, p. 135). The preamble established that the rapid social transformation of Spanish society has left the bureaucratic apparatus unprepared and not flexible enough to address instances of poverty, inequality, and structural discrimination (NSRF, 2007, p. 6). Emphasis was placed on a lack of integrationist instruments, incentives, and flexible procedures needed for generating equitable and accessible public services. As explained by one of the designers of the NSRF:

> Our institutions continue to be largely underequipped to address the new public demands and the complex realities of the Spanish society, such as an increased immigration, the disentanglement of family support system,

changing gender roles, and urban poverty. Our anti-discrimination schemes continue to be quite limited and potential innovations of public interventions are constrained by the procedural complexity and inertia.[10]

The majority of interviewed policymakers involved in the design of SF programming insisted that SF were considered an expedient tool for developing a strategy of 'competitiveness with a human face'. The Andalusian authorities added that through the regional OP they had earmarked funds for accelerating reforms of the 'sluggish' bureaucracy and developing a high-quality anti-discrimination framework.[11]

It is important to point out, however, that Spanish SF programming conceptualized 'participation in socio-economic life' almost exclusively in terms of labour market activities. The analysis of institutional barriers presented in NSRF was undertaken mainly in the domain of employment policy. The diagnostic section explicitly mentioned that the 'inability to access meaningful employment opportunities generates high unemployment rates, income inequality and poverty, the main drivers of social exclusion' (NSRF, 2007, p. 118). Neither the NSRF nor the regional OPs emphasized the multidimensional and relative aspect of exclusion. Institutional shortcomings in other areas, including housing, health, and education were side-lined with five key priority axes pertaining solely to employment themes. The officials insisted that such narrow focus was imperative for preserving a clear policy focus and secure a concentration of funding. The head of the department of the Administrative Unit of the ESF (MA for the ESF) explained:

We decided to focus on the most prominent shortcomings of our economy, and according to our research, unemployment and exclusion from employment indeed dwarf our economic and social development [...] We need to mobilize all our recourses to tackle this enormous and complex issue [...] of course we do realize that some areas are neglected, but ESF is simply too small in scope to address them all.[12]

The reductionist definition was translated into ESF OPs, which all used the concept of *social exclusion* and *exclusion from the labour market* interchangeably. The Andalusian General Directorate for European Funds and Planning insisted that a focus on the economic aspects of exclusion avoids the stigmatization of certain regions and groups as it does not link 'social or cultural position in the society to poverty and destitution'.[13] In the midst of the economic crisis, securing employment for marginalized groups was also deemed pivotal by many of the interviewed grassroots representatives:

Unemployment among the Roma in Spain grew nearly threefold between 2005 and 2011, it now reaches almost 37%. The economic crisis is rocking Spain and hurts everybody, especially the traditional open-air markets where so many Roma work as vendors. If the government doesn't prioritize employment, we are all going to starve – even the more educated Roma.[14]

Nevertheless, the prioritization of employment began to be strongly criticized by independent commentators who questioned the neoliberal emphasis on insertion into paid work, and the limited focus on the application of anti-discrimination measures in other policy areas:

> We got this 'great' anti-discrimination framework, but what use does it have if it only talks about employment, what about the erosion of human rights, the inequalities people experience when accessing social support, housing, healthcare. Spanish support system is crumbling down and we keep on telling people that once they work all will be fine.[15]

In contrast, the framing of social exclusion articulated in the Slovak SF programming outlined an array of exclusionary dynamics taking place across all major policy fields. The NSRF stated that exclusion 'is a multidimensional phenomenon, comprising in addition to the income dimension also other important aspects, such as the level of satisfaction of fundamental needs, access to employment, access to education, housing, healthcare, law and culture' (NSRF, 2007, p. 23). The document also stressed the unequal access to rights protection and insufficient political and civil participation (NSRF, 2007, p. 24). In reference to the Roma minority, the emphasis was placed on spatial segregation, dismal living conditions, health problems, and intergenerational poverty (NSRF, 2007, p. 24). As stated by a manager working for the Office of the Slovak Government Plenipotentiary for Roma Communities:

> Extreme levels of poverty among Slovak Roma are well documented and acknowledged by the Slovak government. It is well accepted in policy circles that marginalization is multidimensional, acutely felt in all the vital policy areas, including employment, education, housing and health. Focusing on only one aspect is simply not possible because these areas are strongly interconnected.[16]

However, the expansive conceptualization of social exclusion has at the same time directed attention away from institutional and wider macro-economic factors. Although the Slovak NSRF described instances of labour demand asymmetries and uneven territorial development, it defined social exclusion in terms of the 'inadaptability of certain groups and individuals' and their 'distance from the mainstream society' (NSRF, 2007, p. 20). The NSRF assessment explicitly stated that while some people 'exclude themselves voluntarily from socio-economic life', others are 'unable, incapable or unwilling to access available rights' (NSRF, 2007, pp. 24, 56, 158). Similar assertions appeared in OPs, pointing out that the unfavourable position of marginalized citizens stemmed from a lack of 'basic competences which often led to helplessness and an inability to guide or control the decisions which have implications for day to day life' (OP E&SI, 2007, p. 47). This framing was defended by the Slovak Ministry of Labour, Social Affairs and Family:

Wlicu talking about marginalization we need to take in consideration issues such as inadequate skills to compete in the labour market, health problems, family situation and area of residence. If we are to use SF in an effective manner these circumstantial factors need to be properly identified and assessed so the projects can be carefully tailored. We already know that a 'one size fits all' strategy does not work in practice, people are different, they deal with different problems and are differently predisposed [...] policy action needs to take this into account.[17]

Conceptualizing strategic targets

The difference in conceptualizing social exclusion and its causes influenced the way SF programmes delineated the main targets of SF allocation. The Spanish NSRF emphasized that SF would be channelled towards public institutions and public agencies in an effort to 'accelerate administrative reforms and advance equality principle' (NSRF, 2007, p. 78). Although regional OPs included a human capital objective – vulnerable groups and people at risk of exclusion – it did not specify exactly who would be the final beneficiaries. The Andalusian authorities insisted that the absence of precisely defined targets was a conscious choice reflecting an Andalusian socialist agenda (loosely based on universality principle) and lack of tradition delivering positive discrimination interventions. Neutrality was also defended on the basis that the transformation of public institutions would indirectly benefit all vulnerable groups:

> The main drive here is to invest in building more inclusive institutions rather than introduce independent projects targeted at excluded groups. It is not unreasonable to believe that once public institutions are prepared to support equality, those who are marginalized will benefit. Programmes directed at excluded groups cannot be successful if governing procedures remain unchanged.[18]

In effect, the priories dealing with social exclusion were not directed at specific social groups but rather at identified socio-economic problems (i.e. long-term unemployment, limited entrepreneurship, early school dropout, and informal employment). They also remained 'ethnically neutral' with no reference made to Roma minorities, their cultural distinctiveness, specific circumstances or even areas of residence. While critics argued that this omission stemmed from the limited political attention given to the precarious living conditions of Roma communities (Bereményi and Mirga, 2012), the designers of SF programming insisted that the introduction of ethnically specific priority axes would go against the region's commitment to social solidarity and universality. They further argued that a neutral approach was considered essential in preventing an ethnicization of poverty, whereby being Roma might be automatically equated with being excluded. A public manager from the Andalusian Ministry for Equality and Social Welfare expressed that some level of neutrality was instrumental in avoiding the promotion of difference over equality and in reducing the risk of isolating the Roma exclusion from the wider political agenda. Essentially this meant that the Spanish SF programming moved away from providing immediate assistance to those most affected by exclusion, opting instead for long-term systemic adjustments.

In contrast, programming adopted in Slovakia was more precise in defining excluded groups. While the diagnostic section stressed that exclusion affected various groups and individuals, it focused predominately on the Roma communities. The NSRF stated that: 'the problem of the insufficient level of social inclusion is most obvious in the case of the Roma ethnic community' (NSRF, 2007, p. 21). Roma people were categorized as a group that faced a greater risk of exclusion than any other group of Slovak society (including homeless and disabled people, and immigrants). Moreover, there was an explicit contention, that their situation was *unique* in its scope and character. The specificity of the Roma question was attributed to spatial factors: residence in disadvantaged and economically lagging regions and in segregated and impoverished settlements. However, the diagnosis did not explain the causes of such disadvantages, in particular, common practices of spatial segregation. The interviewed NGOs attested that this omission gave rise to the false conviction that Roma intentionally choose to reside in isolation or are themselves responsible for inadequate living conditions:

> Public authorities continue to focus on Roma culture and behaviour, despite a lack of data on that topic, the marginalized Roma communities are often viewed as the source of all evil where pathology and self-imposed isolation are on the rise threatening the well-being of Slovak mainstream society [...] Instead of accounting for wider socio-economic problems, the authorities engage in rhetoric that present Roma communities as the main barriers to cohesive development and not the victims of unjust and ineffective policies.[19]

Indeed, the role of Roma culture in perpetuating exclusion was emphasized throughout the entire SF programming. While the NSRF stressed that: 'different cultural characteristics serve as barriers to meaningful integration' (NSRF, 2007, pp. 21, 23) the OPs linked the cultural behaviour of the Roma to circumstances of exclusion stating that: 'natural socio-hierarchical rules of social life in Roma communities pose a risk for building up and maintaining communication barriers' (OP E&SI, 2007, p. 63). The OP Education has ventured as far as to explain the inadequate education attainments of Roma children with a 'low value of education among Roma communities' (OP Education, 2007, pp. 35, 62). In this manner, SF programming mirrored widely held political perceptions that the Roma need to change in order to benefit from systemic provisions.

Recognizing structural discrimination

Where the two SF programmes differ most substantially is in their acknowledgement of structural discrimination. The diagnostic section of the Spanish

NSRF and all relevant OPs explicitly recognized that: 'social exclusion is generated by systemic discrimination particularly entrenched in the area of employment' (OPA, 2007, p. 26). This acknowledgement prompted the creation of the thematic multi-regional OP FAD that presented *discrimination in the labour market* as the main and most immediate cause of poverty and exclusion (OP FAD, 2007, p. 13). As explained by the Intermediate Body (IB) for the OP FAD:

> Negative perceptions about groups and individuals prevent them from obtaining the same employment opportunities as the mainstream society. This is the single most important barrier to meaningful participation in the economic spheres of life. It is an institutional shortcoming that needs to be prioritized in all SF and other public interventions.[20]

Nevertheless, the diagnosis fell silent on the intersectionality of discrimination, and inequality axes, such as ethnic origin, race, or area of residence were altogether ignored. The interviewed Spanish anti-discrimination advocates maintained that such conceptualization of discrimination failed to capture racism and intolerance directed specifically at the Roma community. However, senior policymakers maintained that discrimination affected all 'different groups in similar manner' (i.e. preventing them from entering the labour market and/or accessing quality public services), and that is why SF objectives focused on discriminatory patterns rather than on group identity. The SF programming director argued that social exclusion framed in terms of institutional shortcomings rather than group dynamics is beneficial to the overall functioning of SF programming:

> Taking into account the characteristics of the problems, and not the types or groups of persons affected by it, forces public authorities to consider structural revisions in service delivery. The aim is making them more accessible and inclusive to all those in need because this effectively prevents stigmatization of certain groups or treating them in separation from mainstream strategies.[21]

Consequently, the SF were earmarked for 'generic anti-discrimination initiatives', aimed at warding off all forms of discrimination in the labour market. Under this approach, the representation of the Roma as a unique socio-cultural category was rendered counterproductive. While critics maintained that such a stance ran the risk of diverting funds from anti-discrimination initiatives tackling anti-Gypsyism, empirical data did not support this claim. In fact, the number of awareness raising campaigns aimed at reducing anti-Roma stereotypes increased (Evaluation of the Impact of the Multi-Regional Operational Programme Fight against Discrimination, 2013).

In Slovakia, SF programming failed to link social exclusion to discriminatory processes. In fact, the diagnosis of Roma circumstances altogether omitted any references to institutional discrimination. As confirmed by a public manager from Eastern Slovakia:

> We talk about multidimensionality, we talk about dependencies and critical living situation, we elaborate and analyze, but if you look carefully you will not find any references to systemic discrimination, as if the escalation of anti-Gypsyism, the deeply rooted prejudice in the Slovak public sector, and well-documented patterns of segregation do not in any way contribute to the marginalization of the Roma.[22]

A reference to discrimination appears for the first time in the prescriptive section of the NSRF, in a statement that all social inclusion actions will 'aim to combat discrimination based on sex, race, ethnical origin, religion and beliefs, disability, age or sexual orientation' (NSRF, 2007, p. 96). Prior to that, discrimination was neither defined nor properly assessed, making it impossible to infer where it was most acutely felt and who the victims and the perpetrators were. The concept was also not elaborated further down in the SF programming, as none of the relevant OPs elaborated discrimination in their assessment of social exclusion. As pointed out by a member of the Monitoring Committee (MC):

> It has been pointed out in numerous meetings with Managing Authorities that patterns of discrimination and unequal treatment should be elaborated on, unfortunately, this has never been realized and in general, there is a great reluctance on part of the authorities to account for discriminatory patterns, especially within public administration, despite strong evidence of such practices.[23]

Consequently, the thematic priorities and objectives inside SF programming failed to elaborate on the need to tackle any forms of discrimination and less than 2% of SF were allocated towards anti-discrimination measures.

Adopting strategic action plans

In the case of Spanish NSRF, the acknowledgement that social exclusion is driven chiefly by systemic factors resulted in the commitment to equality mainstreaming, albeit solely in the area of employment (NSRF, 2007, p. 135). During interviews, policymakers affirmed that the social inclusion action plan was aimed at tackling discrimination in employment and consolidating the principle of equal opportunity inside public services (predominately unemployment agencies and integration bodies). This aim was articulated under the priority: *construction of a working environment free of discriminatory practices, committed to the principles of equal opportunity, transparency and economic as well as social innovations.* The emphasis was placed on the need to adjust public services and administrative procedures in order to 'strengthen attention to diversity and equal opportunities' (Evaluation of the Operation Programme ESF Andalusia 2007–2013, 2010, p. 138).

As confirmed by the manager from the General Directorate for European Funds and Planning, the IB of the OP ESF Andalusia:

> We expect that all potential beneficiaries demonstrate how their initiatives will cater to diversity and equal access and how they will address discrimination, without such elaboration the proposed intervention is automatically rejected. To aid the process we set up equality indicators, time-frames and public budgets, we also designated bodies responsible for monitoring and evaluation to invest in equality research and information exchange.[24]

The interviewees, including local NGOs, were in agreement that mainstreaming equality could bring attention to the long-term impact of policies and projects and facilitate expedient systemic changes (albeit rather slowly). Although criticisms arose regarding the unsystematic evaluation of mainstreaming, the OPs established equality indicators, measures supporting cognitive activities, awareness raising campaigns, and the exchange of good practices. Practical information and concrete tools were provided to the MAs in order to ensure that mainstreaming became an integrated part of their everyday work. While this process was not free of delays all interviewees insisted that at least it was put in place. In an interview, a senior manager from the MA ESF in Madrid confirmed that SF programming aimed to support a working environment free of discriminatory practices, committed to the principles of equal opportunity, transparency, and innovation:

> The aim is to really bring about changes in the way thing are done, this is not an easy task and we struggle against great bureaucratic inertia, but we believe that SF can really jump-start and sustain institutional transformations. What is important is that all objectives and measures adhere to the equality principle and that the proposed projects delineate how they will address discrimination and how they will contribute to greater cohesion.[25]

On paper, the equality principle was incorporated into the main objectives pertaining to the development of social inclusion programmes and services. The two multi-regional OPs – OP FAD and OP E&A[26] – called for the construction of a working environment free of discriminatory practices, committed to the principles of equal opportunity, transparency, and economic as well as social innovations. The regional ESF OP emphasized the need to adjust public services and administrative procedures in order to 'strengthen attention to diversity and equal opportunities' (OP ESF Andalusia, 2007, p. 138). While a number of critics insisted that these were window-dressing commitments,[27] concrete regulations were implemented to secure non-discrimination principles during the distribution phase. The selection criteria were made conditional upon the adherence to the equality principle, and all projects had to include equality indicators. As confirmed by the manager from General Directorate for European Funds and Planning, the IB of the OP ESF Andalusia:

We expect that all the potential beneficiaries demonstrate how their initiatives will cater to diversity and equal access and how they will address discrimination, without such elaboration the proposed intervention is automatically rejected. To aid the process we set up equality indicators, time-frames and public budgets, we also designated bodies responsible for monitoring and evaluation (MCs, Equal Opportunity Thematic Group, ESF Forum, and Social Inclusion Network), and invest in equality research and information exchange.[28]

In Andalusia, SF have been used to create a unit where all other council areas or departments could draw expertise and methods for introducing equality principles into the Community Support Framework for 2000–2006.[29] This unit provided training, information, and tools to the entire Administration in Andalusia to ensure that non-discrimination becomes an integrated part of all initiatives co-funded by Europe. The prioritization of anti-discrimination measures was further secured through budgeting. The MAs and IBs for regional ESF OPs were required to earmark a concrete amount of SF for measures addressing discrimination in the labour market, while the central and regional authorities were to provide co-financing from a pool of the public budget reserved exclusively for promoting equality measures and non-discrimination (NSRF, 2007). The OP ESF Andalusia, under Priority Axis 2 (promotion of employability, social inclusion, and gender equality) assigned €73,130,561 for measures tackling discrimination – the second largest amount within the axis[30] – a sum co-financed by the aggregated budget of central, regional, and local authorities. In effect, over 80% of SF projects introduced in Andalusia, addressed directly or indirectly barriers to equal opportunities in employment.

The endorsement of mainstreaming has largely ousted approaches targeted at specific groups or communities, an approach strongly criticized by Roma activists.[31] Out of 15 thematic objectives, only one aimed to 'improve the employability of people at risk of exclusion' through targeted measures. However, these were 'ethnically neutral', with no explicit mentioning of the Roma minority as a target group (OP ESF Andalusia, 2007, p. 237). No references were made to cultural distinctiveness,[32] particular circumstances, or even area of residence. The few proposed targeted measures called for customized itineraries of insertion. Even in this case, however, the specification of group membership was avoided and the measures proposed it more as an additional component to be anchored within implemented projects than a systemic approach. While some commentators saw this as a way to combine mainstreaming with the targeted approach, critics maintained that targeting which does not take into consideration group dynamics is strictly cosmetic with limited leeway to really address the specificity of discriminated groups.[33]

In the case of Slovak NSRF, the focus on individual adaptability informed the adoption of a targeted approach. The majority of interviewees asserted that SF were seen as tools for developing 'insertion' projects targeted at specific and well-defined groups. Social inclusion objectives within the OPs called for preparing and training excluded groups so that they could participate in all aspects of socio-economic life. The strategy relied on slogans such as 'catch up', 'activate', or 'motivate', all of which accentuated the need for the behavioural change of the target group. As commented by a public manager working for the MA for OP E&SI:

> SF can be a great tool for helping vulnerable groups develop their potential so that they can partake in socio-economic activities on an equal footing with other citizens, SF projects can equip them with necessary skills, for example, help them to complete secondary education.[34]

The conceptualization of *social exclusion* as a multidimensional phenomenon meant that targeting had to be realized in various policy fields. For this reason, Slovak authorities established a number of thematic ESF OPs (OP E&SI, OP Education, OP Health, and OP RD) which all incorporated horizontal priorities, labelled HP MRC.

The HP MRC aimed to strengthen and increase the efficiency of targeted activities and aggregate financial resources for tackling Roma exclusion. The Plenipotentiary Office became the coordinator of the HP MRC, responsible for drafting the 'complex projects' aimed at increasing the employment and education level within MRC, and improving the living conditions (including health and housing). Although there was no specific financial allocation for this priority, an estimated €200 million was expected to be drawn from six OPs, two financed through the ESF and the rest from the ERDF. However, upon closer scrutiny the design of HP MRC appeared excessively vague, lacking precise objectives, output indicators, and instructions of how cooperation among different OPs was to be realized. Moreover, the Plenipotentiary Office neither received an additional budget for its new coordinative responsibilities, nor was granted decision-making authority. While some commentators noted that this 'vague' design was caused by limited administrative capacity to develop complex governance programmes, it could also be attributed to the general neglect of long-term thinking about institutional reforms. As expressed by the manager from the SDF (IB for OP E&SI):

> It really seemed that designing nice and comprehensive strategic documents, in line with EU regulations and recommendations was a priority; whether and how objectives embedded in these documents were to be realized was of lesser concern [...] as long as EC gave a check mark and accepted the NSRF; that what was important not what will happen in the far and unknown future.[35]

Perhaps the gravest shortcoming of the targeted approach was its silent treatment of discrimination. None of the OPs stressed the need to tackle discrimination and systemic inequalities. No specific objectives were set up, let alone an entire OP, that dealt explicitly with structural inequalities or discrimination. Overall co-financing of anti-discrimination activities from the state budget has been limited, accounting for less than 4% (CSES, 2011b) and supporting exclusively

awareness raising projects. In instances where attention was brought to administrative modernization, it pertained to investments in innovative technologies
and infrastructure, with no mention of how equitable access to services will be
provided for. In an interview, a civic association manager from Eastern Slovakia
contended that SF were used predominately to strengthen the institutional setting
for business elites and not for regular citizens or the excluded groups:

> The SF are improving conditions for large businesses and entrepreneurs,
> which is needed of course, but no money is earmarked for programmes which
> could make public services more inclusive or more accessible. The current
> programming fails to address instances of discrimination and rights violation
> [...] it really does not reflect the fact that for the most vulnerable groups sys-
> temic barriers continue to be extremely high.[36]

Moreover the OP E&SI emphasized the need to invest in human development in
order to break patterns of dependency and assist excluded groups in accessing public services and benefit from advancement mechanisms (OP E&SI, 2007, p. 45).
The objectives called for the 'integration of excluded groups and individuals' into
the institutional landscape, with references made to adaptability, adaptation, and
activation. The focus fell on the provision of special care services and curatorship to
excluded groups with an aim to prevent pathologies, improve personal competences
and living conditions (OP E&SI, 2007, p. 142). OP Education also emphasized the
need to improve the skills and attendance of vulnerable pupils while OP Health
called for the creation of special health awareness initiatives among excluded groups.

The attainment of these goals was to be achieved through national and demand-
driven projects, targeted at specific thematic areas and groups. In the specific case
of MRC, the endorsement of soft affirmative action aimed at delivering additional financial assistance. The NSRF stated that: 'the circumstances of MRC are
addressed separately [...] as projects need to be tailored to specific community
needs' (NSRF, 2007, p. 95). The OP E&SI set up national programmes targeted
specifically at Roma communities (i.e. field social work, community centres)
while OP Education channelled funds to programmes supporting Roma teaching
assistants. The selection criteria asked potential beneficiaries to demonstrate how
their projects will assist or include persons of Romani origin and applications
would receive a higher score for accounting for Roma beneficiaries. As expressed
by MA of OP E&SI 'we need to motivate project managers to tailor their initiatives towards the Roma that is why we provide financial incentives'.[37] The critics,
however, pointed out that the selection procedures were strictly symbolic, limited
to 'checking the MRC box on the application'. There were neither clearly outlined
evaluations indicators, nor monitoring. As expressed by a member of the MC:

> Targeting of Roma in projects was done in a superficial manner, which in fact
> led to situations where projects that had one Roma participant were consid-
> ered examples of good practices [...]. Moreover, selection processes favoured
> projects like training or consultation, which could be easily evaluated, hence

localities, instead of devising long-term complex projects aimed at institutional changes, submitted something 'quick and dirty' with the word Roma slapped on to it.[38]

Thus, while governing authorities and many Roma advocates tended to support the targeted approach, the manner in which this strategy was executed only further distanced Roma inclusion initiatives from general regional development strategies (this had severely negative consequences which will be discussed below). Commentators attributed this to weak administrative capacities, but also to a sheer neglect of the structural dimension of Roma exclusion that: 'rendered the targeted approach of little value'.[39]

Structuring effect of policy design on SF outputs in Spain

Thus far the chapter has demonstrated that the Spanish and Slovak SF programming conceptualized social exclusion differently, which in turn influenced the content of proposed solutions. What follows is an attempt to demonstrate how these differences structured SF outputs.

Quantitative assessments of Spanish SF programming demonstrated that Spain committed a significant proportion of estimated spending on ESF measures towards social exclusion and equality (55.4%).[40] At the same time, its ESF absorption rate was above the EU average (Spain 46.3%, EU average 41.1%).[41] Country reports largely confirmed the efficient implementation performance free of excessive delays, mismanagement, and cancellations. The ESF MA in Madrid ascribed these achievements to the narrow focus and coherent objectives:

> Focusing on one theme allowed us to streamline administrative resources [...] we were able to work more efficiently because we didn't have to design multiple project-calls directed at different sectors and different organizations. If that was the case we would need to come up with different evaluation methodologies, different time-frames and eligibility criteria, and this would substantially strain our administrative capacities.[42]

The IB for OP ESF Andalusia echoed this sentiment stressing that the clear unilateral focus led to the increased efficiency and streamlining of selection procedures:

> We were able to intensify our efforts to deal with the identified condition [...] instead of introducing numerous project-calls we have opted for two major calls, one directed at public organizations and the other at private and social ones [...] Given that the calls were thematically focused we avoided the inflow of miscellaneous applications, this speeded up the selection process.[43]

Although the final beneficiaries, particularly the civil society organizations, remained rather sceptical of these postulations, and complaints about excessive bureaucracy came up in numerous interviews, the general view was that the application procedures were consistent, and the state's administrative support was stable if not widely accessible.[44]

According to SF stakeholders, the delineation of concrete (if frugal) objectives further contributed to the effective allocation of SF by allowing for the aggregation of funding. Well-articulated priorities and comprehensive equality indicators were seen as a means to consolidate the mainstreaming of the equality principles and prevent the fragmentation (or redirection) of SF interventions. The very creation of the multi-regional OP FAD was considered an important step in anchoring mainstreaming methodologies. The total budget of €208,068,774 fortified the regional ESF OPs' strategic focus on discrimination and delivered essential cognitive support to civil societies and public institutions. Moreover, close to 89% of all OP FAD initiatives were aligned (in terms of objectives, priorities, and targets) with initiatives introduced by regional ESF OPs (Evaluation of OP FAD, 2013). This allowed for the introduction of projects larger in size and with extended time-frames (allowing projects to continue into the next funding period). What needs to be pointed out is that the MAs tended to circumvent complex initiatives in favour of simple and focused projects. As explained by the Fundación Secretariado Gitano (FSG):

> We generally feel that it is better to implement a smaller number of projects but of greater size and capacity. The small, localized projects are useful in providing immediate practical aid, but to facilitate real transformations and policy impacts we need ambitious, large-scale, and result oriented initiatives [...] We also strongly believed that such projects should be relatively 'easy' to manage. From our experience as IB, the complexity of the management and control system discourages the usage of SF altogether.[45]

Looking at the fiches of Spain ESF projects it appears that they were predominately large-scale, multimillion-dollar initiatives, implemented by public authorities with substantial co-financing from the public budget. For example, a total budget of €41.7 million was allocated to the labour insertion programme Acceder in the 2008–2013 period, in total €72,222,833 has been invested since 2000 (EURoma, 2010). In Andalusia, the majority of labour inclusion projects run by regional OP ESF, possessed budgets reaching €5 million or more (Evaluation OP ESF Andalusia, 2010). The majority of winning initiatives outlined strategies for tackling discrimination and developing methodologies for the 'inclusion of vulnerable groups'.

The effective outputs were further reinforced by the strategic focus on inducing institutional changes. The 2013 evaluation of the OP FAD demonstrated that SF contributed to enhancing institutional quality by anchoring anti-discrimination methodologies and equality principles among public and civil society organizations.[46] As such, it created social, economic, and institutional conditions to prevent exclusion, making it an emblem of the principle of equal opportunity. The evaluation also emphasized that the focus on institutional improvements has advanced quality management, control, and monitoring inside the MAs. For example, in the period 2006–2011, the amount of resources that were returned to the ESF by ineffective management was only 0.07% of the expenditure incurred, while managed funds that did not exceed the control of different audits was less than 2% (Evaluation OP FAD, 2013, p. 60). Finally, it was attested that institutions have increased the amount and quality of professional resources, which allowed them to develop more effective projects in line with the equality principle. The foundation Once expressed that:

> Institutional quality should not be viewed as an end in itself, but a means to create accessible and cohesive public services and inclusion projects, using SF as an instrument for improving the way institutions deal with exclusion is imperative and such style of work should be prioritized in the future programming periods.[47]

Nevertheless, the neglect of the ethnic dimension of poverty (or intersectionality) was criticized by Roma inclusion advocates. The criticisms stressed that the neutral treatment of excluded groups runs the risk of bypassing the most marginalized communities.[48] Bereményi and Mirga (2012) argue that the use of the ESF for the Roma in Spain has been rather limited to the nationwide programme Acceder and that its existence served as a disincentive for regional authorities to programme meaningful Roma-related activities in their ESF OPs. These criticisms were rebuked by the interviewed SF stakeholders who stressed that real changes take time and lack of ethnic indicators in the SF has not meant that Roma benefited less than other groups. The ESF MA attested that the focus on institutional reforms was instrumental in raising the number of social exclusion initiatives and providing greater assistance to all marginalized groups including the Roma.[49] A director of the Secretariat for Roma Community within the Andalusian Ministry of Equality and Social Welfare argued that:

> The international reports often put a lot of emphasis on the number of beneficiaries while neglecting to account for institutional changes that take place. Exclusive targeting of Roma is simply not feasible, not only because of the fluidity of the Roma identity but also due to legislative restrictions regarding the collection of ethnic data. That is partly why we focus on creating services and procedures that cater to all excluded and discriminated groups. Although the impacts of our initiatives are not immediately evident this does not mean that Roma do not benefit. We've seen a flourishing of Roma activism, a growing number of high school graduates, and falling number of ethnically driven hate crimes. These improvements are directly related to changes in procedures and regulations and numerous SF projects such as social enterprises.[50]

Managers of SF projects introduced in Andalusia confirmed that SF had 'jump-started' changes in the mentality on the part of the public administrations, business sector, and society at large. They also asserted that the modernization of employment offices led to the flexibilization of procedures and hence greater initiatives for working with vulnerable groups. In particular, Andalusian support for social enterprises[51] was viewed as a positive development, as extremely effective in providing employment opportunities for the most excluded persons.

Structuring effect of policy design on SF outputs in Slovakia

Slovak suboptimal outputs have been well documented in studies and evaluation reports (Hurrle et al., 2012; OSI, 2009; EP, 2011; CSES, 2011b). The SF programming was criticized for excessive bureaucratization, acute inefficiencies, low absorption, and a redirection of SF from envisioned goals. In particular, the HP MRC and the Local Strategies of Comprehensive Approach were assessed as failures given that only some €16 million out of the allocated €200 million had been contracted (Hurrle et al., 2012). This state of affairs could be directly linked to the design of the SF programming, particularly to its wide conceptualization of social exclusion, which lacked strategic focus and clearly stipulated objectives. The MC members commented that the intent to address all dimensions of social exclusion has reinforced the fragmentation and diffusion of funds:

> The money was allocated to various OPs, each with their own objectives, priorities and interests. In effect, we had numerous integration strategies not linked to one another in any way. HP was supposed to serve as a coordination tool, but without any political clout, budget or actual management plan it was really unable to do anything [...] we ended up with miscellaneous project-calls, prone to cancellations and overlaps, some even contradicted one another [...] managerial efficiency was simply lost.[52]

In addition, the diffusion of funds among mixed and disparate objectives and measures reinforced the creation of small initiatives of dubious effectiveness (over 85% of the competitive allocations did not exceed a budget of €500,000) (Grambličková, 2010). The reliance on small initiatives was also tied to a lack of secured co-financing from the public budgets (only the minimum 15% was provided) and meagre administrative support provided for project managers. In practice entities competing in project-calls needed to amass their own funds and operational capital (even the NGOs had to contribute expected 15%). This impeded the participation in project-calls of small impoverished localities and privileged 'small and simple' interventions. As explained by a project manager from Banská Bystrica:

> All projects directed at Roma communities were to be implemented by local authorities or local NGOs [...] neither the central nor regional authorities contributed their expertise or co-financing. Not surprisingly the poorest of the poor failed to compete on equal footing with the well-off localities [...] those who did manage to get funds were only able to manage simple highly localized initiatives, nobody aspired to contribute to larger changes.[53]

The ambiguous focus has also prompted inefficiency during the selection processes. According to the MC, the eligibility criteria within project-calls were excessively vague and open to wide interpretations. This generated a great interest and overflow of miscellaneous project proposals.[54] The MAs were not technically prepared to meet such a demand, which, as a result, generated further delays and legitimized the superficial selection process, whereby applications were scored strictly on meeting the technical standards and not on feasibility or policy contribution. In an interview, a senior employee of Regional Development Office stated that due to the inflow of an 'excessive number of applications' there was no time 'to evaluate each and every project in greater detail'.[55] SDF pointed out that selection committees were often confused as to which policy area or theme should be prioritized when dealing with Roma exclusion. In general, the consensus was that: 'any intervention is better than none' as long as Roma communities are presented as a target group.[56] However, rather than promoting complex approaches, the tendency was to introduce one-dimensional, minor assistance services (i.e. training, social curatorship, setting up of community centres, or infrastructural repairs). As stated by the Roma Institute:

> This is what happens when you are under pressure to spend the money on time, but you are not really required to contribute to social integration in a wider sense. People go for projects that are easy to realize, whether such initiatives are actually helpful in generating integration is of little regard. As long as you can show that the money was spent as promised you are safe, everything else is just an unimportant detail.[57]

The critics have also pointed out that the targeted approach so strongly supported by the SF stakeholders has neither curtailed the pervasive redirection of SF away from the MRC nor contributed to a larger number of social exclusion projects or higher number of Roma beneficiaries (Hurrle et al., 2012). By and large, this could be attributed to a purely rhetorical articulation of the HP MRC and lack of clear indicators or conditionalities. The Regional Development Agency in Prešov argued that the targeted approached was designed without a clear understanding of the on-the-ground conditions:

> Public servants simply lack extensive knowledge about the MRC, thus the indicators are designed according to technocratic rationales rather than assessments of the situation. There is this push to change or improve the circumstances of Roma, but it cannot work if the people responsible for designing and managing initiatives do not know what exactly needs to change. It is like working in the dark [...] this also kills the morals of the bureaucrats who become convinced that the situation is hopeless, and nothing can be done to improve it.[58]

However, the failure also stemmed from the excessive *problematization* of Roma behaviour – the ethnicization of social exclusion – and the neglect of wider structural inequalities and discrimination. Overall, the objectives stressing the need for institutional modernization fell silent on the issues of discrimination, while the Roma inclusion initiatives were confined to measures lacking any structural component (i.e. training and consulting). Numerous stakeholders argued that the adherence to the targeted approach in fact only reinforced the exclusion and stigmatization of the Roma population. A member of the MC stressed that the pervasive focus on strengthening the adaptability of minorities legitimized the separate approach, disconnected from wider socio-economic developments.[59]

Finally, the analysis of project reports shows that the majority of implemented initiatives did not internalize anti-discrimination or equal treatment goals; according to the 2011 Country Report, less than 2% of implemented projects addressed (directly and indirectly) structural discrimination. According to Roma activists, this further dwarfed the effectiveness and legitimacy of SF projects:

> For a long time, we've been saying that what needs to be targeted are the structures of exclusion and not only the excluded people, this might sound insensitive but offering training to people who live in segregated communities and face daily discrimination in employment and pretty much all other areas of life, well that is just throwing money out the window. SF should be used to change policies, tackle discrimination, promote equality...we don't have projects like that.[60]

Concluding remarks

This chapter demonstrated empirically that the framing of public problems influences the process of policy implementation and its final outputs. The analysis has confirmed that Roma exclusion is largely a constructed concept, underpinned by normative contentions about the causes of poverty and marginalization. While policymakers rely on empirical assessments to formulate the definitions of Roma exclusion, these assessments tend to be mediated by the existing cognitive and moral maps that orient their actions and routines. In turn, these politically accepted definitions legitimize a specific course of action, even if it is not needed or demanded by the final beneficiaries.

In the case of Spanish SF programming, the framing of social exclusion in terms of structural barriers prompted the adoption of a mainstreaming approach for funds allocation. The analysis confirmed that institutionalization of mainstreaming generated an array of anti-discrimination measures that directly and indirectly benefited Roma communities. The absence of targeted strategies and negligent attention to the specificities of Roma exclusion generated a counterintuitive result, as the expected redirection of SF away from the Roma did not take place. In fact, the 'ethnically neutral' approach fostered stronger political attention to patterns of social exclusion and allowed for a higher allocation of SF to Roma people.

In contrast, the Slovak SF programming framed social exclusion in terms of individual or group adaptability with negligent attention given to general institutional inequalities and structural discrimination. This neglect enforced channelling of funding towards measures that aimed to change the behaviour of target groups – Roma communities. The adopted targeted approach was supposed to offset the pervasive practice of redirecting funding from the most marginalized communities, instead leading to the isolation of Roma measures from regional and local development strategies. This had the effect of reinforcing the redirection of funding to other priorities. While targeting appeared sensitive to the specificity of the conditions in the Roma settlements, it in fact contributed to the ethnicization of the problem. As confirmed by SF stakeholders the opportunity for systemic transformation was effectively lost, and the Roma people could benefit only from short-lived training and consulting activities that were not linked to public services or poverty reduction programmes.

These findings challenge the perceived positive influence of the targeting approach, championed by the EU and numerous international Roma advocacy organizations. It appears that targeting SF at minority groups without resources provided for institutional 'transformations' – in particular the enhancement of anti-discrimination principles – is counterproductive as it leads to the ethnicization of the problem and its separation from mainstream policies. This often leads to disenchantment and de-legitimization of the entire SF programming. In fact, if one looks more closely, an increase in the allocation of SF towards Roma integration priorities in Slovakia has actually generated greater contestation of their usefulness in facilitating inclusion.

Given the evidence, the importance of policy design cannot be underestimated in understanding the causes of implementation success and failure. However, it must also be remembered that the implementation of SF strategies rests in the hands of numerous stakeholders, who hold considerable discretion over actual planning and development of strategic documents. Given that governance of SF is realized through complex networks and third-party arrangements, it is necessary to scrutinize who the main participants are and how they influence or interact with strategic action plans. The analysis needs to pay special attention to the participation of Roma minorities in shaping and realizing public interventions. It has been well documented that the Roma continue to face extensive barriers in influencing decision-making processes (McGarry 2010; McGarry and Agarin, 2014; Trehan, 2009). Consistent disenfranchisement considerably weakens the impact of social inclusion policies, as the voice of those most affected rarely informs public interventions. Thus, it is prudent to expect that the institutionalization of mechanisms that bring these voices into all phases of SF programming will substantially shape the effectiveness of SF outputs in terms of quality of allocations and their legitimacy.

Notes

1 De Rynck and McAleavey (2001) analysis of Maastricht Treaty's Articles demonstrates that the strategies that target the economic development of underperforming regions continue to be held in check by inexorable territorialization and that human resource development targeted at specific groups plays a secondary role in cohesion policy.

2 This disconnection was addressed during 2011 negotiations, mainly in response to the impact of economic and financial crisis on cohesion goals (Berkovitz et al., 2015). Hence, the final legal framework of the 2014–2020 cohesion policy funds, adopted by the EP and the Council in December 2013 on the basis of the Commission proposal of 2011, aims to close the gap by providing support (through cohesion policy) for the delivery of structural reforms. Within the broader set of country-specific regulations cohesion policy now targets those that are appropriate to address with multiannual investments within the scope of the European Social Investment Funds. The changes in regulations show that cohesion policy is now more committed to channelling funds at systemic reforms. In practice, this has meant that cohesion policy provides support for (through conditionality and thematic concentration of funding) institutional adjustments/developments in the labour market, public administration, business, research and development, energy, and education policies. While it is too early to determine the effectiveness of these reforms, they have been considered a positive and very much needed development (Berkovitz et al., 2015). At the same time cohesion policy continues to support targeted measures directed at the most marginalized communities and individuals.

3 Participation was conceptualized mostly in terms of a greater access to the offered programmes (EC, 2010). Less emphasis was placed on political aspect of participation – taking part in decision-making over the shape and aim of programmes and projects to be delivered.

4 Surdu's (2016) in-depth examination of the academic and expert discourse about the Roma shows that 'report literature' commissioned by various international/political organizations constitutes to be the main voice on Roma issues. This policy orientation often corresponds to the marginality of Romani research *within* the major disciplines (sociology, political science, or economics). It also stultifies the potential for the critical analyses of the status quo. It appears that academic researchers working with the concept of *Roma inclusion* eagerly borrow from the discourse of experts and political organizations, often legitimizing ideologically charged data as scholarly work.

5 Interview #78, 3 October 2014 (Brussels).

6 Presently evidence-based policymaking has put extreme pressure on public bureaucracies to devise programmes which can quickly deliver visible outputs and outcomes. The channelling of funding to one-dimensional targets has been widely accepted as a strategy to secure visible impact (Bachtler et al., 2017).

7 Mounting evidence shows that the economic crisis has weakened overall commitments to gender mainstreaming at both the supranational level and national level (Karamessini and Rubery, 2014).

8 Generally, in European policy language, applied both in legal and policy documents, anti-discrimination, equal opportunity, and equality mainstreaming are often used as synonyms. This creates major difficulties in developing and implementing efficient policy tools for ensuring equality on different grounds and fostering policy learning.

9 The formulation of this principle merges two related but different equality considerations in a single reasoning. The first consideration advocates for social inclusion actions from which the Roma benefit but which do not exclude other people who share similar socio-economic circumstances. This is to avoid creating new inequalities or injustices by leaving behind some unprivileged. The other consideration rehearses the core idea of mainstreaming as to lace the Roma inclusion interventions in broader policies and decisions. In this approach, the transformative impacts of the policy measures reach out to the majority society as well (Kóczé et al., 2014).

10 Interview #4, 14 June 2011 (Madrid).

11 Interview #11, 22 June 2011 (Seville).

12 Interview #1, 7 June 2011 (Madrid).

13 Interview #9, 22 June 2011 (Seville).

14 Interview #73, 3 October 2014 (Seville).

15 Interview #76, 3 February 2015 (Madrid/Skype).
16 Interview #53, 26 July 2011(Bratislava).
17 Interview #43, 13 May 2011 (Skalica).
18 Interview #11, 22 June 2011 (Seville).
19 Interview #69, 23 July 2011 (Bratislava).
20 Interview #23, 13 June 2011 (Madrid).
21 Interview #23, 13 June 2011 (Madrid).
22 Interview #54, 28 July 2011 (Kosice).
23 Interview #59, 03 March 2011 (Bratislava).
24 Interview #9, 22 June 2011 (Seville).
25 Interview #1, 07 June 2011 (Madrid).
26 It is important to note that the two OPs set the priorities and objectives of all regions, a strategy adopted to reflect the explicit acknowledgment that even in the 'better off' regions structural barriers to employment exist and need to be addressed (Ministry of Employment and Immigration, 2011). As such the two OPs have earmarked the ESF for anti-discrimination measures undertaken in phasing-out regions as well.
27 Interview #75, 3 October 2014 (Seville).
28 Interview #9, 22 June 2011 (Seville).
29 Extended to 2007–2013 and subsequently to 2014–2020.
30 This amount was earmarked on top of funds channelled to Andalusia through the OP FAD (Mid-Term Evaluation Report, 2011).
31 Interview #38, 19 June 2011 (Granada).
32 The only place where culture is mentioned is in the context of education, where it is prescribed that all educational activities should be sensitive to diversity and cultural differences (Thematic Priority No. 72). The OP ESF Andalusia specifically calls for the 'mainstreaming of cultural diversity' inside the education system (58).
33 Interview #8, 16 June 2011 (Madrid).
34 Interview #47, 11 May 2011 (Prague).
35 Interview #50, 26 July 2011 (Bratislava).
36 Interview #68, 26 July 2011 (Bratislava).
37 Interview #46, 26 July 2011 (Bratislava).
38 Interview #59, 3 March 2011 (Bratislava).
39 Interview #62, 23 July 2011 (Bratislava).
40 Surpassed only by Germany and Poland (see Inside Europe, 2014, available at: http://insideurope.eu/taxonomy/term/204).
41 Data up to the end of year 2012 at: www.qren.pt/np4/np4/?newsId=3198&fileNam e=novos_Gr_Site_012013.pdf.
42 Interview #2, 07 June 2011 (Madrid).
43 Interview #9, 22 June 2011 (Seville).
44 Interview #30, 27 June 2011 (Madrid). Interview #36, 23 June 2011 (Servile). Interview #39, 16 June 2011 (Granada).
45 Interview #22, 6 June 2012 (Brussels).
46 While there is no expansive data to confirm this, it does appear the working of OP FAD served to reinforce the efforts of the Spanish state to expand its anti-discrimination legislation.
47 Interview #30, 27 June 2011 (Madrid).
48 Interview #8, 16 June 2011 (Madrid).
49 Interview #1, 7 June 2011 (Madrid).
50 Interview #11, 22 June 2011 (Seville).
51 In 2007–2011, SF allocation prompted the creation of over 300 social enterprises in Andalusia, benefiting over 30,000 people, an unofficial estimate points out that more than 12% of the beneficiaries were of the Roma background.
52 Interview #60, 2 March 2011 (Kosice).
53 Interview #72, 26 July 2011 (Banská Bystrica).

54 In an interview the Regional Development Office confirmed that for one-project call, the demand exceeded expected prognosis by 200%. Interview# 51, 26 July 2011 (Bratislava).
55 Interview #51, 26 July 2011 (Bratislava).
56 Interview #50, 26 July 2011 (Bratislava).
57 Interview #61, 26 July 2011 (Bratislava).
58 Interview #55, 26 July 2011 (Prešov).
59 The 2012 UNDP Report has demonstrated this empirically (Hurrle et al., 2012).
60 Interview #73, 14 May 2011 (Skalica).

5 Working through partnership
Who, how, to what effect?

The previous chapter showed that the discursive aspects of policy design plays an important role in structuring the implementation process. Hence, the analysis of programmatic outputs needs to begin with a critical examination of the ways in which policy proposals produce 'social exclusion' as a particular kind of problem. That is, policy responses need to be understood as part of a discursive construction of the 'problem'. However, policy implementation is not simply an interplay of words and ideas, but a complex process involving a growing number of actors bound by various interests, norms, and institutionalized routines. Inside cohesion policy design, new forms of public participation are emerging as stakeholders seek opportunities to actively participate in shaping the policies that affect their communities. In response, member states are exploring new ways to inform and include civil society and private interests in vital decisions over funding and development. In many ways, wider participation becomes paradigmatic of accountable governance. In the context of the ongoing decentralization, policy outputs are becoming contingent on collaborative arrangements. As such, the analysis of SF programming needs to venture beyond the discursive elements of funding schemes and focus on untangling the networks of power invested in controlling and managing EU financial transfers.

Partnership is now a core principle of SF programming (Regulation (EEC) 2052/88). In recent years it has informed successive waves of reforms aiming to involve an increasingly wide range of stakeholders in the planning and implementation of OPs, which account for the needs and priorities of stakeholders and final beneficiaries on a local level. A model of effective and legitimate governance, partnership aims to draw on the knowledge and expertise of an array of public, private, and social actors and contribute to the accountable development of local capacities. Partnership is often presented as a rational tool tied to the principle of subsidiarity and the principle of proportionality governing the exercise of the EU's competences. However, the requirement in the Council Regulations for member states to designate the most representative partners for SF management indicates that cooperation arrangements have strong normative underpinnings. This chapter investigates the practice and quality of partnership in Spain and Slovakia, with the aim of inferring which mode of participatory policymaking has proved the most conducive to successful SF outputs. The critical analysis attends to the normative concept of *representation*, highlighting the conflicting notions of who should represent the interests of MRC and through which means. The central thesis of this chapter is that the consolidation of partnership is a project orchestrated by the state and not the result of grassroots mobilization. As such, the analysis pays attention to the way governments frame the purpose of participatory arrangements and enable (or prevent) local communities to take an active part in SF programming.

The governance literature presents partnership either as a tool for accessing knowledge and expertise of a wide array of actors (Conway, 1999; Rhodes et al., 2003; Osborne and Gaebler, 1992), or as a highly political instrument with the faculty to empower disenfranchised groups and improve the democratic workings of the state (Geddes, 2006; Taylor, 2007; Finn, 2000; Fung, 2004). Each consideration brings to light important questions regarding the impact partnership may have on effective, legitimate, and equitable governance. What this chapter problematizes is the notion of legitimate representation: whether SF partnership should directly include members of the marginalized community (people directly affected by exclusion) or professionals and policy experts trained in specific themes and adherent to dominant political ideologies. The advocates of Roma integration call for the mandatory involvement of Romani voices, arguing that only when Roma people themselves partake in all aspects of policymaking, and have the authority to make vital policy decisions, can public intervention bring about effective results (Guy, 2013). Minority rights advocates insist that partnership should not only strive to generate informed policymaking but also support the very empowerment of marginalized communities (Richardson and Ryder, 2012; Cohen et al., 2018). In short, only through enabling the Roma people to partake in policymaking can power hierarchies be equalized and real progress take place. Considering these debates, this chapter asserts that the partnership design most likely to promote successful SF outputs must account for the presence of marginalized interests (by inviting community representatives to take an active part in decision-making processes) and facilitate sustainable collaboration between these interests and a cadre of policy experts and development specialists. In order for such dynamics to develop, the state needs to support less resourced organizations (and local authorities), and be able to cede power to social and local stakeholders.

The empirical section of this chapter analyzes the partnership practice developed in Spain and Slovakia along two important dimensions in which mechanisms of participation vary. The first dimension concerns who participates, whether recruitment is open to all who wish to engage, or those powerful interests who are summoned and resourceful service delivery organizations. The second dimension examines the institutionalization of partnership arrangements, focusing on the amount of decision-making the authorities ceded to new participants, and the availability of enabling resources provided to marginalized interests. It then explores the link between partnership design and successful policy outputs. The findings show that each country developed a distinct partnership design reflective of governing norms and the dominant framing of social inclusion. Spain extended partnership to carefully selected policy experts and service delivery organizations who received considerable decision-making authority and technical support. The resulting co-productive modes of partnership improved implementation of funding, even though they largely failed to empower Romani voices and strengthen minority claims. In Slovakia, the opening of partnership to all interested stakeholders, corresponded with reluctance to cede decision-making authority over strategic action plans and to provide technical support for less organized interests. This not only weakened the managerial effectiveness of SF initiatives but also, more importantly, diminished the input of Roma-led organizations and grassroots Roma rights activists. Overall, the findings demonstrate that in a highly bureaucratic system of European financial transfers, expertise and professionalism are more valued (and indeed are more likely to secure successful outputs) than the equal representation of minority interests. At the same time, while the endorsement of partnership principles by SF schemes creates participatory spaces, these are carefully orchestrated by the national and regional authorities, who maintain the final decision over who participates and through what means.

Representation at crossroads: expertise versus political voice

As shown in Chapter 3, governance literature upholds the idea that the complexity of modern public problems necessitates a range of inputs from the experts involved in delivering social, economic, and infrastructural programmes (Conway, 1999; Rhodes et al., 2003; Osborne and Gaebler, 1992; Osborne, 2010; McQuaid, 2010; Nelson and Zadek, 2000). It is now a norm to present partnership working as an expedient tool for tackling various causes, as well as the symptoms, of complex public dilemmas. The scholarship on collaborative policymaking upholds that partnership is a particular type of institution, a technical device with the general purpose of carrying a concrete concept of the *politics/society relationships* sustained by regulations (Osborne, 2010; Bache, 2010). This conceptualization is driven by an omnipresent conviction that policymaking is a rational, evidence-based process focused on finding optimal solutions to well-defined issues and problems. As such, governance theorists invested in cohesion policy expect that policymakers and the ruling elites voluntarily recruit organizations that hold specific merits, thematic orientations, and policy resources, which will enhance the effectiveness of public interventions (Brinkerhoff, 2002; Jordana et al., 2012). McQuaid (2010) argues that governments seek partnerships which allow for the pooling of resources (i.e. increasing the number of budget-holding organizations involved in delivering solutions), improving efficiency (i.e. avoiding duplication in service delivery) and sharing knowledge and expertise (i.e. to maximize the appropriateness, quality, and efficiency of provisions). The flexible nature of partnership can also facilitate a process of comparison and appraisal so that governments can identify best practices and evaluate alternative options. Inherent in these convictions is an explicit understanding that partnership should *enhance* policymaking rather than bring about *political change*. This instrumentalist perspective falls silent on issues of empowerment or grassroots mobilization, as it does not consider these dimensions conductive to territorial cohesion and consensus making over development strategies (Crescenzi and Giua, 2016).

Few scholars refute the positive value expertise brings into policymaking. However, critics point out that the prioritization of technocratic efficiency (the 'added value' for policymaking through drawing on the knowledge and skills of experts) actually destabilizes transparency and democratic accountability (Bauer, 2002, Derkzen and Bock, 2009; Newman, 2001; Gittell, 2001; Rahman, 2016). Peters and Pierre (2004) describe the trade-off between efficiency and democracy as a 'Faustian bargain' whereby the reliance on expert organizations marginalizes the role of elected politicians and local community leaders and obscures accountability to voters and local jurisdictions. Rahman (2016) contends that policy expertise should offer insights, but not a resolution because to do otherwise is to reduce citizens to 'passive observers' and mere beneficiaries of properly rationalized decision-making. 'Experts can provide information, advice, and knowledge as inputs into democratic debates, but it is the democratic public that must hold sway to check guide and channel the use of expert knowledge' (Rahman, 2016, p. 100). The move to open weighty matters of public concern up to political and democratic judgement is not a rejection of expertise, but rather an effort to place expertise in its proper place.

Advocates of community-focused governance also challenge the professionalization of partnership, arguing that it does little to empower marginalized voices. Goetz (2009, p. 240) insists that existing patterns of privilege and the uneven distribution of resources are not necessarily altered just because there are new participants in the system. The rise of heterarchy and the diffusion of power are just as likely to reinforce hierarchies by masking underlying power relations. Extensive empirical studies validate these normative claims by showing that the participation of the poorest and most socially excluded is far from straightforward and that a number of preconditions exist for entry of the poorest people into participatory institutions (Rigon, 2014). Impoverished communities have limited lobbying capacity and are often unable to bring to the table the needed (or expected) resources. Many of the new spaces created became bureaucratic arenas where 'one-size-fits-all', unable to take into account people's contexts and, therefore, failing to empower participants, de facto legitimizing decisions taken by others. Putting structures of participation in place is not enough to create political institutions that respond to the priorities of the people living in poverty. The analyses of partnership arrangements in cohesion policy show that only a few are accountable, inclusive, and representative of poor communities and fewer still go beyond funds management or delivery to impact on law and policy (Polverari and Michie, 2009, Dąbrowski, 2013). Far more often, partnership with social actors is little more than a façade as governments maintain full control over funding allocations (Dobbs and Moore, 2002; Kröger, 2008; Guy, 2009).

Advocates of Roma rights have been the severest critics of expert-driven partnership, actively pushing for a shift in the site of decision-making from a close group of experts to the community organizations and citizens directly affected by exclusion and discrimination (Kóczé and Trehan, 2009; Jovanović, 2013;

Surdu, 2016). They argue that engaging Roma community representatives and minority rights advocates in policymaking could be a meaningful way to curtail paternalistic attitudes and oust the tokenistic interventions delivered by the state (Jovanović, 2013). The Roma activist, Rudko Kawczynski (1997), takes a more radical stance arguing that there is no substitute for the involvement of the community itself at all levels of the political process. In his opinion, the Roma people need to engage in grassroots mobilization anchored in a civil rights movement and aimed at changing the attitudes and structures of the majority, rather than at changing the behaviour of the minority. McGarry (2010) in turn argues that participation in mainstream policies and programmes could not only create new approaches to marginality, but also instigate an enabling environment for political struggle, which may allow excluded Roma communities to exercise agency through the institutions, spaces, and strategies they make and shape for themselves. In short, the participation of Roma representatives in policymaking, not only implies their recognition as fully-fledged citizens and capable contributors to the development of society, it also contributes to more legitimate and informed social inclusion policies. In this sense, partnership is not an end in itself but a means for expanding the overall democratic quality of public governance and ceding power to the communities.

Architecting representation in cohesion policy

The inclusion of historically disenfranchised communities in governing processes is not a straightforward matter. First, an important differentiation to make when discussing community participation is to clarify whether we are talking of *organic* or *induced* participation. Organic participation refers to civic groups acting independently of, and often in opposition to, government (e.g. civil rights movements, collective action against particular interventions, and ethnic/racial mobilization). Organic participation generates the so-called claimed spaces, spaces that powerless or excluded groups create for themselves (Fung, 2006). These spaces range from ones created by social movements and community associations (networks, fora, communes, etc.), to those simply involving common spaces where people meet to debate outside of the institutionalized policy arenas. In contrast, induced participation refers to participation promoted through the policy actions of the state, responding to popular demands, international pressure, or shifts in policy. There is often some overlap between organic and induced participation. For example, a government may decide to scale up the efforts of small-scale organic initiatives and thus turn them into induced initiatives. However, they remain in conflict over access to and control over indigenous resources.

Roma involvement in cohesion policy very much resembles induced participation, which in the last decade has become synonymous with effective and legitimate policy interventions (EC, 2011). All major stakeholders, including the EU, expressed their concerns with the disenfranchisement of Roma people from the socio-political sphere of influence, calling for the involvement of Roma people at every stage of the policymaking process. The 10 Common Basic Principles for Roma Inclusion explicitly calls for the active participation of Roma in the design, implementation, and evaluation of policy initiatives (Principle 11). The main idea is that member states should support the full participation of Roma people in public life and aim to stimulate active citizenship of the Roma people, as well as to develop their human resources. While the way to achieve such an active participation is not very well specified, the EC and international advocacy bodies request consultations with the communities, the use of community knowledge and expertise (i.e. through scaling up good practices), and capacity-building initiatives (i.e. global grants and training). What comes across from the mounting volumes of recommendations and policy briefs, is that the involvement of Roma people should be 'induced and nourished by the state', an assumption often challenged by scholars and activists invested in collective mobilization.

In fact, many Roma activists cynically refer to the state's sponsored participation as the 'Gypsy industry', which they contend, enriches the participating individuals but leaves most Roma unaffected (Trehan, 2001). However, ethnic mobilization of Roma communities remains weak and cramped inside the NGO sector (Sobotka, 2002). The ethnographical diversity of the Roma population combined with severe levels of discrimination and lack of resources within marginalized communities effectively curtails efforts to gain political influence (Vermeersch, 2006; McGarry, 2010). In effect, many Roma activists themselves insist that 'local and national politicians must understand that it is their responsibility to change the existing game' (Daróczi, 2017, quoted in European Economic and Social Committee, 2017).[1] However, the harvesting of political will to include Roma representatives in policymaking has proven problematic. Governments continue to rely on carefully selected thematic experts who manage Roma inclusion programmes according to pre-designed action plans. While many of these experts are now recruited from a growing pool of Roma, critics point out that these so-called 'Roma-in-charge', not only lack decision-making authority but are far removed from the realities of local communities (Richardson and Ryder, 2012; Nicolae, 2012). As commented by the Director of the Roma Initiatives Office at the OSFs, Željko Jovanović (2013, p. 198): 'while a degree of institutional participation has been granted to us, we have no political power to enforce change.'

The superficial inclusion of community interests has also been attributed to the pervasive view that Roma make difficult partners because of their assumed low level of professionalism and political experience (Trehan, 2001; Surdu, 2016). However, the EU's limited efforts to promote community empowerment are not restricted to Roma people and are reflective of the general conceptualization of *partnership* in cohesion regulations. The overall prerogative of the regulations was one of 'increased partnership working, with greater involvement of sub-national bodies, economic and social partners and other organizations among the member states' (EC, No. 229/2008). However, national governments maintained the authority to select the most 'competent' bodies (Article 9, Council Regulation 183/2006). As such, the new governance spaces, as Cornwall (2004) reminds us, are spaces to which partners are invited by the state and which are created and defined by the state (*invited spaces*) as opposed to spaces created and defined by citizens (*popular spaces*). The top-down approach is virtually incompatible with grassroots mobilization unless the former aligns its goals with those of the state. In a time of austerity and with the normalization of far-right discourse, voices of impoverished and racially oppressed groups have little chance to gain political support.

Hence, despite the progressing decentralization and consolidation of multi-level governance in the sphere of cohesion policy, government officers still hold the power to arbitrarily open or close participatory spaces and give importance to (or withhold importance from) social interests and the claims made by them. As pointed out by Jones (2003), central government is more willing to open up partnership to resourceful agents who can take over certain duties (i.e. service delivery) than to engage actors who challenge the governing status quo and seek to re-shape existing approaches to regional development. Empirical research confirms that many national and regional governments act as gatekeepers and exclude organizations that do not adhere to a dominant policy discourse/practice or are not in possession of needed resources (Kröger, 2008; Parker and Clements, 2012). In many instances, the emergence of partnership arrangements enhances the prominence of a small, professionalized and elite group of local/social actors. The elitist character of partnership often remains even if the elite is a more inclusive one than before, for example, through the inclusion of community interests (Geddes, 2006) and/or the provision of capacity-building resources to weakly-organized localities (Zadek and Radovich, 2006). However, as observed by Kurzydlowski (2013), these invited (and/or supported) community organizations often function more like public service deliverers rather than representatives of specific social interests, invested in empowering local communities. As such, they often deliver projects designed in offices far removed from the local contexts.

In sum, partnership within cohesion policy does not resemble a level playing field where all 'invited' stakeholders engage with one another directly as equals and reason together about public problems. According to Fung (2006), the sole expression of participants' interests or endorsements of community consultations does not guarantee that different interests and requests will translate into actual decisions over policies. Governance theorists maintain that a partnership capable of transforming community interests into effective policies must nourish local participation through enabling efforts (i.e. technical, administrative, or cognitive). However, as argued by Cornwall (2004) and Fung (2006), to avoid paternalism the enabling governance needs to cede decision-making authority to local agents as well as cultivate deliberation and consensus making. Of course, whether these partnership arrangements generate successful implementation outputs is not to be assumed, but to be researched empirically. Spain and Slovakia both realized their commitments to partnership in a substantially different manner – the difference very much reflecting domestic approaches to social inclusion and equality. To understand the impact partnership arrangements had on the implementation of European funding, the analysis focuses on the purpose and institutionalization of collaborative modes of governance, as well as the political and technocratic motivation to recruit the most competent partners.

However, the reality of Local Social Partners (LSPs) (to deal with them first) does not necessarily bear out these hopes. The emergence of the LSP tends to enhance the prominence of a small elite group of local actors (notwithstanding the fact that there may be significant differences as to who is in and who is outside the charmed circle). The elitist character of LSPs remains even if the elite is a more inclusive one than before, for example through the inclusion of 'community' interests. Moreover, the business of the LSP is largely conducted behind closed doors, with only very limited public or democratic transparency or accountability. In this, LSPs reflect wider concerns about the transparency and accountability of network governance (Bailey, 2003, p. 455). There are also limitations to the extent to which LSPs, in reality, bring together the interests of the public, private, and voluntary, and community sectors in a more pluralist and discursive process. There are a number of points here (see also Lowndes and Sullivan, 2004).

In the first place, the lines of communication between the individuals serving on the LSP, and the wider constituencies, which in principle they represent in some way, are often tenuous.

Shaping partnership in Spain and Slovakia

In Spain, partnership principles need to be analyzed through the prism of progressive regionalization processes, which commenced after the transition to democracy in 1979 (Pi-Sunyer, 2010). The creation of 17 ACs and the adoption of the principles of the autonomous process by Constitutional Court (1983) prompted a rapid devolution of expenditure powers and legislative transfers (including healthcare, education, and social services). Decentralization progressed through bilateral commissions, in which political negotiations determined the competencies and costs of sustaining services for each AC (see Sanz, 2010). In this context, cohesion policy, especially the partnership principle, acted as 'an added resource for regional mobilization strengthening ACs position vis-à-vis their struggle for more constitutional power' (Ladrech, 2010, p. 111). However, the redefinition of the central state's relations with historical regions left local and social actors outside the sphere of influence. As explained by a senior public servant from the Andalusian Ministry of Local Administration and Institutional Relations:

> Andalusian authorities, as well as other ACs, found it difficult to accept that their newly gained powers should be shared with an array of new actors. Since the 80s ACs were lobbying for a greater say in the use of SF and considered local involvement a threat to their bargaining power. The administration viewed cooperation with social partners in a more relaxed manner, mostly because it did not challenge the political gains of regions. In fact, public managers thought that the third sector could bring in expertise and resources, desperately needed for development of regional services, without hijacking political power. Yet, in the 1990s, nobody dreamed that one day NGOs would determine the shape of OPs let alone NSRF.[2]

The recognition that the Spanish institutional framework is not well prepared to address acute socio-economic problems (see Chapter 4) meant that the central and regional authorities were in dire need of resources and expertise (Morata and Popartan, 2008). Partnership proved a useful tool for enhancing bureaucratic knowhow. In an interview, the manager of the Central ESF Administration Unit confirmed that the unit decided to extend partnership to local agents (including city halls and NGOs) to instigate knowledge transfer from deprived areas to public administration. However, regional stakeholders treated the political dimension of partnership with caution and remained reluctant to cede decision-making authority or support local activism.

> We need to cooperate with these actors [local authorities and social partners] to learn more about on-the-ground realities and concerns, so our responses can be more effective. At the same time, we want to maintain discretion over funds allocations; we want to make sure that funding is used to support our political priorities.[3]

Despite intensifying lobbying efforts of local interests to secure 'fair' representation in decisions over funding, partnership maintained its vertical and exclusive character (Leonardi, and Nanetti, 2011). The central and regional administrations maintained full control over the strategic dimensions of SF programming, recruiting actors with long-standing experience working in delineated priority areas. Prospective partners (including IBs, supervisory bodies, consultants, and project managers) were expected to have well-developed networks of influence (in the local communities and professional sectors), a 'good record' of performance (demonstrable outputs, outcomes) and capacity to propose innovative interventions derived from successful pilot projects.[4] Even the composition of MCs, which in theory was to reflect a variety of interests (NSRF, 2007, p. 218), was restricted to service-providing organizations well-connected to public institutions (i.e. members of Sectoral Networks or Social Pacts[5]). As stated by the department head of the ESF Administrative Unit: 'it is important to work with experienced partners whom we can trust, who can engage in constructive dialogue and who are open to compromise'.[6] While, commentators criticized the approach based on trust for reinforcing political patronage, an evaluation of organizations serving in MCs confirmed that indeed all recruited members had substantiated experience in service delivery, management of social inclusion projects, and were the key leaders of professional networks.[7] Still, while the MAs insisted that they worked with a diversity of social and private entities who engage in innovative approaches to social exclusion, the analysis of the consolidated partnership demonstrates that most of participating organizations aligned their goals with regional development strategies and championed conventional approaches. Hence, few (if any) organizations that directly challenged the status quo received an invitation to collaborate. As confirmed by MA representative:

> It should be remembered, that we need partners who can help us penetrate areas traditionally bypassed by our welfare provisions, so we look for

organizations that have documented experience in delivering assistance [...]. At the same time, we need to work together and not challenge one another; this requires some common ground or what we call organizational fit [...]. The state uses SF to improve its workings, not to cater to political interests [...]. If people are not satisfied, we have numerous political channels where such dissatisfaction can be expressed.[8]

The Andalusian authorities shared this position confirming that they preferred to work with partners who held complementary social inclusion goals (i.e. improving access to public services) and were directly involved in the provision of employment and education services. This was visible in the OP FAD, which was realized by organizations with solid records of service provision to groups at risk of exclusion (including the Roma people), at once pushing out organizations advocating for minority rights and grassroots mobilization efforts.

Critics attested that the recruitment of professional service providers over community activists stemmed from a deeply embedded fear that the representation of minority interests at the strategic level of SF programming could set off nationalistic sentiments, and reinvigorate independence movements in Catalonia and Basque Country. In fact, the central government considered involving a minority rights organization detrimental to social solidarity and the overall ('ethnically neutral') socio-economic objectives of SF programming. When asked about the state of Roma representation in SF partnership, the Seville Provincial Office insisted that ethnic representation is not vital for legitimate and effective use of funding:

> This idea that services for the Roma should be designed and delivered by Roma-led organizations might sound good in theory but in practice, it simply reinforces societal division [...]. Organizations with membership linked exclusively to ethnicity are often unable or even unwilling to provide services for other groups [...]. We receive only a small share of SF, and we think it is best to use it for projects that aim to improve the situation of all vulnerable groups [...] of course community input is important but from our experience, public funding is best used by organizations that account for wider socio-economic issues affecting all impoverished and excluded citizens.[9]

This sentiment was echoed in interviews with central and regional stakeholders, who insisted that effective social inclusion programmes do not need to be delivered by people identifying with a specific race or ethnicity; 'commitment to equality and cohesion this is what we need, progressive thinking and accountability is what we value, who brings these to the table is not all that relevant'.[10]

Interestingly, this stance has not resulted in a total ousting of organizations working predominately with Roma communities. In fact, the FSG, a well-established foundation promoting access of Spanish Roma to rights, services, goods, and social resources on an equal footing with the rest of the citizenry, undertook a key role in the strategic phase of SF programming. However, the recruitment of the FSG reflected the general trend of involving partners who are willing to work 'for' the government and are skilled in the delivery of innovative services.[11] FAD adeptly aligned its organizational goals with the priorities and objectives of the authorities, a process that guaranteed its place at the decision-making table. As explained by the director:

> We knew that we needed to follow government's lead if our efforts were to be taken seriously by them, we had to convince the government that we have what they need – resources, community networks, and trust of the people we work with.[12]

In 1997, the FSG ran a pilot project, INTEGRA, presenting it to the central authorities as a template for employment inclusion interventions. The multicultural approach and the structural aims of the project (i.e. working closely with public employment offices to enhance existing employment insertion programmes) fitted well with government's plan to increase employment rates and tackle discrimination in the labour market:

> The FSG proposed a feasible and innovative project, which greatly aligned with our goals and priorities. Given that the pilot resulted in favourable outcomes, the ministry was inclined to put its resources behind the initiative. FSG commitment to serving all needy citizens together with its extensive networks with other NGOs and local groups made them an ideal partner for developing labour inclusion projects, the fact that they provided services to Roma communities was an additional asset.[13]

FSG involvement in employment initiatives (later expanded to education programmes) did not escape criticism. Minority rights advocates, more critical of the government's agenda, argued that the FSG's unidimensional focus on employment did not account for the wider needs and interests of Roma communities. As one member of the Gypsy Association in Granada stated: 'they [FSG] are simply pleasing the state, they cater to the neoliberal agenda that's what they do, they don't represent Roma interests, they represent interests of the state'.[14]

Despite these criticisms, the work of FSG demonstrates that 'professionalized' NGOs working closely with the public authorities were willing and able to offer vital assistance to the most marginalized groups. In fact, the solidarity of professional NGOs with Roma communities has been a prominent feature of Spanish civil society, and the so-called 'Spanish model' for Roma inclusion (Rodríguez Cabrero, 2011). The State Council of Social Action NGOs, the EAPN-Spain, the Volunteer's Platform, and SOS Racism have all sought to incorporate Roma issues into civic dialogue and create links with local Roma-led organizations and associations. This expression of solidarity has played a key role in anchoring Roma issues in the state's political agenda, even amidst the rampaging economic crisis. As expressed by a member of EAPN-Spain: 'Gitanos are full-fledged Spanish citizens, so yes, we call on to the government to make sure that Gitanos are treated as equal citizens'.[15]

In Slovakia, the mobilization of the partnership principle has taken a different course, strongly influenced by the unsystematic decentralization process. Since the transition to democracy and separation from the Czech Republic, the Slovak incumbent parties have been supporting a centralized model of governance taking steps to empower the central authority at the expense of self-government and civil society (OECD, 2014). The decentralization attempts undertaken in the 1990s were severely curtailed by a weak administrative capacity, a low level of cooperative culture, and a tradition of excessive reliance on bureaucratic control and command structures (see Bailey and De Propris, 2002; Davey and Gábor, 2008). In this context, the central administration maintained full control over regional development, almost singlehandedly setting the strategic outlook, key priorities, and management methods. The role of regional administration and local self-government remained minuscule, with all MAs (including the MA for OP Regional Development (OP RD)) working under the jurisdiction of central administration (Bassa, 2007). The influence of civil society was even weaker, characterized by ad-hoc interactions, which took place outside the institutional framework. The government recruited MC members in an ad-hoc manner, handpicking individual members without providing a concrete rationale for their choices (Batory and Cartwright, 2011). As late as 2006, there was no concrete strategy for civil society involvement in SF programming.

In the 2007–2013 funding period, the situation began to change due to strong EU pressure and the lobbying efforts of Slovak civil society (and to a lesser degree, local authorities) to formalize partnership arrangements. The government set up MCs for all the OPs, which became sites for peer learning, the exchange of best practices, and the discussion of common problems. This was true for both the representatives of regional authorities and various NGOs. In short, MCs became a platform for informal networks to emerge among actors who otherwise might never have come into contact (Batory and Cartwright, 2011). Moreover, a coalition of CSOs (civil society organizations) at the Governmental Council for NGOs (an advisory body of the government) proposed a uniform system for delegating MC members and for increasing the number of participants. Despite numerous setbacks, the selection process became more transparent and standardized. A member of MC noted that:

> MCs are far from ideal, however considering the previous funding period we [social actors] made substantial progress. The selection process if anything is more transparent and representative of the diverse societal needs. It is also open to all those actors who take interest and are eager to contribute their voice.[16]

Overall, the prevailing discourse on partnership championed the notion of 'voice' over 'expertise'. During interviews, both social actors and local authorities insisted that partnership was an entitlement and a tool for advancing pluralist democracy. While the central managers emphasized that NGOs' contributions were relevant to the shared goal of the successful absorption of EU development funds, they were excessively vague on what specific knowhow or resources these actors could bring into policymaking.

> Some of NGOs serve as our trusted experts, they provide substantive suggestion and help us to articulate important issues better [...]. We need these actors to stay closer to the people we are supposed to serve.[17]

In fact, SF programming made no reference to the experience or expertise needed to strengthen the design and delivery of social inclusion interventions,[18] instead emphasizing the need to engage a wide assortment of voices (NSRF, 2007, p. 9). The main eligibility criteria for participation reflected this omission, accounting mainly for the legal status of organizations, thematic interests, and ethnic status (i.e. Hungarian, Romani).

Not surprisingly, MCs gathered a wide assortment of representatives operating in different policy fields (i.e. employment, human rights, disability, environment, minority, etc.). Among the participants, a growing number of Roma-led organizations began to take an interest, a development greatly praised by the international community (see Schreier, 2015). Working groups included Roma organizations that managed community centres, promoted civic rights activism, and/or organized cultural events. They also included providers of education services, housing developers, legal issues specialists, and charities (Batory and Cartwright, 2011). This organizational congestion was justified on the grounds that as a diverse ethnic minority, the Roma people need wide-ranging representation. Some stakeholders even insisted that given the size of the Roma population, and the scope of the problems they face, the representational sample was still too small.[19]

Discussions on the 'legitimate' representation of Roma in partnership arrangements placed a strong emphasis on the ethnic identity of selected leaders and organizations. According to the OSF, this focus was in fact supported by the authorities mainly because of international pressure (i.e. from the EU and international advocacy groups) demanding 'genuine' Roma representation in all aspects of SF programming.[20] International expert groups and advocacy coalitions maintained that tailored Roma inclusion interventions could only be successful if designed, delivered, and monitored by the Roma themselves (EURoma, 2011). The Office of the Slovak Government Plenipotentiary for Roma Communities became a key agency for securing Roma representation in SF programming, while MCs provided 'extra spaces' for Roma-led organizations. The presence of Roma representatives aimed to curtail 'ethno-business' dynamics whereby experts (mostly non-Roma) pushed out Roma-run initiatives and prevented the formation of grassroots social capital. As attested by a Roma-led NGO:

> The state treats Roma people as a target group, but nobody asks us about what it is that we need or that we want. We are bombarded with initiatives that at times appear simply absurd: computer classes for illiterate people or refurbishing segregated classrooms. This form of help is simply not effective, promoting passive attitudes. If the Roma are given a chance to organize and

build necessary organizational capacities, they can then contribute as managers and consultants, not only recipients.[21]

However, in practice, the envisioned benefits of Roma representation have failed to strengthen the 'true' voice of excluded citizens in SF programming. According to the interviewees (from both public and social spheres), recruited Roma-led organizations could rarely demonstrate involvement in the communities they were claiming to represent. Many commentators openly questioned the legitimacy of Roma participants, arguing that they seldom hold community support:

> For the authorities, anybody who claims to be a Roma is automatically a legitimate leader; nobody bothers to check who they represent and what they do in real life. Those with money can travel to Bratislava and make claims for people they do not even know, and they get money because the government can then say that Roma are being helped.[22]

> This whole participatory talk is strictly superficial, they include Roma organizations to appease international watchdogs, but nobody bothers to engage communities in true dialogue.[23]

At the same time, SF authorities maintained that it was not their responsibility to ensure or verify the legitimacy of Roma leaders. As bluntly expressed by a senior public servant:

> We open the door for all those who want to participate, [...] if the people consider the Roma leaders to be illegitimate it is up to the communities to delegate somebody else. But Roma say one thing and then say something different, that's the fact. People who want to get heard need to organize and set their priorities first, we are not able to interact with groups who simply expect to have a voice in public matters without contributing their own resources. Roma want a lot but are not willing to work for it.[24]

This explicitly racist statement, shared by many of the interviewed MA members. It demonstrates that the government placed the responsibility of 'getting involved' on the interested groups or localities, with that giving strength to the already widespread notion that the Roma communities needed to take care of their own matters. The emphasis placed on the ethnic dimensions of partnership combined with racist sentiments diminished the potential to form coalitions between Roma and non-Roma organizations and stakeholders. Interviews with various MC members confirmed that most participating Roma representatives were not part of any larger networks or policy coalitions, and often did not hold a common stance on policy action or strategy.[25] The mainstream NGOs were not prepared (or willing) to incorporate Roma issues inside their agendas. A frequent reason provided by the NGOs was that Roma-led organizations were keen to address issues affecting only their communities (or families) and were not interested in working on wider strategic objectives.[26] At the same time, Roma representatives claimed that mainstream NGOs and local authorities were unwilling to place Roma interests on their strategic agenda.[27] This reluctance was also reinforced by the notion (held by both Roma and non-Roma stakeholders) that patterns of Roma social exclusion differ substantially from the general population and thus should be addressed by the Roma themselves. This view legitimized the off-loading of public responsibilities onto the communities and their representatives, who often held little direct experience delivering complex socio-economic projects and were not resourced well enough to interact with a complex and often hostile bureaucratic apparatus.

Institutionalization of partnership

As Slovakia opened-up partnership to a wide assortment of actors including minority representatives, Spain maintained exclusive partnership arrangements reserved for expert organizations with experience in service delivery. These different approaches to recruitment influenced the way the authorities in the two countries consolidated Roma interests inside wider policy networks and decision-making over SF allocations. This, in turn, had a serious impact on the outputs of SF programming.

An important feature of the Spanish partnership arrangements was that both the national and regional governments provided substantial technical support for the enhancement of inter-agency collaboration. In the 2000–2006 funding period, the OP Technical Assistance (TA) made 'support for strengthening administrative and cognitive capacities of SF partners' its main objective. It earmarked funds for research activities (i.e. situational studies, household surveys and impact evaluations) as well as communication and information exchange channels (i.e. the creation of networks, thematic groups, forums, and seminars). The assistance sought to improve the quality and effectiveness of the SF operational system (coordination, allocation, evaluation, management, and monitoring) and promote lesson-learning and best-practice exchange. The bulk of technical resources went to the MAs, the paying authorities, and supervisory bodies. Although the localities and civil society organizations were not direct beneficiaries, they were eligible for research grants and subsidies for training and communication (i.e. networks, forums, awareness raising, etc.). Between 2007 and 2013, OP TA spent close to €64 million (in convergence regions) on capacity-building interventions. Additionally, technical assistance constituted an objective in all the OPs, earmarking funds for planning, implementation, evaluation, and internal audits.

A key source of technical support directed at third-sector organizations came in the shape of programmes financed by general taxation (0.5% of income tax payments explicitly targeted by taxpayers in their annual income tax statements) global grants, and public subsidies. The central and regional authorities earmarked 5% of public budgets for providing material infrastructure and human resources assistance to selected NGOs (mainly through training initiatives, information exchange, and consultancy services). Annual reports of key NGOs active in SF programming demonstrated that state support was the main source of their funding,[28] a dynamic criticized for generating the explicit co-option and infiltration of civil society by political interests. Indeed, as demonstrated by Verge (2012), public funding succeeded in shaping the civil society organizations' goals and objectives, creating a formalized professional non-profit sector for the delivery of service provision. The ESF MA confirmed that they granted technical assistance predominately to service delivery organizations, to enhance their presence in the sector of social policies, which laid in the jurisdiction of the AC.[29] Although NGOs maintained some critical voice, their capacity to act as vital watchdogs and whistleblowers remained weak. Yet, while it is difficult to reject the co-optation thesis, the collaboration between public authorities and NGOs did grant the latter an unprecedented influence over SF programming design (Leonardi and Nanetti, 2011).

The involvement of NGOs in SF programming came into force in the 2000–2006 funding period. For the first time, five national NGOs were nominated as IBs in two multi-regional OPs, OP FAD and OP TA (these included Foundation Once, Luis Vives, Caritas, the Red Cross, and the FSG). While commentators insisted that this decision was made to pacify ACs' fears that multi-regional OPs would re-centralize social policy and stall or even reverse the decentralization processes (Arriba and Moreno, 2005), the unprecedented allocation of managerial control was also a result of unified efforts undertaken by the key NGOs, who negotiated the terms of involvement using *one voice*. In 2007–2013, the IBs became responsible for overseeing the design of the OP priorities, formulating selection criteria, implementing, and evaluating in-house projects, as well as initiatives co-financed by the ACs and municipalities. Although the IBs did not hold a veto power, the decisions over strategic design were deliberated and made through consensus. Interviewed IBs asserted that the MAs were receptive to the proposed ideas and allowed the IBs to steer the discussions.[30] They also admitted that their capacity to participate in deliberations on an equal footing with managerial bodies stemmed largely from state subsidies:

> Of course, it was difficult to convince the authorities and push our agenda, but we were all well prepared. We had procedural knowledge and access to information and we invested a lot in preparation and consultations with professionals. Overall, the authorities were not explicitly trying to stall our efforts, and they were actually quite willing to hear us out. At the same time, we need to be honest and admit that without technical assistance from the government we simply would not be able to hold our ground.[31]

The MC also held substantial decision-making authority, especially at the strategic phase of programming. The MC members contended that all meetings were organized around specific agendas with delineated thematic focus. The MAs provided information packages to all participants, who could then prepare their stances in advance. While such guided itineraries allowed for constructive debates, members often maintained that it hindered discussions about intrinsic local matters, forcing participants to discuss themes preselected by the authorities. As one of the participants said.

> We were expected to comment and deliberate on issues, which predominately mattered to the authorities, it was incredibly difficult to discuss local matters, especially those that did not reflect the main objectives [...]. Maybe such narrow focus helped us to engage in fruitful discussions and allowed for compromise, but it prevented us from talking about new ideas [...] it appeared that the only problem we really talked about was unemployment, other issues were simply ignored.[32]

Despite these criticisms, all the interviewees positively assessed the operation of MCs in the 2007–2013 period, pointing out only minor procedural quandaries.

While partnership remained restricted to service delivery organizations, the government set specialized forums where non-members could express their concerns and gain access to strategic documents, minutes from the meetings, and assessment of the debates. This, at least on the surface, induced some degree of transparency and accountability. However, what truly enhanced accountability for general SF outputs was the involvement of the participants in both the strategic phase (designing strategies) and implementation phase (project delivery). This essentially meant that both the MAs and IBs saw the implementation of SF from the beginning to the end, and were entrusted with managing inclusion strategies, which they themselves helped to design.

Overall, Spanish partnership design was based on co-productive arrangements, which operated through stable networks of communication institutionalized between SF management and third-sector actors. Social partners benefited from capacity-building assistance derived from the public authorities (both at a central and regional tier) and were able to influence the decision-making processes. By getting involved in the early stages of project selection (i.e. advising MAs on eligibility and selection criteria), social partners could assess the take-up capacity and needs of the final recipients, thus contributing to a more accurate and legitimate allocation of SF. In many ways, acting in co-productive arrangements has allowed NGOs to act as a 'linchpin' between the state and local communities.

Nevertheless, the co-productive arrangements strongly resembled corporatist forms of governance, privileging some interests over others. As such, the partnership logic of the Spanish state did not generate political activism and stopped short of accelerating community empowerment. In many ways, the Spanish approach traded the political empowerment of local actors for the efficient delivery of services, and in doing so muzzled the critical voice of Spanish civil society. Interviewed Roma activists warned that such an approach reinforced power asymmetries and diminished mobilization efforts among the communities:

> Sure, SF are delivered faster if only a few actors decide their fate, but a system that treats citizens as passive beneficiaries of bureaucratic endeavours, even if these appeared quite effective, does not contribute to building local

capacities, does not really make people feel like full owners of these provisions, it does not even allow one to criticize public actions [...]. This in the long run dramatically reduces political awareness and activism.[33]

However, even the most vocal critics, tended to agree (if reluctantly) that while funding did not contribute to community empowerment it did indeed arrive at the doorsteps of the most impoverished localities.

In contrast, the Slovak government provided residual and unsystematic capacity-building assistance to actors interested in collaboration. Among the central authorities, there was an intrinsic understanding that legislating partnership principles alone made it equally accessible to all interested organizations.[34] The government did, however, recognize that public administration would indeed need additional resources for transposing cohesion regulation and developing effective SF strategies. For that reason, newly established MAs now develop technical assistance objectives incorporating them in all OPs in order to strengthen the coordination and management of SF allocations. Yet the envisioned goals were vague, lacked strategic dimensions, and earmarked budgets. While the establishment of the specialized OP TA (2007–2013) aimed to streamline budgetary procedures, coordination remained weak. As explained by a public manager working for the Ministry of Construction and Regional Development (MA for OP TA):

The USI principle (unify, simplify, increasing effectiveness) was not comprehensively implemented, we continued to struggle with a high rotation of staff and insufficient experience in spreading the information about the SF to the implementing bodies and the public. This caused serious delays and slowed down the absorption of available funding. The money was available but not well managed.[35]

The inefficient management of the OP TA strongly affected the managing capacities of the MAs and IBs. In the interviews, managers all raised concerns about under-staffing, procedural congestion, and insufficient resources (both human and financial). In turn, the NGOs represented in MCs insisted that communication with MAs is not transparent. During a High-Level Event in Bratislava (2011), the MA faced severe criticisms from local and civil society representatives for not providing sufficient information regarding administrative procedures, and for delaying project-calls, the selection processes, and the actual transfer of funds.

Technical support for localities and civil society organizations was even more scattered and unsystematic. Most of the local authorities gained access to resources (usually basic legal training and IT infrastructure) via taking part in tender calls, which essentially meant that they had to invest time and their own resources just to be considered. This almost immediately disqualified the most impoverished and under-resourced localities. Civil society organizations had an even harder time getting access to public grants, prompting them to seek funds from international donors (e.g. the OSI). As commented by one Roma NGO:

It is hard to say what the government has been trying to do in the last decade. While funding was in fact provided to the mushrooming Roma civil society organizations, the criteria for the allocations were vague. Every ministry, every agency held some different idea of what the role of the civil sector should be, and unfortunately, clientelism and tokenism prevailed.[36]

The ad-hoc support failed to strengthen the capacities of both public and third-sector stakeholders. However, even more detrimental was the consistent reluctance of central authorities to provide new partners with influence over the strategic stage of SF programming. For example, while the Plenipotentiary Office served as a link between public authorities and local communities, it lacked the resources, expertise, and actual political influence to fulfil its obligations. As noted by the Plenipotentiary himself:

> At best, we can oversee what was being done, give some ideas hoping that somebody would listen, but most of the time final decisions were taken without our presence - sometimes we were actually the last ones to know. Our budget could only support small-scale activities, offer some small scholarships or consultancy services, but this was not enough to mobilize the fragmented and impoverished Roma community.[37]

This dynamic was reflective of the general politicization of Slovak bureaucracy and inefficient budgetary management (see Meyer-Sahling and Veen, 2012). However, what also contributed to the weak authority of the Plenipotentiary Office was the widely shared notion (among the SF bureaucrats) that as a 'Roma agency', working exclusively for the benefits of Roma communities, it did not need extensive power over the general workings of the SF.[38] In the interviews, the SF managers contended that what MAs offered to the Office was 'enough' to fulfil its coordinative obligations. In an interview, a public servant from OP RD directly dismissed Plenipotentiary's complaints, stating that:

> They deal with one specific objective, the MRC, we deal with all of them, they can't expect us to provide more support than we already give them. What they need to do is work more efficiently and stop the internal infighting.[39]

In fact, many interviewees (both public bureaucrats and Roma activists) seemed anxious about the professional shortcomings and bureaucratic imbroglios inside the Office. They contended that the Plenipotentiary Office had become a strictly symbolic agency invested in its own survival and political opportunism.[40] Interestingly, the same interviewees seemed less concerned about ongoing corruption scandals and mismanagement of funds by central ministries,[41] they also failed to recognize ongoing political ostracism directed at the Plenipotentiary. Whatever the cause, the weakness of the Plenipotentiary Office meant that Roma communities became disconnected from the SF bureaucracy, with no mediating organizations working in their interests. This disconnection was further reinforced by the limited advocacy for Roma issues undertaken by mainstream NGOs and local authorities. Even the SDF (an IB for OP E&SI) which is very invested in reaching out to Roma communities, was not able to inspire mainstream organizations to take an active interest in Roma issues.[42]

While the attitudes among the MA managers towards working with MCs and NGOs improved in the second programming period, the interactions continued to be weak, allowing only for information exchanges among the participants with no opportunities granted for deliberation. The reliance on strict consultations became the main *modus operandi*, as explained by an NGO manager:

> The MAs would invite opinions from the third sector however it was strictly a one-way process. We delivered our insights usually in a written format and the authorities either used it or discarded it; of course, we were never informed about these decisions. For example, during the formulation of the OP E&SI, we meet on many occasions, providing a list of recommendations. The MA seemed very accepting, yet in the final version, the OP did not reflect any of our recommendations.[43]

While local and social partners held little influence over programming design, they were the ones implementing and managing SF projects on the ground. The institutionalization of demand-driven project-calls shifted the sphere of influence over implementation from MAs onto the winning contenders. The role of MAs in the delivery stage was limited to procedural oversight (the selection of winning projects, contractual documentation) with no designated oversight over the actual implementation and its outputs. This meant that MA were often more concerned with a quick allocation of funding than with the actual workings of individual programmes. Whether the selected projects contributed to the general goals of inclusion was often side-lined under the assumption that the 'general selection process on its own was effective in picking up the right candidates'.[44] However, given that the criteria were not informed by local knowledge and the less resourced agents were unable to compete in tenders on an equal footing with well-organized interests, the delivered initiatives were prone to bypassing the impoverished communities. The study conducted by the UNDP (Hurrle et al., 2012) confirmed that this trend was indeed characteristic of Slovak SF allocations.

In sum, the Slovak government institutionalized a pluralist approach to partnership, which in theory provided a participatory space for a wide diversity of actors. However, the insubstantial provision of technical resources (to both MAs and social actors), a lack of transparency, and lack of distribution of decision-making authority, curtailed meaningful input and knowledge transfer. The interests of MRCs received limited attention from more powerful organizations, being instead passed over to the Plenipotentiary Office, itself ill-equipped to play a representative role. At the same time, a practice of off-loading of responsibility for SF delivery onto local and social partners through tender calls further disadvantaged Roma communities from gaining ownership of the funded projects.

Partnership and SF outputs

The above analysis showed that partnership principles take different forms in different national contexts, both in terms of who participates and through what modes. It also demonstrated that the manifestation of participatory governance is often a carefully architected project constrained by prevailing institutional frameworks and indigenous approaches to social inclusion. What follows is an analysis of how co-productive partnership developed in Spain and pluralist approaches championed by Slovakia structured both the implementation process and its outputs.

While co-productive partnership design endorsed by Spain has failed to mobilize grassroots Roma interests and strengthen minority claims, it has proved extremely effective in securing the efficient management of SF. The recruitment of a limited number of actors who shared organizational cultures and objectives has facilitated a constructive dialogue largely liberated from a deep-cutting conflict of interests. This has sped up the deliberation processes, avoiding delays and decisional impasses. Moreover, restrictive membership has prevented the fragmentation of SF interventions, albeit at the expense of more locally driven approaches reflective of diverse community needs. Surprisingly, however, exclusive partnership has not diverted SF from marginalized groups and Roma neighbourhoods. Programmatic evaluations have proved that SF assistance for Roma people has been growing, a pattern that could be attributed to the systematic investment in the capacity building of organizations with an extensive record of working in Roma communities. As explained by an MA manager:

> Marginalized groups often lack a strong voice and representatives championing their interests and the sad truth is that the state is not always willing to cater to their weak demands, thus a 'buffer' organization can at once inform policymakers about the actual needs of these groups and put greater pressure on the authorities to address them [...]. While community activism should be the ultimate goal of any underrepresented group, in the bureaucratic system such as the SF, it is more pragmatic to rely on the support of well-resourced and well-connected organizations.[45]

The mediatory role of the FSG in SF programming has confirmed this view, as it managed to convince the authorities to allocate a substantial (if not particularly impressive) proportion of funds to social inclusion schemes. The evaluation report assessed these interventions as effective and legitimate (Villarreal, 2013), although critics maintained that disproportionate focus on employment undermined the severity and multidimensionality of Roma exclusion (Laparra et al., 2013). Nevertheless, the anchoring of wider exclusion themes in the SF agenda has strengthened the sustainability of efforts undertaken:

> Perhaps Roma issues are not the main priority of the state, but the fact that civil society stands behind the Roma population means that the issues stay

on the political agenda and do not disappear under the weight of other interests. Only through solidarity and collaboration can we make sure that the
authorities pay attention. Working in isolation is simply not effective or even
counterproductive.[46]

Indeed, even with the progressing economic crisis and consolidation of austerity
governance, the government was reluctant to abandon Roma issues, and the FSG
continued to receive public subsidies for its ongoing operations (FSG Annual
Report, 2013). The clear allocations of decision-making authority to the members
of partnership has in turn allowed for converting ideas and recommendations into
sustainable measures. This enhanced the legitimacy of delivered outputs.

The involvement of MAs and IBs in the actual implementation of SF projects
further contributed to more legitimate SF outputs. These managerial bodies have
remained accountable for each SF intervention, providing an imperative oversight and communicating government goals to local beneficiaries. They also possess managerial capacities and a co-financing ability to scale up and sustain local
efforts. As explained by a project manager from the Foundation Once:

> When SF are allocated via competition schemes, the MA are only responsible
> for the allocation of funding and are not involved in the implementation of
> winning projects. In the case of the OP FAD, all parties [MA, IB, tenders]
> were involved in designing, planning, implementing and evaluating under-
> taken initiatives. This meant that all parties held similar priorities and worked
> for a common goal, and they could not easily pawn off responsibility onto
> somebody else. This is really how partnership should work.[47]

Finally, while SF were not channelled directly into community activism, it could
be argued that the sustainable allocation of SF combined with the financing of
research and awareness raising campaigns has indirectly strengthened the capacity of the Roma to articulate their own interests. While concrete data is not available, interviews with Roma associations from Granada and Madrid confirmed that
they considered SF useful in forming thematic networks (with other Roma organizations but also with local authorities and other non-Roma NGOs) and developing
their own managerial capacity:

> We don't view it [EU funding] as a magic wand, after all, it is designed and
> managed mostly by the government, and as we know the government cares
> little about the people. But, in a way we do benefit from this money, it allows
> us to interact with resourceful organizations who help us put our vision into
> practice. We learned a lot about the way this system works and now we can
> better subvert it (laugh). We are far away from any real progress, but hey
> sometimes you need to see positive in what is happening around you.[48]

The impact of partnership institutionalized in Slovakia has been less than satisfactory, in fact often redirecting funds away from the most marginalized

communities. The well-intended opening up of participatory channels to a wide range of stakeholders paid little attention to the actual merit of the incoming partners. This, in the longer run, has dwarfed constructive debates and the formation of common ground among conflicting interests. Many MC members contended that the discussions were fragmented, not free of personal insults and unjustifiable grievances.[49] The MA's lack of mediating ability only reinforced this fragmentation, hindering effective planning and decision-making at a strategic level. As pointed out by an MC member:

> While we fought to have more meetings and working sessions, the way these were conducted was, I am sorry to say, a simple waste of time. There was no clear agenda, people come unprepared, and most of the time we did not really agree on anything. Moreover, discussions were often hijacked by one or two speakers, while everybody else did not contribute at all.[50]

Although it is not surprising that wider participation complicated deliberations, the fact that extended partnership has neither secured greater input from marginalized communities nor more substantive allocations of SF to MRC objectives is more astounding. The findings show that this failure stemmed from the residual and unsystematic capacity-building assistance, which left less resourceful actors fully outside the area of influence. Those who were 'included', such as the Plenipotentiary Office, lacked the necessary decision-making authority to influence the design of SF and were in fact rarely considered 'legitimate' representatives by the very people they were supposed to represent. In effect, the shaping of SF was left in the hands of bureaucrats who often had little knowledge of the on-the-ground situation and who themselves struggled with inadequate managerial and administrative capacities. As admitted by a senior public manager:

> We lack input from the communities. The truth is that besides the mapping of Roma communities we have very little information about the actual needs and dynamics inside these communities. At the same time, we are really not able to engage in planning and assessment considering the overload of work and high rotation of our staff. To be honest we are the ones who need more resources and then perhaps we could cater to more interests, help more people.[51]

Not surprisingly, the proposed objectives and measures, as well as the issued project-calls, did not reflect the documented needs of the Roma communities (Hurrle et al., 2012). Ironically, the execution of these sterile aims was placed in the hands of local authorities and small NGOs (more or less representative of local interests). This, rather than reinforcing legitimate outputs, led to opportunism and the blunt mismanagement of funding.[52] Moreover, given that the implementers had to come up with considerable co-financing[53] and operational capital, many opted out from participating, which in turn reduced SF absorption. As explained by a member of the Civic Association for Support and Development of the Regions in Slovakia:

> The burden of implementation rests on our shoulders. We are expected to navigate the excessive bureaucratic process of application, aggregate funding, do impact assessments and more. While the central authorities do little to help us out [...] for us it simply doesn't make sense to invest so much in the application process when we know we can't sustain the implemented initiatives.[54]

The negative influence of Slovak partnership design was most acutely visible during the planned implementation of the local strategies (Making the Most, 2013). In 2008, the authorities issued a call to all localities with MRC inviting them to prepare local strategies, which the government would support with SF. The main champions of this initiative included the Office of Plenipotentiary, the Roma Institute, and the Ministry of Labour, Social Affairs and Family. The initiative, envisioned as an affirmative action, reflected the Slovak assertion that Roma issues should be addressed through specific programmes and targeted projects. According to SDF the call generated great interest given the low criteria for acceptance and promised technical support.[55] However, it quickly became evident that the Office had no capacity to coordinate the selection process and review a growing pile of local strategies (the Office at that time had only ten full-time and two part-time employees). Many inquiries were thus left unanswered, communication channels were blocked and deadlines not respected.[56] This situation not only generated frustration among the localities but also jeopardized the transfer of funds earmarked by the MA for the HP MRC. The Plenipotentiary Office without any decision-making capacity or strong political allies was unable to compel the government to provide the critically needed assistance or even to delay the deadlines for the open-call. The bureaucratic overload was aggravated by little cooperation among the localities and weak collaboration between Roma-run NGOs and mainstream organizations. In the end, respectable MAs redirected most of the earmarked funds to other calls, generating further frustration and resulting in mutual accusations and finger pointing.

Concluding remarks

This chapter showed that different partnership arrangements play an extensive role in shaping SF outputs. The analytical focus on who participates and through what means proves that cohesion policy partnership is underpinned by ideological convictions and a normative understanding of public problems (in this instance the social exclusion of Roma people). The most important and indeed surprising finding of this research is that partnership regulations are not conducive to local mobilization and local empowerment (despite the EU's insistence that member states should use partnership exactly for this purpose). The very complexity and bureaucratization of SF programming mean that its implementation is best assured when partnership is exclusive and well resourced, incorporating the input of experts and service delivery organizations and not necessarily involving those affected by marginalization and poverty.

The success of the Spanish SF programming was indeed contingent on co-productive partnership arrangements, whereby central and regional authorities recruited a few experienced service delivery organizations (rather than community representatives) and granted them generous capacity-building resources and decision-making authority. These architected 'powerhouses' were able to secure efficient implementation, free of the extensive delays and mismanagement so common in Slovakia. Surprisingly, they also managed to uphold the socioeconomic interests of Roma communities. This needs to be attributed to the 'ethnically neutral' framing of exclusion, which has proved conducive to network building and solidarity among various excluded groups and localities. While critics point out that the recruited partners acted more as an agent of the state than true community representatives, their role in safeguarding funding for exclusion goals should not be fully delegitimized. In many ways national NGOs established themselves as 'buffer zones' between the state and the communities, using their status and acquired resources, to channel local knowledge into public bureaucracy, thus contributing to more informed programmes and projects. Many grassroots Roma associations admitted that working with 'bureaucratically savvy' organizations opened-up access to funding opportunities which would otherwise be out of their reach. However, very few saw SF as an instrument for engendering community control over development and growth. The local activists remain cynical about partnership in general, commenting: 'this is the state's show, we take what we can, but much more is needed to set in motion any real change, this whole partnership thing only masks a lot of what's wrong with government policies'.[57]

In contrast, the Slovak all-inclusive approach to partnership initially appeared as a genuine mechanism for bringing Roma voices into policymaking. However, the official commitment to harbour community representation proved superficial, with neither resources nor decision-making capacities provided to the recruited partners. The omnipresent notion that the Roma should take care of their own interests and compete for funding on equal footing with others remained blind to drastic power asymmetries, pervasive discrimination, and lack of resources at a local level. The case of Slovak partnership design proves that the promotion of a wide partnership when devoid of any real decision-making authority, not only leads to managerial inefficiencies but in fact diverts funding away from those who need it the most. Ironically, the systematic neglect to engage expert organizations with strong ties to the communities and experience in delivering social inclusion services put funding in the hands of technocratic agencies who lacked local knowledge and remained unaccountable for the delivered projects. Separated from influential policy networks and powerful agents, Roma communities remained on the fringes, and once again were blamed by both the government and a larger public for either misusing funds or not showing interest in integration measures. Not surprisingly, a feeling of defeat and jadedness became widespread among grassroots Roma activist groups, with one leader summing up the interview by saying: 'we get the money it's bad, we don't get the money it's bad, whatever we do we lose out, Gypsy karma'.[58]

Notes

1 Quoted in European Economic and Social Committee, 19 September 2017.
2 Interview #14, 21 June 2011 (Seville).
3 Interview #2, 7 June 2011 (Madrid).
4 Interview #19, 14 June 2011 (Madrid).
5 In 2003, Andalusia reached an agreement with social partners and representatives of local municipalities called The Social Pact Agreement of Andalusia. The agreement resulted in the creation of 114 new offices spread around the rural territory in the region. These offices, called Territorial Units for Employment and Technological and Local Development, were financed by the regional government and managed by means of an agreement with local authorities (mainly municipalities) and social partners. With time, more than 85% of involved organizations became members of the MC and were asked to contribute to the design of SF programming (Evaluation Andalusia, OP ESF, 2010).
6 Interview #1, 7 June 2011 (Madrid).
7 The ESF Administrative Unit allowed the researcher to examine membership reviews conducted by the Chair of the MC for the ESF in 2013, given that this information is confidential, it will stay anonymous.
8 Interview #4, 14 June 2011 (Madrid).
9 Interview #15, 24 June 2011 (Seville).
10 Interview #9, 22 June 2011 (Seville).
11 Some critics also insist that recruitment of the FSG stemmed from the EU's increasing pressure to engage Roma-led organizations, but most of all from the Spanish government's determination to hide the detrimental effects of ongoing public funding cuts (interview).
12 Interview #22, 6 June 2012 (Brussels).
13 Interview #9, 22 June 2011 (Seville).
14 Interview #38, 19 June 2011 (Granada).
15 Interview #79, 3 February 2015 (Skype).
16 Interview #58, 3 March 2011 (Bratislava).
17 Interview #43, 13 May 2011 (Skalica).
18 This tendency is characteristic of ESF strategies. ERDF programming has placed more emphasis on engaging experts, particularly from the private sector.
19 Interview #61, 26 July 2011 (Bratislava).
20 Interview #63, 23 July 2011 (Bratislava).
21 Interview #72, 26 July 2011 (Banská Bystrica).
22 Interview #73, 14 May 2011 (Skalica).
23 Interview #71, 23 May 2011 (Bratislava).
24 Interview #51, 26 July 2011 (Bratislava).
25 According to OSF Bratislava in 2009, there were more than 260 registered NGOs identified as Roma-led. Only a few of them provided sustainable services in the communities (housing, employment schemes, health centers, etc.). The intercultural approach continues to be absent in many areas and there are very few 'mixed' local NGOs that work with the Roma. Although the situation has been slowly changing in the first funding period there was almost no collaboration between Roma and non-Roma NGOs. In fact, there was very little networking among NGOs dealing with Roma issues in general. Interview #69, 2011 (Bratislava).
26 2nd Annual Round Table Debate, EU Politics, Budapest 2012.
27 Interview #70, 27 July 2011 (Banská Bystrica).

28 While in recent years the majority of benefiting NGOs have managed to diversify their funding it is still explicit that the central government is the main supporter (see FSG Annual Report, 2016).

29 Interview #2, 7 June 2011.

30 Interview #22, 6 June 2012 (Brussels); Interview #28, 12 June 2011 (Madrid); Interview #29, 27 June 2011 (Madrid).

31 Interview #23, 13 June 2011 (Madrid).

32 Interview #20, 21 June 2011 (Seville).

33 Interview #41, 27 June 2011 (Almer).

34 High-Level Event on the Structural Funds contribution to Roma integration in Slovakia, Bratislava 2011.

35 Interview #48, 4 October 2011 (Bratislava).

36 Interview #69, 23 July 2011 (Bratislava).

37 Interview #52, 5 October 2011 (Bratislava).

38 This conviction was expressed by all interviewed MA managers.

39 Interview #51, 26 July 2011 (Bratislava).

40 Interview #70, 27 July 2011 (Banská Bystrica); Interview #72, 26 July 2011 (Banská Bystrica); Interview #73, 14 May 2011 (Skalica).

41 Few interviewees, for example, mention the incident (which happened one year before the interviews were conducted) when the Ministry of Education gave €600,000 of EU money, that was earmarked for educating the Roma community, to two soccer teams.

42 Interview #50, 26 July 2011 (Bratislava).

43 Interview #69, 23 July 2011 (Bratislava).

44 Interview #51, 26 July 2011 (Bratislava).

45 Interview #1, 7 June 2011 (Madrid).

46 Interview #22, 6 June 2012 (Brussels).

47 Interview #30, 27 June 2011 (Madrid).

48 Interview #80, 2 October 2014 (Granada).

49 Interview #58, 3 March 2011 (Bratislava).

50 Interview #60, 2 March 2011 (Kosice).

51 Interview #51, 26 July 2011 (Bratislava).

52 It was common practice to write a project application to meet selection criteria, without accounting for its operational costs or long-term impacts. Interview #62, 23 July 2011 (Bratislava).

53 Even the NGOs were by law expected to provide 15% of the co-financing, an amount that often exceeded the resource capacity of smaller grassroots organizations.

54 Interview #68, 26 July 2011 (Bratislava).

55 Interview #50 26 July 2011 (Bratislava).

56 Interview #53 26 July 2011 (Bratislava).

57 Interview #74, 1 October 2014 (Granada).

58 Interview #73, 14 May 2011 (Skalica).

6 Safeguarding programmatic synergies

The last two chapters explored the way policy design and participatory arrangements influenced implementation outputs. The key argument, put briefly, was that it is impossible to explain policy success or failure without teasing out the representation problem logged inside policy proposals and unpacking modes of partnership responsible for the planning and delivery of action plans. The analysis focused on probing SF programming as it developed across different stages of the implementation process. What remains unexplored is the way EU funding strategies interact with or complement domestic policies, budgetary plans, and administrative protocols. As an external tool, the SF is expected to comply with a grander European vision associated with multi-annual strategic planning, broad and diverse key stakeholder involvement leading to new partnership arrangements, shared objectives, and a systematic and structured approach to programme management procedures and inclusiveness (EC, 2000). At a conceptual level, the debates over the tailoring of SF concerns the issue of the 'added value' broadly understood as 'a positive effect of cohesion policy management on the implementation of Member States' own policies for regional development' (Mairate, 2006, p. 168). Such an approach is bound to generate an array of coordinative challenges, as governance structures multiply and intersect. How member states conceive and manage programmes, which transcend organizational boundaries and entail additional administrative input, is likely to affect the entire implementation processes. As such, the analysis in this chapter explores the synchronizing dynamics instigated by the Spanish and Slovak government, to demonstrate how different coordinative strategies and joined-up efforts impact final SF outputs.

To capture these complimentary dynamics the chapter first turns towards the debates on the 'added value' of SF programming, a concept directly related to the benefits stemming from interventions on the ground. It is difficult to provide an uncontroversial definition of the concept of '*added value*' and set out its related evaluation criteria. Perceptions of 'added value' differ according to different levels of government, between organizations within and outside the EU regional policy system, and even between actors within the same programme, depending on their position and interests (Bachtler and Taylor, 2003). Nevertheless, in general, 'added value' involves an assessment of the extent to which SF interventions are likely to add value to programmes carried out by other administrations, organizations, and institutions, i.e. in being complementary to, and coherent with, them. Cohesion scholars maintain that a 'tight' strategic alignment tends to generate effective and sustainable interventions while meeting the growing demands of accountability vis-à-vis the budgetary authorities and thereby European taxpayers, about the use of SF (Mairate, 2006). This chapter upholds this assertion. However, it also critically analyzes the potential of 'added value' to generate innovative policy responses to social exclusion. A pertinent question that is explored is whether the merging of EU funds with public expenditures contributes to systemic reforms (reflective of the Lisbon Agenda) or reinforces domestic political interests and accepted ways of doing things. The chapter goes on to explore how Spanish and Slovak governing elites conceptualized the *'added value'* of cohesion policy and what coordinative regimes they put in place to consolidate programmatic synergies and maximize the impact of EU funding. The attention falls on the dynamics of 'joined-up government' understood as the connection and interchange between programmes or service delivery by different public agencies. The empirical analysis shows that in Spain political motivation to use the SF as a tool for improving and reinforcing existing approaches expedited the construction of the coordinative regime, based on joined-up government methods. While these efforts generated effective and sustainable outputs, they also reinforced existing practices leaving little space for innovation and policy experimentation. In other words, SF were used to buttress 'traditional' approaches not always able to keep up with the changing socio-economic landscape. In turn, the Slovak government proved less committed to the complementary approach and less able to coordinate the fragmented administrative landscape and induced joined-up efforts. By and large, the implementation of SF took place in isolation, without any linkages to domestic policies and programmes. The consolidation of a 'double-tier system' proved particularly detrimental for Roma inclusion initiatives, which were once again sidelined from public budgets and wider domestic reforms plans. It also led to the duplication and incongruity of delivered SF interventions, while muddling accountability for allocated funds. Overall, the findings bring about rather pessimistic conclusions regarding the potency of SF to foster innovative approaches to social inclusion. The impression is that SF outputs are more likely to be effective in places where domestic social exclusion strategies and policies are already in place. When such strategies are missing or are relatively unfledged the potency of SF to foster institutional development and modernization appears surprisingly weak.

Cohesion policy: complimentary and 'added value'

European cohesion policy explicitly calls for the complementary use of SF, to improve administrative capacities and trigger modernization processes within the territorial administration of member states (Mairate, 2006). Quintessentially, this means that to deepen and widen policy convergence, member states must synchronize SF programming with national development plans. The additionality principle regulates complementarity through Article 15, which states that: 'EU SF may not replace the national or equivalent expenditure by a member state' (Article 15, No. 1083/2006). The aim is to create a co-financing system whereby European funding is channelled into initiatives partially funded by the national, regional, or local authorities (within the convergence objective the co-financing ceilings for public expenditure amount to 75% for both the ERDF and the ESF). Although the cohesion framework encourages member states to channel the acquired funds towards innovative approaches, there is an overt expectation that SF initiatives will also support ongoing public schemes, and SF will have a leverage effect on public and private sources of funding as well as domestic development strategies (Bachtler and Mendez, 2007). For example, for inclusion programmes targeted at the Roma minority, the EC recommends using SF for both strengthening the existing national Roma inclusion strategies and developing innovative interventions particularly at a local level (EC, 2008, 2011, 2016).

The quest for complementarity is not limited to the amalgamation of financial resources. The EC expects that national interests, values, and procedures will subscribe to the overarching cohesion objectives and its *modus operandi*. How such complementarity should best be achieved has not been clearly specified in the past, allegedly to give member states considerable leeway in designing appropriate coordination measures. In a way, the EC assumed that 'adjustments' of domestic governance will happen automatically as member states will restrain their domestic interests in order to benefit from generous EU financial transfers.

However, this assumption was enfeebled by Europeanization and cohesion policy scholars who demonstrated that the level of compliance with EU regulations tends to be fairly inconsistent (Falkner et al., 2008; Börzel et al., 2007). It became clear that some member states were not, in fact, using SF in a prescribed additional manner. Scholars tended to ascribe this inconsistency to the strength of domestic interests and accepted norms (Sedelmeier, 2008). However, it could also be argued that it stems from the vague and rather incongruous expectations of the EC that the SF should simultaneously support existing approaches and re-shape them to fit and succour supranational goals. Such duality is difficult to reconcile, especially when the use of SF might challenge the status quo or when SF objectives do not have a counterpart inside the national strategies (thus new approaches and administrations need to be created) (Méndez et al., 2007) The lack of clear guidelines from the EC only strengthens this contradictory pull. Not surprisingly research shows that member states tended to adopt a hybrid strategy – in some policy areas SF constitute an 'added value' to existing approaches while in others SF are channelled towards new-fangled programmes (Toshkov, 2012). The question that arises is which approach is actually more conducive to successful SF outputs. Theoretical debates concerning the perceived benefits and shortcomings of synergies can help to generate some normative assumptions.

Synergies and joined-up efforts

Issues concerning programmatic synergies began to dominate discussions on effective governance, as the ongoing public sector reforms moved governing away from the centre of the conventional politically-driven public sector. In this process, the rhetoric and reality of governing were transformed and many conventional (hierarchical) styles of governing were abandoned in favour of a complex system of networks and horizontal interdependent interactions. Metagovernance scholarship, in particular, tried to assess the functional value of working across organizational boundaries over the customary working in silos (Clarke and Stewart, 1997; Peters, 2010). Ling (2002, p. 620) observes that comprehensive public programmes cannot be delivered through the separate activities of existing organizations but neither can they be delivered through the creation of a new 'super agency'. As such, there is a need to align incentives, structures, and cultures of various bureaucratic units to comprehensively address critical tasks that cross organizational boundaries. The boundaries could be inter-departmental, inter-tier, or sectorial (corporate, public, community). However, what is essential is that they are erected because of distinctive procedures, aims, controls, and values held by each organization or cooperative arrangements. For example, SF programming is managed by autonomous agencies (MAs and IBs) which often espouse idiosyncratic controls, procedures, and aims that tend to differ from those held by departments dealing exclusively with domestic policies. Such a complex bureaucratic amalgamation needs joined-up action to diminish the protective and exclusive tenacity of organizational boundaries without actually removing the boundaries themselves.[1] However, as pointed out by Sorenson (2006), joined-up efforts require deep-cutting changes (including changes to organizational culture) and substantial resources which might, in fact, discourage coordinative undertakings. Yet, a growing scholarship on metagovernance does show that the benefits of joining-up are likely to outstrip the initial costs and long-term investments.

Simplifying service delivery

Perhaps the most regularly developed argument in favour of joined-up efforts is that they can make access to services seamless – rather than fragmented – for the individual and society, which in turn reduces the need for citizens to understand the way in which government is structured in order to gain access to the services they need (Peters, 2010). This is critical since citizens (especially those affected by exclusion) have difficulties accessing a wide range of government agencies, often located at different tiers of government, because of resources (including time and money) and capabilities necessary to navigate complex bureaucratic procedures (Carey and Dickinson, 2017). It has been demonstrated that navigating a bureaucratic 'labyrinth' can discourage those seeking public assistance, thus breeding apathy, inaction, or blunt non-compliance with official rules and regulations (Weaver, 2009). Joined-up government is seen as a provider of 'common responses' that facilitate better access to public services and interventions. In the context of SF programming and social exclusion, such common responses based on established links between SF inclusion objectives and public inclusion services (i.e. SF training initiatives designed to fit the requirements of public employment offices) can facilitate the delivery of comprehensive assistance rather than unilateral and short-lived projects. This strategy is crucial given the multidimensional aspect of social exclusion requires multifaceted approaches provided by different agencies working together towards similar goals (Ringold et al., 2005).

Joining-up can also facilitate the simplification of procedures, an important aspect to consider in the excessively bureaucratized SF allocation and absorption procedures. Administrative streamlining can strengthen the absorption capacities of organizations contending for SF (in particular local authorities or NGOs) by aligning existing procedures (i.e. federal transfers, public grants) with those guiding SF programming.[2] It may ease the difficulties in navigating SF procedures and requirements. Moreover, it may allow the organizations contending for SF to exploit their knowledge and experience accumulated through applying for public grants and subsidies. While, this may not be of much help to organizations or communities which historically have been prevented from interacting with public authorities (as in the case of the Roma people), the potential for simplifying the bureaucratization of funding applications could at least, in theory, provide a more user-friendly environment, accessible to less organized interests.

Managerial efficiency and accountability

Another related argument explores the positive influence that joined-up government has on safeguarding efficiency. It has been pointed out that when policies aimed at exclusion are sectorial, their reciprocal influence and contradictions are often poorly evaluated (Mulgan, 2005). Thus, when tensions between different approaches arise, they often remain unresolved (or are simply ignored). Joined-up government may, in fact, decrease the risk of such contradictions. Pollitt and Talbot (2004) demonstrate that the coordination of organizational objectives, values, and procedures spreads the knowledge of existing approaches to public problems (i.e. social exclusion) and their inherent interdependencies among all policy stakeholders and delivery agencies. As such, the lead organizations and key participants can gain an end-to-end view of the programme and its performance against expectations, and can respond more appropriately to performance issues.

Joined-up efforts can also strengthen incentives for the creation of joint funding applications and pooled budgets, and can link payment to joined-up targets. Such practices at once streamline budgetary procedures, cutting costs tied to management and allocations, and facilitate the amalgamation of funds. Of course, the consolidation of such practice depends on the capacity and willingness of the central authorities to mediate various interests and to dispense the necessary incentives (both negative and positive, i.e. conditionality and administrative resources) (Pollitt and Talbot, 2004). In the case of cohesion policy, linking SF programming goals and interests with those of domestic departments could enhance the capacity to secure co-financing by bringing in funds from various sources (allowing for aggregating funding that goes beyond the mandatory 15%). The amalgamation of funds in return can facilitate the creation of larger projects without running the risk of the duplication or implementation of unsustainable projects. Finally, it can facilitate the comprehensive evaluation and endorsement of necessary adjustments, since all actors involved subscribe to common input and output indicators.[3]

While joined-up government can promote the more efficient management of SF programming, it is not self-evident that sole efficiency gains will translate into a greater allocation of SF towards inclusion objectives or high-quality projects. A key question put forward by literature on metagovernance is how one can have joint action, common standards, and shared systems, on the one hand, and vertical accountability for individual agency performance on the other (Per et al., 2014). The challenge is to achieve a better balance between vertical accountability to central government, horizontal accountability to local government and thematic agencies (i.e. MA), and responsiveness downwards to users and clients. Peters (2010), as well as major top-down implementation scholars (Mazmanian and Sabatier, 1989), contend that clearly designated responsibility can strengthen accountability and reinforce the achievement of organizational objectives. Certainty about competencies and mutual responsibility can eliminate confusion about who is accountable for what.

Accountability problems may also be resolved through the introduction of common frameworks and reporting mechanisms for shared programmes (Mulgan, 2000). A well-executed joined-up government, which aligns organizational goals as well as procedures, can thus improve accountability by ensuring that there is a clear understanding and appreciation of the roles and responsibilities of the relevant participants in the governance framework. In the context of cohesion policy, clearing up expectations and reinforcing credible reporting can promote the sharing of reliable information and data, but perhaps, more importantly, bring SF and domestic agencies' accountability into alignment. Such linkages can reinforce collective responsibility for the performance and outputs of individual SF projects.

Striving for innovation

Finally, it is argued that joined-up government facilitates the testing of new and innovative approaches to policy problems (Mulgan, 2005, 2007; Lekhi, 2007). A quest for policy or systemic innovation has been widely endorsed by various states and public agencies trying to keep up with the demands of a rapidly changing society. Innovation has been placed at the heart of the European 2020 strategy for tackling major societal challenges, including social exclusion, unemployment, and resource scarcity. It is thus not a coincidence or isolated impulse that within the cohesion policy framework, innovation of public administrations has been strongly prioritized. It has been argued that joined-up government with its strategic leadership, rather than micro-management is needed if government is to effectively improve public services (Lekhi, 2007). The coordination of a range of different policy perspectives can, in itself, produce a greater dynamism through the sharing of ideas, expertise, and practices. When actors at all levels and sectors coordinate their planning and objectives to live up to their common responsibilities, they are more likely to gain fresh inputs and ideas and create new policy instruments and methods (Pollitt and Talbot, 2004). This reduces the risk of encapsulating innovative ideas in isolated spaces thus dwarfing their potential to infiltrate policymaking routines. In terms of SF programming, which in many ways aims to induce policy innovation, strong coordinative measures may ensure that these aims are effectively harboured inside the domestic institutional setting. This is particularly important in the area of Roma exclusion where there is a persistent demand for innovative strategies and approaches delivered by relevant stakeholders and agencies.

Although it is difficult to refute the positive impact that coordination may have on the design and delivery of public services, it must be recognized that its institutionalization requires extensive efforts that can put a great strain on central authorities (in terms of time and resources). The existence of many bodies with overlapping functions, and the tendency for groupthink, can severely limit the envisioned benefits of joining-up. Perhaps that is why Pollitt (2003) has argued that well-defined vertical and horizontal organizational boundaries should not be seen as a symptom of obsolescent thinking, but as mechanisms ensuring stability and professional specialization. Division of labour and specialization are inevitable features of modern organizations and can provide needed constancy and clear-cut direction. Working horizontally is a very time- and resource-consuming activity that is not always able to satisfy diverse demands and needs, or deliver timely responses to critical situations. Moreover, there must be a genuine willingness on the part of the bureaucratic elites to counteract the common tendency to retreat into policy silos and nurture path-dependencies. Such willingness is hard to come by, considering that certain laws, rules, and institutions create heavy disincentives for change because so much has already been invested in the existing ways of doing things (Pierson, 2004). Thus, costs of joining-up and path-dependencies should be kept in mind during the investigation of synergizing efforts and their influence on implementation outputs.

What comes out of this discussion is that while joining-up has a strong potential to improve the overall operation of public bureaucracy, it is a costly venture that needs time and long-term commitment. Nevertheless, in the context of cohesion policy, the creation of synergies appears almost axiomatic, given that cohesion policy regulations urge member states to exploit the 'added value' of European funding. The next section analyzes the empirical data in an effort to expose joining-up practices undertaken in Spain and Slovakia and the effects of synergies on implementation outputs.

Before exploring the form of programmatic synergies in Spain and Slovakia, it is important to take an in-depth look at the way these two countries understand and exploit the 'added value' of SF programming. The EC's regulations on the 'added value' of SF leave considerable room for manoeuvre, predisposing national actors to interpret them according to their own needs, interests, and institutional settings. In effect, each member state has its own idea about the way EU funding can or should contribute to local development. How member states understand the purpose of SF influences the character and strength of programmatic synergies.

Spain political consensus on complementarities

In Spain, all consecutive democratic governments have shown a strong political proclivity to align SF programming with existing national and regional development strategies. Following accession to the EU (1986), Spanish authorities made a uniformed political decision to use the SF (particularly the ESF) as a tool for the consolidation and modernization of welfare programmes and equality policies (Royo, 2007). For this purpose, inter-departmental committees were established to synchronize the Spanish NSRF with National Reform Programmes (NRP).[4] All major ministries, including the Ministry of Labour (1988), Ministry of Social Affairs (1988), and Ministry of Health (1989) endorsed SF as an instrument for strengthening NRP's key objective to 'reduce gaps in access to social protection and employment and enhance visibility to the problems of certain social groups'. While the central government sought to earmark SF for the development of innovative approaches to equality and social inclusion, it maintained that SF must 'add to rather than replace' existing legislative frameworks (Leonardi and Nanetti, 2011). The Ministry of Education, for example, used SF to support the implementation of Article 63 of the Organic Law for the General Ordering of the Education System (1990), aimed at 'promoting equal opportunity in the education of students from unfavourable contexts'.[5]

The additive character of SF were outlined in the first paragraph of the 2007–2013 NSRF, which stated that SF were 'indirect tools of influence that are not necessarily meant to produce a direct impact on social policies but rather aim at easing reforms and improving existing public interventions' (NSRF, 2007, p. 4). According to the Ministry of Employment and Social Security, SF were compelling tools for buttressing political support for the planned reforms:

> We use European funding primarily as financial reinforcement for our welfare reforms and employment initiatives. Our aim is to use external funding to safeguard the sustainability of the domestic reforms and programmes. Yes, in many ways we are reluctant to use SF to create novel approaches and interventions, mostly because many policymakers feel that it could generate opposition from the bureaucratic cadre and increase the costs of implementation [...]. We try to achieve a delicate balance between sustainability of current programmes and their innovation.[6]

The designers of SF programming elaborated the 'added value' priority in the key objectives of the multi-regional ESF OPs. The OP FAD stressed the need to: *equip mainstream employment and welfare policies with interventions sensitive to different situations of discrimination and inequality* (FAD, 2007–2013, p. 45), while the OP E&A contained a clause regarding: *the need for innovative approaches which could ease the labour market reforms and enrich existing approaches* (OP E&A, 2007–2013, p. 20).

Similar dynamics took place at the regional tier of the government. Here too the political commitment to exploit the potential of SF for strengthening existing approaches surpassed calls for experimentation or deep-cutting reforms. A spillover effect characterizing the decentralization of social policies in Spain has only further strengthened the propensity for aligning the SF programme with regional reforms. As explained by a senior public manager:

> The modernization of the social protection system was the main priority of all the ACs endowed with this new responsibility. It is almost a competition, who could modernize faster and better. SF programming was moulded in such a way so it could help increase regional budgets earmarked for initiatives already in operation; nobody thought it would be wise to channel funds towards projects that do not directly contribute to regional reforms or go against party agenda.[7]

This view is reflected in the OP ESF Andalusia, which incorporated an explicit clause calling for SF initiatives to 'complement and reinforce' existing regional development plans and contribute to the consolidation of cohesive welfare policies (i.e. OP ESF Andalusia, 2007–2013, p. 2). The same commitment was incorporated into the Regional Reform Programme (RRP) and in the manifestos of all relevant regional ministries and public agencies. An interviewed public manager, not directly involved in the management of SF, confirmed that the ESF funding was above all seen as a reinforcement of operating social inclusion programmes and services:

> We see SF as additional resources, and we use them to strengthen the elevation of existing programmes and inclusion services. We do not want to use SF to build fully new programmes. The funding periods are simply too short to generate lasting impacts, and we need to remember that soon Andalusia will lose the convergence status. EU funding is a complimentary budget, not the main source for the things we aim to do and that we are doing.[8]

Slovakia: an ambiguous commitment

In Slovakia, the commitment to use SF in a complementary manner was at best ambiguous. The government presented the 2007–2013 NSRF as a central strategic document for 'defining and linking together all relevant components of individual and autonomous, yet coherent strategies of the EU, the Slovak state, regional authorities and individual policy sectors, with the aim to achieve greater synergies and the highest efficiency' (NSRF, 2007, p. 137). However, within state administration, the articulation of this commitment remained weak. In fact, different ministries and agencies held conflicting notions about the contribution SF should make to domestic initiatives. While the Ministry of the Interior expressed a preference for using SF as a buttress for the needed modernization of public administration, the Ministry of Labour, Social Affairs and Family was more vocal about the need for innovation, experimentation and piloted interventions (especially in the area of social inclusion).[9] The overall political discourse on cohesion policy fell silent on the potential of SF to reinforce existing public interventions around social inclusion. Instead, the NSRF amplified the need for innovation and experimentation with novel approaches, particularly in the area of social inclusion and minority treatment. The focus on modernization was partly reinforced by EU conditionality, requiring all the new member states to improve minority treatment, transpose anti-discrimination legislature, and devise national inclusion schemes. However, the political affinity for novelty and vicissitude also aimed to address the well-documented ineffectiveness of indigenous inclusion strategies, particularly those targeted at Roma minorities. As explained by the senior manager from SDF:

> It is difficult to think of SF as a tool for the reinforcement of existing practices, in an institutional landscape that lacks evidence-based social inclusion policies, and really cannot account for achieved progress or even minor improvements [...] it should not be surprising that there is a strong anticipation that SF will help to jump-start innovative ways of thinking about social problems.[10]

The thematic OPs have also reflected the inclination to earmark SF for the development of pioneering approaches. Although 'additionality' and 'complementarity' appeared in all the preambles, these concepts were neither elaborated on nor developed later in the documents. Instead, different axes emphasized the need for 'setting up novel approaches' (OP E&SI, 2007–2013, p. 142). This was particularly visible in sections delineating social inclusion measures. The OP E&SI explicitly supported innovative approaches and projects under the framework activity:

> Promoting increased access to, quality and effectiveness of care services (social services and measures of social and legal protection and social curatorship) that improve the access of the at-risk and marginalized groups of the population to the labour market and society.
>
> (OP E&SI, 2007–2013, p. 145)

The OP Education followed suit stating that EU funds will be geared towards initiatives which 'support the development of innovation in all aspect of education' (OP Education, 2007–2013, pp. 24, 69, 84). The SDF office confirmed that:

> The use of SF is perhaps the only incentive available, which could prompt central authorities to engage in the creation and implementation of integration initiatives, especially directed at Roma communities.[11]

However, it was the local authorities who proved the chief enthusiasts for SF supporting the innovation and creation of new services. As expressed by a local mayor:

> We are excited about the inflow of extra funds. Our locality for years has been in deep need of new infrastructure and modern services. The money

allocated from the national budget was never enough to realize our ambitions. We hope that European money will allow us to test new grounds and design novel ways of addressing the dilemmas of our jurisdiction.[12]

When asked about the potential for SF to reinforce ongoing reforms and existing projects, most mayors confessed that there were no inclusion initiatives in operation and the existing services were not suited for addressing problems experienced by MRCs and other vulnerable groups (including the disabled and long-term unemployed). An analysis of the National Regional Development Strategy of Slovak Republic 2008–2012, showed that the articulation of complementariness or overlaps with SF programming pertained to their mandatory co-financing only.

Spain: decentralization, consensus, and soft approaches

The political motivations for using SF as a buttress for existing approaches was reinforced by the ongoing regionalization of the Spanish state. The ceding of power to ACs prompted the central government to fortify vertical coordination as a means to maintain a degree of control over social policy and the modernization processes. The reliance on deliberation and negotiation between the central government and the newly empowered autonomous regions somewhat eased coordinative challenges, although in the beginning interactions were strictly bilateral.[13] The launching of the Sectorial Conferences (1982) aimed to break the bilateral harness, and maximize inter-region and inter-departmental cooperation. By 1999, 24 Sectorial Conferences were set up, including one for 'European Affairs', which brought together high-ranking officials and political representatives from both the central and regional governments. At first, the regional authorities showed concern that the Sectorial Conferences would transform into a mechanism controlled by the central administration and used to intervene in areas of regional competences. Gradually the uneasiness subsided, paving the way for more 'trusting' interactions (Arriba and Moreno, 2005). It needs to be highlighted that these conferences served exclusively as communication platforms with a limited focus on actual joint decision-making. Thus, policy analysts viewed them as a mechanism of 'institutional courtesy' (Grau and Creus, 2000) that paved the way to cooperative regionalization and the reduction of inter-tier cleavages. In the context of ESF, the European Affairs Conference was pivotal in strengthening the motivation of regional authorities to align their reforms with NSRF.[14]

Since accession to the EU, the central authorities in Spain have seen cohesion policy as a potent instrument for maintaining some level of supervision over the rapidly decentralizing system. During the first programming periods (1989–1993), the management of SF was in the hands of the central administration, which controlled the preparation of the regional programmes through its Public Investment Committee, an informal committee dependent on the State Secretary of Economic Planning. The regional authorities took part in the formulation of regional OPs but were not included in the final decision. In many ways, this allowed the central government to anchor the complementary approach which called for channelling EU funds towards the modernization of existing approaches and inclusion services. With time complementarity became the leading norm guiding all the following funding periods. Rather surprisingly it did not meet with considerable resistance. In the long run, the channelling of funding towards existing programmes dwarfed efforts to introduce policy innovations and ignored all the actors seeking considerable change to the status quo (i.e. grassroots NGOs, human right advocates, immigrant associations). The EU exerted little pressure on the Spanish authorities to continue with state reforms and the development of innovative approaches (at least not to the extent it did in CEE region).[15]

From 1993 onward, the institutionalization of vertical interactions between the centre and the regions strengthened ACs' discretion over the management of SF programming. Simultaneously, inter-departmental contacts multiplied, culminating in a regular exchange of information concerning funding goals and corresponding measures. From 2000, the role of localities and social actors also crystallized, as partnership regulations gave the municipalities managerial responsibilities over SF programming (Arriba and Moreno, 2005). Once again, the late-coming of the sub-national stakeholders indirectly eased the alignment of organizational goals to those put forward by the central government and ACs. It appeared that by acquiring greater decision-making power over the management of SF, the key stakeholders were more inclined to join-up efforts, at least at the planning stage. While the organizational goals of sub-national agencies were streamlined according to the central blueprint, the decision over the design of specific measures was nested inside the IBs of regional OPs. The Spanish Ministry of Economy and Finance became responsible for the coordination of the application and management of the SF via the General Directorate of Community Funds of the General Secretariat of Finance and Budgets. However, once the money was parcelled out (according to convergence and axes criteria), the administrators of regional OPs became responsible for designing project-calls and selecting winning proposals. Despite these developments, 60% of ESF funds remained under central control while 40% were passed to the ACs (NSRF, 2007). There, the central administration retained a broad margin to manoeuvre in distributing and managing the funds. The positing of central goals for the public departments and granting decision-making over their execution strengthened compliance and collaborative tendencies.

However, what truly strengthened the coordinative process was the introduction of tangible mechanisms which fused the work of domestic agencies with those managing the SF. These had a character of 'soft instruments' and were meant to serve as a forum for the exchange of knowledge and expertise to ensure transparency and consolidate a common direction. One such mechanism was the Cohesion Policy Forum which facilitated interaction among all the stakeholders, including the MAs, IBs, and ministries dealing with social policy, education, and health. Under this forum, specific task groups were organized to assure that all actions planned for each priority in the OPs would complement one another (including those not benefiting from SF). Although the key stakeholders criticized the fact that the forum met only once or twice a year, they agreed that it improved their understanding and knowledge of the work conducted by different ministries and agencies.[16] The forum was also instrumental in building consensus regarding the need to use the ESF for the continuous modernization of social services according to the principle of equal opportunity and non-discrimination (Law 43/2006 of 29 December; Royal Decree 395/2007).

In agreement with the ACs, the central government also introduced coordination committees with the sole purpose of analyzing the complementarity of SF with national, regional, and local measures. The committees brought together MAs, relevant bodies of general state administration, line ministries, and regional agencies. They were responsible for analyzing the contribution of SF to regional development and issues concerning actions that could benefit from aggregated funds. Their work was in turn supplemented by sectorial networks, i.e. the Network of Urban Initiatives, Network of Equality Policy, and Network for Social Inclusion, which maintain a permanent secretariat in charge of disseminating information to its members and organizing thematic meetings. Despite ongoing resistance to joined-up initiatives (i.e. the resistance of the bureaucratic cadre and constraining legal procedures), the committees developed a culture of reporting, which in many ways strengthened transparency and accountability. As noted by a senior manager from the Ministry of Education:

> It brought together parties which would otherwise not feel obliged to communicate, it is too early to talk about joined-up government, but the ground has been laid out, most importantly transparency and some degree of reciprocity has seeped into the highly compartmentalized bureaucratic apparatus.[17]

Overall, the Spanish coordinative efforts managed to create lasting links between SF authorities and general administrative apparatus. While not free of challenges, and resistance of the bureaucratic cadre and also local stakeholders, the synergies were formed and sustained.

Slovakia: centralization, top-down command, and fragmentation

Slovakia has not fully realized the alignment of SF with national and regional social inclusion strategies. Although at the beginning of the first funding period (2004–2006) political discourse called for the orchestration and use of EU funds to reinforce a nationwide modernization of services, such rhetoric subsided over the following years. Faced with EU conditionality Slovakia concentrated on building management infrastructure for SF programming. In this process, it neglected to emphasize the need to create synergies with existing public administration. According to the interviewees, political aspirations to develop new structures and measures diluted concerns about the need to re-evaluate existing interventions and connect them to SF programming.[18] In effect, the newly established agencies for SF management (i.e. MAs, the Plenipotentiary for the Reform of Public

Administration, MCs) held their own organizational goals and worked in isolation from the line ministries and managers of social programmes and services. In short, Slovakia developed a two-tier system, one which separated SF management apparatus from domestic policymaking bodies.

As a centralized state, Slovakia had little experience with horizontal governance and inter-departmental coordination. Generally, policymaking leant towards a vertical chain of command with the highly inconsistent involvement of sub-national actors and civil society (see Chapter 5). However, upon the accession to the EU (2004), the Slovak central government was no longer able to exert full control over the expanding bureaucratic apparatus. Accession conditionality required the state to decentralize administrative units, establish new public management units, and create the Nomenclature of Territorial Units for Statistics (NUTS) instrumental for SF delivery mechanisms and for locating the area where goods and services subject to European public procurement legislation are to be delivered. These changes often exceeded the capacities and expertise of public management boards (Kusá and Gerbery, 2007). Perhaps for that reason, rather than pooling resources, the Slovak government set up new agencies whose mandate was restricted to the management of SF programming (i.e. setting action plans, administering tenders, selecting winning proposals, etc.). The new cadre of bureaucrats and 'European experts' adhered to procedures and norms dictated by the European conditionality, which differed substantially from the traditional administrative *modus operandi*. For example, the social inclusion priorities articulated in SF programming were not reflective of existing social policy legislation (i.e. the Act on Social Assistance, Act No.45/2004). Hence while SF programming called for a greater allocation of funds to tackle the multidimensional aspects of exclusion, domestic reforms induced extensive welfare cuts (Drál, 2008). This incongruity meant that innovative measures contained in SF programming often could not be implemented (or scaled up) as the required legislative provisions were lacking.[19]

Coordination within the institutional setting responsible for cohesion policy was more substantial. Shifting the responsibility for regional development from the Ministry of the Interior to the Plenipotentiary for the Reform of Public Administration strengthened cross-sectorial cooperation in regional policy.[20] However, there was a considerable reluctance on the part of national ministries to delegate control over EU funds to the lower tiers of government, let alone to social actors operating outside public administration. At the same time, the central ministries lacked the capacity to control and discipline the crowded bureaucratic apparatus. The practice of gatekeeping created an atmosphere of mistrust, confusion, and bureaucratic pedantry, stifling learning processes and the flexibility needed for designing appropriate local measures. A lost opportunity for goal alignment only further consolidated these confusing dynamics, reinforcing the reluctance of front-line stuff to take on responsibility. As noted by a senior public manager working in regional administration:

> Everything was dictated from the top but with little concern for existing procedures used by us and other specialized agencies [...] we were supposed to

adjust but no guidelines were provided as to how [...] we entered a period of double checking and triple checking, and at one point it was evident that nobody was exactly sure what rules applied to what [...] it slowed down everything, and on some issues we entered a total stalemate.[21]

This is not to say that the involvement of sub-national actors in SF programming has not taken place. However, the Slovak central government failed to devise concrete mechanisms for cross-sector planning, decision-making, and the management of public funds. Rigid departmentalism characterizing Slovak bureaucracy obstructed the creation of a coherent social inclusion strategy, which could serve as a lynchpin or a guideline for the convoluted administrative apparatus. As such, OPs nested within different ministries were not interconnected – neither with one another nor with the ministerial portfolios. Paradoxically, ESF social inclusion priorities, specifically those targeted at MRCs, emphasized the need for horizontal, multifaceted, and highly integrated approaches (NSRF, 2007). Such a comprehensive approach was simply not feasible in the system characterized by working in silos. As explained by a senior public manager from the Ministry of Interior:

> The SF programming was pushing for the multidimensional approach in an institutional setting that was not prepared to accommodate it; it was simply assumed that different public agencies will work together so no oversight or guidance was provided [...] everybody continued to pursue departmental objectives, that more often than not contradicted each other, a culture of blaming was rampant as well as avoidance of responsibility.[22]

Problems related to the lack of coordination were in fact well acknowledged. The NSRF for the period of 2007–2013 explicitly stated that:

> Based on the experience from the previous programming period it is necessary to concentrate on better coordination of relevant policies and higher concentration of public funds to priorities than in the period 2004–2006. Better coordination and concentration of resources should lead to higher efficiency and effectiveness of SF contributions and help the country to progress'. However, the coordinative efforts were undertaken predominately within the SF programming framework often in an ad-hoc and highly politicized manner.[23]

In fact Slovakia has created numerous coordination agencies and units (not linked to one another) each responsible for specific priority axis. Thus while the horizontal priority MRC was coordinated by the Deputy Prime Minister's Office for European affairs and the Plenipotentiary Office, the coordinative responsibility for Horizontal Priority Equal Opportunities rested in the hands of the Minister of Labour, Social Affairs and Family. This bureaucratic congestion contributed to further fragmentation, especially since many of the coordinative bodies were under direct political influence and held limited decision-making power over the actual priority axis. As noted by the Plenipotentiary:

> The Office was not granted any decision-making authority, its influence depended fully on personal relations with individual Ministries, yet the Ministries themselves held very different ideas about needed action. Moreover inter-departmental cooperation was virtually absent thus actions taken by the Office were often simply ignored; we could not count on any rules or mechanisms to fall back on.[24]

In sum, the Slovak administrative apparatus remained excessively departmentalized without tools which could enforce inter-departmental collaboration and ease information flow. In effect, Slovakia witnessed the emergence of a double-tier system, in which SF programming and its social inclusion priorities were isolated from socio-economic legislation and domestic reform plans. This isolation, as will be shown below, played a significant part in diminishing the effectiveness of implementation processes, encroaching heavily on the sustainability of the implemented projects.

Programmatic synergy and SF outputs in Spain

The Spanish commitment to complementarity realized through the introduction of 'soft' coordinative mechanisms had a decisive effect on SF outputs. Firstly, political pressure to exploit the 'added value' of SF facilitated the alignment of departmental goals, not only easing tensions but also intensifying information sharing. The MAs, nested within ministries, adhered to the same protocols and subscribed to one 'grand vision' of tackling social exclusion albeit amidst tensions and contestations. Nevertheless, the expectation was for the governmental bodies applying for SF to propose an intervention in support of domestic programmes and delineated domestic strategies. Additionally, applicants had to ensure that their programmes or projects adhered to legislative regulations. The interviews with claimants for funding confirmed that these expectations were taken seriously and despite cases of political favouritism, the 'added value' of SF was the main criterion for accessing funding:

> Of course, the ability of an agency to lobby for funds was an important factor, as was its wealth and political affiliation, however, even these preferential candidates needed to demonstrate the added value of their proposals. They were required to show how their programmes contributed to regional reforms or wider national legislation. Without that there was a serious risk of losing some of the funding. This has been the case with our Advice Body, which was unable to make appropriate references and interlinks. We proposed a strictly innovative approach not fully in line with existing legislation, and that was a mistake.[25]

The same criteria applied to all open tenders for NGOs and private organizations who had to demonstrate how their proposals added to mainstream policies and programmes. Interventions closely aligned with the central state's actions guaranteed a higher score during the selection process. While such complementarity guaranteed cohesive approaches, it also meant that innovative pitches were often rejected:

> The obsessive drive to improve rather than replace the state's policies actually thwarted the competitiveness of innovative proposals. It also, from the start, put the new or independent actors at a serious disadvantage. The contenders had to convince the authorities that they could benefit from the proposed schemes, that they could compound them with their own interventions. We were able to do that, but we had to re-think our initial proposal. Hopefully, we will be able to push for a change in the approach to the social enterprises in our region, but it is a tricky game.[26]

The data on projects implemented between 2004 and 2011 (CSES, 2011a) shows that more than 75% of the ESF social inclusion initiatives were complimentary of the national/regional programmes completed under three main axes: *the increase and improvement of human capital* (NSRF, Axis 3, 2008), *the improvement in the efficiency of public administration and competitiveness* (NSRF Axis 5, 2008), and *the enhancement of the job market and social dialogue* (NSRF, Axis 6, 2008). This symbiosis allowed for the amalgamation of funding and in many ways increased the sustainability of implemented interventions. For example, projects aimed at tackling discrimination in the labour market, introduced through OP FAD, faced little problem in securing co-financing and administrative resources from regional and local authorities, allowing project managers to devise long-term objectives (going beyond the five-year funding period). Implemented projects were also strongly connected to social services (i.e. beneficiaries needed to be registered with an employment office, or SF training projects included the labour insertion component managed directly by public agencies) strengthening inter-agency cooperation and policy learning (Rivero et al., 2013). Projects targeted at the long-term unemployed, including the Roma communities (i.e. Acceder, the Seville street vendors' initiative, and the women's integration projects run by the Roma Women's Association, ROMI), were coordinated with regional and local welfare provisions (including child benefits, unemployment payments, and health insurance). While these projects improved access to public services (especially for groups faced with high levels of oppression and discrimination) they did not induce far-reaching institutional changes. As asserted by a community leader in Seville:

> We managed to work out legal permits for flower vendors in the city [majority Roma families] this was a huge thing, but that's as far as we could go, we cannot lobby for greater legal change, we are too dependent on the authorities to challenge the way they do things.[27]

Nevertheless, consolidation of the complementary approach curtailed the duplication of efforts and overlaps. In many ways, demands for innovation was overridden by the quest for the efficient allocation of funding. As expressed by a senior public servant working in Seville:

> Efforts are made to reduce duplication and increase efficiency. Although more work needs to be conducted to strengthen the alignment of our work with SF programming, we have made considerable progress on eliminating the greatest overlaps, in particular between measures provided by OP FAD and the Andalusia Plan for the Roma Community [...] Sometimes not everything that is new works, we need to remember that institutional memory is useful and we can and we should learn from our mistakes.[28]

This stance echoed across public agencies, in one way or another benefiting from EU funds. Moreover, all interviewed stakeholders insisted that linking SF with domestic services strengthened overall accountability for the results of implemented projects, and facilitated inter-departmental, inter-sector learning. An FSG regional manager noted that:

> Our knowledge about the ongoing public programmes allowed us to structure our own measures accordingly. It also gave us leverage when negotiation co-financing proposals with local stakeholders. At the same time, the authorities were happy to assist us seeing that we are contributing to their efforts rather than taking over.[29]

Similar opinions were expressed by agencies within the Andalusian government as well as the local authorities. As noted by a public servant working in the social services department in Granada City Hall:

> Although we are mostly responsible for localized social assistance services, we also have access to information regarding SF projects, which makes decisions over co-financing and potential contributions easier and more transparent.[30]

Moreover, the strategic management provided by the central government – in the form of inter-departmental conferences and workshops (which always included actors responsible for domestic and European programmes) allowed for the clarification of evaluation criteria and sharing of best practices. This, in turn, fostered 'check and compare' approaches, where leading stakeholders were motivated to continuously re-assess their achievements against the laid-out framework:

> Constant re-assessment was indeed strongly endorsed by the bureaucrats. Of course, reluctance was rampant as departments were not eager to admit failure and we struggled with setting up coherent indicators. Nevertheless, this not only helped us see acute inefficiencies but in a way made everybody more accountable and more willing to improve their outputs.[31]

As mentioned above, the institutionalization of synergies has lengthened the lifespan of individual projects, increasing the potential for policy impact. The data shows that close to 80% of the social inclusion projects (with Roma people as direct or indirect beneficiaries) introduced in the 2000–2006 funding period, continued in 2007–2013 (CSES, 2011b). Moreover, some of the projects (i.e. Acceder, GranadaEmpleo) actually grew in scope and scale, increasing the number of beneficiaries (EURoma, 2010). However, once again the stability and longevity have dwarfed the opportunity for innovation. Although, theoretical assumptions maintain that joined-up actions can reinforce the dissemination of innovative ideas, the case of Spain appears to contradict these assertions. Even though the information flow was fairly open and accessible to social inclusion stakeholders,[32] the strong proclivity to use SF as a reinforcement for existing approaches impinged on the creative processes and experimentation. As commented by an NGO worker:

> The procedures successfully barricaded initiatives which were not reflective of national goals and interests. The imperative to channel SF for interventions that were already linked to public services severely disadvantaged truly innovative, grassroots projects such as participatory research [...] if you wanted to introduce projects with no counterparts run by public administration you could not count on European provisions.[33]

Another NGO worker noted:

> We work on small-scale individual-based projects in the area of multicultural education, however, our methodology is not in line with approaches undertaken by mainstream education. We quickly found out that we are not eligible for available financial assistance unless we compromise on our objectives and working methods.[34]

At the same time, numerous public managers, as well as the leading NGOs, maintained that synergy has effectively prevented the dispersion of funds to miscellaneous projects, which were believed to provide immediate charity-like assistance without contributing to longer-term integration aims. While opinions about the effectiveness of the existing approach were fractious, all sides were in agreement that experimentation and innovation have not been strongly promoted by the Spanish SF programming. Instead, SF reinforced already well-developed domestic strategies without considerable efforts made to promote innovative pathways or initiatives. Critics insisted that in some cases SF were used to buttress interventions that held no real value for the community and did little more than consolidate status quo.[35]

Synergies in Slovakia and SF outputs

The emergence of a double-tier system dichotomized the public bureaucracy into domestic and European-focused agencies. This system reduced the overall efficiency of the SF programming while also having the effect of lowering morale among the bureaucratic esprit de corps involved with Roma policy.[36] The lack of coordinative mechanisms and strategic oversight locked public agencies inside silos, with no incentives provided for information sharing, mutual learning, or reciprocity of resources.[37] In effect, the interaction among MAs and domestic agencies (including line ministries) was residual and strictly formalistic.[38] The departmentalization dynamic was reflected in the project-calls and selection criteria. An analysis of social inclusion project-calls issued between 2004 and 2013 showed an evident lack of 'added value' criteria, or focus on the reinforcement of domestic practices.[39] The demand-based allocation procedures were not linked to national or regional development objectives and they did not introduce selection criteria reflective of the upcoming (planned) reforms.[40] Moreover, it was common for applicants to propose a short-term intervention, which subscribed solely to organizational vision, with no specification on how the projects would contribute to existing social inclusion action plans. As explained by a senior public servant working for the MA OP Education:

> During the selection process, we really lacked clear guidelines as to who would be the best recipient and what approaches were really in demand. The MAs guarded their own interests focusing on meeting internal goals and requirements, often behind closed doors. We couldn't really learn from them [...] No efforts were made to foster resource reciprocity, when faced with criticism agencies simply pointed fingers at other stakeholders or refused to take responsibility for their actions [...] we all worked in isolation, hiding behind our own protocols.[41]

Fragmented selection processes (dispersed among various MAs located in different ministries) facilitated the implementation of miscellaneous projects which quite often contradicted domestic political agendas and approaches. For example, in the midst of welfare cuts and intensifying anti-Gypsyism (Marušák and Singer, 2009), numerous competitors (particularly social actors) proposed ambitious projects dependent on generous social provisions and an expansive safety net (i.e. the construction of social housing, social assistance programmes). The incompatibility with general social policy trends confined the duration of the projects to a five-year funding period (often only one or two-year initiatives were introduced) and hindered the scaling up of local initiatives (even those which delivered positive results). As commented by a leader of a grassroots NGO:

> Even if the SF project is successful there is no interest to make it part of the political agenda. There is no interest to promote Roma issues because the authorities have very different plans and priorities. They often say that since we got the European money we should not expect anything else. Or claim that the legislation does not allow for the project to be scaled up. And yes it is true that a lot of projects are ambitious, but if we stick with what the government is doing for integration, well we will have nothing to do.[42]

The weak (or in many instances non-existent) synchronization of social inclusion action plans raised concerns about co-financing. The majority of implemented ESF projects targeted at MRC only received 15% co-financing from public budgets (the minimum amount stipulated by cohesion regulations), and in some cases, the entire intervention was financed by SF, in full breach of the additionality principle. In fact, in many localities, the SF were viewed as an 'additional pool of money', which could replace municipal budgets. As explained by a member of the MC:

> I must say that the OPs were designed to serve as a source of financing for a litany of miscellaneous measures; money would be allocated to anything from minor infrastructural improvements, cultural activities to field social work, health training or even waste collection. It rarely happened that these measures in anyway reinforced one another and worse they seemed to really replace programmes which should be financed from the public budget in the first place.[43]

The progressive fragmentation of efforts compounded by the lack of effective steering mechanisms contributed to the spectacular failure of the comprehensive local strategy (discussed in Chapter 5) championed by the key Roma inclusion stakeholders, including the OSF, Roma Institute, and the SDF. The ideas to support marginalized localities while they prepared comprehensive long-term inclusion strategies was neither buttressed by an overarching strategy nor coordinated in a systematic manner. As already noted in previous chapters, the Plenipotentiary Office possessed little authority or capacity to reinforce cooperation or provide an oversight of a severely departmentalized system of governance. However, the immediate failure of the proposed intervention stemmed from its vague design and preoccupation with a 'quick fix' to a complex problem. As commented by a manager working in the Plenipotentiary Office:

> The strategies were vague on how they will promote integration, instead they often listed an array of things that need to be fixed in the localities – from sidewalks to community centres, to leaking pipes [...] however this should not be surprising given that nobody really presented these contenders with a general blueprint of what is acceptable and what is not. There was no conditionality, no common indicators [...] so everybody proposed what they thought was most important to their locality, not to the entire country or even region.[44]

The Office further argued that there was little motivation to introduce comprehensive integration efforts requiring longer time-frames, aggregated budgets, and partnerships. In particular, the measures directed at the Roma population were fully isolated from existing services. It is important to highlight that numerous localities had never run projects or programmes targeted at Roma integration

(Hurrle et al., 2012). Hence, they tended to present inclusion plans as an 'extra' component of the proposal or a 'one-time' investment scheme. Not surprisingly, even on paper, the proposals were neither sustainable nor legitimate in the eyes of Roma beneficiaries.

The absence of coordinative and oversight mechanisms also negatively affected the accountability for the majority of SF initiatives targeted at social inclusion. As the organizations' objectives were not aligned, a common purpose (or strategy) was not formalized. Different agencies with their own interests had no clear understanding of the work performed by other agents. As noted by a manager from SDF:

> Although public agencies were all aware that social exclusion requires a comprehensive approach, putting it in motion became virtually impossible [...] A lack of communication, incongruent procedures and the politicization of Roma issues meant that consensus was hard to come by [...] However, it was the lack of guidance from the centre that allowed for this fragmentation, the top-down approach failed to provide direction or oversight [...] in many instances the localities were simply unaware of larger social inclusion plans or policies.[45]

The absence of coordinative tools meant that the ministries were reluctant to earmark funding for comprehensive Roma integration strategies and often did not feel responsible for the results of SF projects implemented in far removed places:

> The responsibility for Roma issues was bounced around different ministries and agencies, but at the end of the day nobody was truly responsible for the delivery of comprehensive approaches [...] any failure was blamed on the implementers, usually small disenfranchised localities, and of course the Plenipotentiary Office. We often joke that the Office was created so the government can blame somebody for all its failures.[46]

As demonstrated in Chapter 5, the MAs were predominantly responsible for the efficient allocation of funds, and not their outputs or impacts.[47] Since they were not involved in the implementation and had limited monitoring capacity, success was measured only in terms of expenditures (i.e. the percentage of money spent on time). Accountability for actual projects rested in the hands of project managers. However, as their projects were rarely connected to an overarching strategy, their effectiveness was difficult to evaluate or monitor. As pointed out by a Roma project manager:

> Many projects claim to help the Roma, but there are no indicators available to check these claims [...] The MAs are not obliged to verify this, the Plenipotentiary has no resources to do it and the MC are not really involved in the monitoring of individual projects. It is a system where accountability is simply lacking, and all is dependent on the goodwill of individuals.[48]

Finally, the erratic coordination of the public sector curtailed efforts to develop and implement innovative approaches to exclusion and integration. While the 2007–2013 funding period saw a considerable inflow of projects proposing innovative methodologies, the project database showed that the majority of winning initiatives paid scarce attention to the multidimensional aspect of social exclusion and proposed standard approaches (i.e. training, individual consultancy, mediation services). While these dynamics were often ascribed to the lack of capacity of the local agents to devise cutting-edge projects, they were also driven by the lack of inter-agency learning and mechanisms for the dissemination and scaling up of good practices. Few of the innovative projects were delivered by NGOs, fully disconnected from regional and local action plans. As commented by the OSF:

> Many pilot projects were in fact quite successful. However, they were not in any way linked to national or regional policies, often did not include public servants in their implementation, and worked against the interest of the localities [...] as such they only lasted for 2–3 years and after the funding period was over they were discontinued.[49]

The lost opportunity for lesson-learning and the inability of the government to coordinate local initiatives negatively affected general attitudes in the public sectors. According to the interviewed public managers there was a widespread sentiment that in the context of Roma integration, 'nothing works', and little can be done to prompt effective integration programmes.

Concluding remarks

This chapter has demonstrated empirically that the creation of synergies has strongly influenced the shape of SF outputs. The findings confirm the assumptions about the benefits and potential shortcomings of joined-up government. The analysis of the Spanish case showed that the alignment of SF strategies and procedures with domestic practices was pivotal in securing effective and sustainable SF outputs. While joining-up was not fully achieved, the central authorities and their regional counterparts were able to steer a complex system of governance so that the public bureaucracy became more open to inter-organizational communication and collaboration. At the same time, the commitment to use SF as 'added value' to domestic programmes, substantially curbed their potential to induce innovative thinking or promote a progressive vision of social inclusion. There was a strong proclivity to allocate funding to initiatives that did not encroach on accepted norms, procedures, or political interests. In that sense, SF programming was co-opted by the national and regional authorities who through adroit coordination were able to use EU funding for securing domestic interests. These dynamics were also made possible, given that Spain already had a well-developed domestic institutional framework for advancing social inclusion action plans. As such, SF, rather than promoting modernization (a difficult and costly undertaking), were used to prop-up existing programmes and services, which on the surface did not require fundamental restructuring or concrete improvements.

The case of Slovakia demonstrates a very different dynamic. Although Slovakia appeared to adhere to the additionality doctrine, the political commitment to use EU funding in a complementary manner was weak. The aspiration to use European funding for the development of new programmes and institutions, compounded with consistently centralized governance practices, reduced motivations and capacities for joining-up. A lack of steering mechanisms, able to induce the alignment of organizational procedures and interests, resulted in the emergence of a double-tier system, disconnecting SF management from the wider domestic bureaucratic apparatus. This, in turn, prompted the excessive fragmentation and duplication of efforts undertaken in the area of social inclusion, and in many cases full-blown incongruity. The overtly bureaucratized system of SF programming was not easily accessible to non-involved departments and agencies, which further prevented the nurturing of common goals, and further consolidated the practice of working in silos. Somewhat paradoxically, Slovakia has appeared eager to comply with EU cohesion objectives and was willing to induce innovative thinking into its public administration. However, the double-tier dynamics severely encroached on these aspirations, as isolated SF interventions were not able to induce wider policy changes or even minor alterations. The fact that Slovakia generally lacked domestic social inclusion strategies and, thus, had to develop new approaches only reinforced the double-tier dynamics. Overall, the funding was used to satisfy an array of localized interests, not always ready or willing to promote cohesive social inclusion strategies.

These findings suggest doubts about the potency of cohesion policy to induce domestic policy changes and foster development of cohesive social inclusion strategies. Looking at the two cases, it appears that SF were first and foremost used to promote domestic interests and policies. While the Spanish success was attributed to the skilful creation of synergies, the fact that existing domestic approaches were in themselves considered valuable is very relevant. It shows that successful SF outputs are strongly contingent on the overall effectiveness of domestic policies. As such they do not present themselves as mechanisms able to introduce innovating thinking or remodel domestic programmes. Considering the enthusiastic promotion of SF as 'mending' instruments and engines for the development of innovative inclusion programmes for vulnerable groups and minorities, such findings severely subvert the normative position of entire cohesion policy.

Notes

1 It is important to highlight the difference between partnership and the alignment of organizational goals and procedures. As partnership seeks to bring different actors together to deliver a particular service or strategy, the alignment of goals seeks to direct diverse action and services (run and delivered through different configurations) in such a way as to avoid overlaps and promote multifaceted services.

2 It has been stated in numerous evaluation reports that the greatest hindrance in accessing funding is overly complex procedures which follow their own logic without taking under consideration the domestic institutional setting (see EURoma, 2016).

3 It has been argued that SF projects targeting the Roma people tend to be evaluated in isolation, hindering the possibility of seeing their actual impact on domestic policies (Hurrle et al., 2012).

4 Apart from Axis 1 of the NRP (strengthening macro-economic and budget stability) which due to its very nature does not relate directly to ERDF and ESF programming, all other NRP axes show a specific association with the actions foreseen in the NSRF.

5 The authority over education issues was progressively transferred to the individual AC, which now regulates and organizes the educational system within the framework of state law. However, the commitment to use SF in a 'supplementary' manner has remained unchanged. Regional authorities of Andalusia asserted that SF will be channelled into initiatives developed under the Solidarity in Education Act (Law 9/1999) including the activities of the Departments of Education and Vocational Guidance which promote 'intercultural education and aid to children faced with vulnerable circumstances'.

6 Interview #3, 7 June 2011 (Madrid).

7 Interview #12, 22 June 2011 (Seville).

8 Interview #76 3 February 2015 (Madrid).

9 Interview #45, 14 May2013 (Bratislava); Interview #46, 26 July 2011 (Bratislava).

10 Interview #50, 26 July 2011 (Bratislava).

11 Interview #50, 26 July 2011 (Bratislava).

12 Mayors for Roma Inclusion Forum Meeting, Skalica, Slovakia 14 May 2011, conference transcript.

13 Often due to an uneven decentralization process, whereby some ACs decentralized faster than others. For a comprehensive account of Spanish decentralization see Keating and Wilson (2009).

14 The case appeared quite different in the area of infrastructure and the ERDF. Madrid's plans for large-scale infrastructure developments were highly contested by the AC who claimed that money was being diverted from the real needs of their populations. Bargaining and pork-barrel politics have prevented the alignment of regional reforms with SF programming. SF strategies were largely imposed on the AC and in many ways changed the way infrastructure reforms were conducted by the Ministry of Transport.

15 The pressure from the EU intensified only in the mid-2000 as an answer to the Spanish 'incomplete' transposition of equality directives (see Bustelo, 2009).

16 Interview #5, 14 June 2011 (Madrid); Interview #20, 21 June 2011 (Seville).

17 Interview #7, 27 June 2011 (Madrid).

18 Interview #43, 13 May 2011 (Skalica).

19 For example, social housing initiatives in OP RD were not designed in line with existing regulations concerning housing and social assistance.

20 Such cooperation was however more pronounced within ERDF programming.

21 Interview #54, 28 July 2011 (Kosice).

22 Interview #44, 14 May 2013 (Bratislava).

23 The majority of interviewees working in the public sector stated that these were executed on paper only.

24 Interview #53, 26 July 2011 (Bratislava).

25 Interview #8, 16 June 2011 (Madrid).

26 Interview #33, 14 March 2013 (Seville).

27 Interview #81 3 October 2014 (Seville).

28 Interview #11, 22 June 2011 (Seville).

29 Interview #25, 20 June 2011 (Seville).

30 Interview #18, 18 June 2011 (Seville).

31 Interview #4, 14 June 2011 (Madrid).

32 In the context of Roma inclusion, it was strengthened by the establishment of the State Council for the Roma People (Royal Decree 891/2005), a collegiate inter-ministerial organ with consultative and advisory powers under the responsibility of the Ministry of Health and Social Policy. It formalised the collaboration and cooperation of the Roma associative movement with the General State Administration. The work of the State Council was evaluated as a 'good practice' as it was noted that the joint work of all relevant stakeholders in the Development Action Plan for the Roma People had greatly improved the quality of the preparation of social policies and specific measures directly affecting the Roma, as Roma NGOs have actively contributed in their preparation (Villagómez et al., 2009).

33 Interview #36, 23 June 2011 (Seville).

34 Interview #37, 23 June 2011 (Seville).

35 Interview#76, 3 February 2015 (Madrid).

36 In the interviews, the majority of senior public managers asserted that they were frustrated with their department and the public sector as a whole since they were often able to identify the problems, but would do little about them.

37 It is important to note that the weak institutionalization of partnership was at the core of these isolationist inter-agency relations.

38 The High-Level Event on the Structural Funds contribution to Roma integration in Slovakia and Košice, 2011, conference transcripts.

39 The 'added value' was granted low priority, thus proposed initiatives, with no articulation on the contribution to domestic plans or services, were not penalized. These dynamics changed in the 2014–2020 funding period with the introduction of the conditionality clause within the ESF.

40 For a database of project-calls, see www.iazasi.gov.sk/en/calls-for-proposal.

41 Interview #49, 4 October 2011 (Bratislava).

42 Interview #72, 26 July 2011 (Banská Bystrica).

43 Interview #59, 3 March 2011 (Bratislava).

44 Interview #53, 26 July 2011 (Bratislava).

45 Interview#50, 26 July 2011 (Bratislava).

46 Interview #50, 26 July 2011 (Bratislava)

47 The only exception was the IB SDF, which was responsible for the allocation as well as implementation of SF projects – in partnership with localities and NGOs.

48 Interview #68, 26 July 2011 (Bratislava).

49 Interview #62, 23 July 2011 (Bratislava).

7 A successful project has many parents but a failure is always an orphan

Structural Funds at a micro-level

We have seen in *Financing Roma Inclusion with European Structural Funds* that SF outputs are structured by factors deeply embedded in implementation processes. The research showed that the diverging performance of SF is very much contingent on the framing of public problems in the overarching strategic design (Chapter 4), the institutionalization of partnership arrangements (Chapter 5) and the harmonization of SF aims with existing public programmes and reforms (Chapter 6). Thus far, the book has discussed these three factors in isolation, mainly to preserve a degree of simplicity and analytical clarity. However, as argued in Chapter 3, any in-depth analysis of programmatic outputs needs to account for the way discursive, participatory, and administrative facets influence and reinforce one another, and try to capture the aggregated influence they have on securing or hindering effective, legitimate, and sustainable results. In other words, the book asserts that an analytical focus attentive to just one factor fails to capture the complexity of causal relationships unravelling across implementation processes and, more importantly, risks presenting a bias (or overly simplistic) picture of either success or failure.

The findings presented in the previous chapter showed that Spanish success has been driven by: a) a clear policy design that recognizes structural dimensions of social exclusion, b) a design of partnership that relies on co-productive interactions that include experts and community stakeholders, and c) the synchronization of SF interventions with domestic policies and exploitation of the 'added value' of SF. At the same time Slovak adherence to an individualistic, ethnically defined framing of exclusion, competitive partnership schemes based on off-loading responsibility for implementation onto under-resourced localities, and construction of a double-tier system which isolated SF from ongoing programmes resulted in a dramatic failure to earmark and utilize funding for acute needs and the interests of the Roma population. The analysis was largely conducted on a meso-level, focusing on the broad design and workings of SF programming. However, to unveil the combined influence of these factors it is useful to move down to the micro-level and explain the performance of individual projects funded through SF. In the multi-level system of cohesion policy, projects are the final beneficiaries of SF allocations and considered the final stage of the implementation process. It is in these micro-cosmoses where the outputs are most pronounced and where compounded influence is most palpable. Moreover, focusing the analytical lens on local contexts with all their complexities allows for the unpacking of the very concept of success and failure to see to what degree general trends and practices are reflected on the ground.

This chapter analyzes six ESF projects implemented in the 2007–2013 funding period. It examines outlier cases that deviated from the population of projects in terms of the outputs (three successful projects in Slovakia and three failing initiatives in Spain). This method is used to demonstrate that policy success is contingent on the presence and performance of the three factors. The examined projects include: PROMOCIONA, Granada Employment, and EDEM in Spain, and National Project Field Social Work, From Benefits to Paid Work, and Integrated Education in Slovakia.

Spain: deviating from the success

The design of the Spanish SF programming emphasized the need to invest EU funds in the development of inclusive public services and the generation of an anti-discrimination framework, predominately in the area of employment (e.g. tackling discrimination in employment and enhancing employment insertion services). Yet, the empirical analysis showed that the implementation process proved efficient and delivered sustainable, and legitimate outputs, albeit not free of contestation. The implementation of SF towards social inclusion strategies was coined a success, with the EU calling Spanish efforts *a model for Roma integration* to be copied by other member states (Smith, 2011). However, at the project level, the success appeared more ambiguous, with numerous initiatives resulting in a blunt failure to construct sustainable access to employment (and other public services) and improve the overall treatment of minorities and impoverished neighbourhoods. The deepening economic crisis accompanied by drastic 'public saving schemes' has left many inclusion projects without basic co-financing and reduced to the pool of human resources. The dismantling of the equality infrastructure (Paleo and Alonso, 2015) and reduction of integration funding (i.e. the Spanish Integration Fund[1]) has severely weakened programmatic synergies, creating an institutional and financial void for project continuation. Nevertheless, the economic crisis offers only a partial explanation of the recorded feebleness of individual projects. It is important to highlight that throughout the entire programming period (2007–2013) ESF absorption and allocation rates remained stable, and despite increasing cuts to public spending, the government did not divert (nor reduce) EU funding away from social inclusion objectives. The major claim made in this chapter is that the ineffectiveness of SF projects stemmed from their non-conformity with consolidated policy frames and standardized approaches of using SF to build social inclusion initiatives.

To illustrate this dynamic, the analysis below scrutinizes three social inclusion projects funded through the ESF, which failed to deliver the expected results. First is PROMOCIONA, a programme introduced as a multi-regional scheme within the OP FAD, targeted at the education of Roma children and youths. Second is an analysis of the Granada Employment Programme, a social inclusion initiative introduced in the province of Andalusia, and funded through OP Employment and Adaptability (OP E&A). Last, it looks at CODE, a local employment initiative introduced in Seville in the marginalized urban districts, co-financed through OP ESF Andalusia. Although the EU had praised the innovative character of these interventions, placing them inside the 'good practice' database (Council of Europe Database; EURoma, 2010),[2] the analysis here challenges this assessment. The analysis shows that services offered by the projects grappled with serious managerial strains and bureaucratic inefficiencies. They also all struggled with outreach, sustaining funding, and inducing institutional transformation. In short, they deviated from the general narrative of success.

PROMOCIONA: targeted education

Previous chapters have outlined the fundamental role played by the FSG in planning and allocating SF to initiatives benefiting Roma communities. Among successful employment initiatives chaperoned by the foundation, PROMOCIONA promised to direct funds to education. Developed in the framework of OP FAD with co-financing from the Spanish Ministry of Health and Social Policy,[3] it served as a response to the concerns raised about the low performance and high dropout rates of Roma students in compulsory secondary education.[4] The key objective was 'to promote equal opportunities in education for Roma students so they could achieve higher rates of academic success in the last cycle of primary education and compulsory secondary education and promote transition into higher education and professional training' (FSG, 2009). The proposed measures (including individual tutorials, group work, and awareness raising campaigns) were to be delivered in close cooperation with educational institutions, neighbourhood councils, and the wider social environment.

In the first two years of its operation, PROMOCIONA was successful in bringing aboard numerous schools and attracting the wider attention of Roma communities. The 2011 mid-term report demonstrated that the programme had worked directly with a total of 1,235 Roma children and youths, 1,076 families, and 476 school centres. At the end of 2011, measures were running in 27 cities in 14 regions of Spain, while the number of beneficiaries rose by 8%. The programme ran training opportunities for educators and community workers (150 actions were introduced for more than 8,000 participants) and developed awareness campaigns for breaking the stereotypes and presenting a positive social image of Roma communities.[5] However, already in 2011, PROMOCIONA had encountered problems in securing funding from local authorities to manage different components of the programme. According to the FSG manager:

> The interest in funding Roma initiatives has subsided and it appears that because of the economic crisis the municipalities are reverting their budgets to other supposedly more pressing priorities. We still have the support of the central and regional governments but the localities are withdrawing one by one.[6]

In 2012, the number of contracts signed with individual schools decreased, and the programme found it difficult to attract experienced pedagogues and community mediators. Moreover, the strategic aim to 'generate equal opportunities and enhance educational conditions' did not engender institutional reforms (or secure political commitment), adding little to the development of intercultural education. While the FSG was fast to attribute these shortcomings to a wider 'assault on education' and lack of political will 'to address Roma education head-on', the very design of PROMOCIONA proved to be the greatest impediment to the programmes' success.

Failing to challenge the status quo

The FSG management team did not hide the fact that the endorsement of PROMOCIONA by the government resulted from a tactical presentation of education as a leading factor in increasing employment among Roma people. This framing, aligned with a wider discourse on social inclusion, allowed the FSG to secure national co-financing and education objectives in OP FAD.[7] However, the wider commitment to equal opportunities was surpassed by a targeted approach, directed more at behavioural rather than institutional change. While the gap between the educational attainment of Spanish Roma people and the rest of the population was assessed in terms of 'an inability to benefit from or access educational services', the cause was attributed to the negative attitudes towards education among Roma minorities. As articulated by a programme manager:

> The Roma population continue to see formal education as a threat to their cultural identity, programmes like PROMOCIONA aim to change this negative perception and encourage the Roma population, both children and adults, to reap benefits of education and to use it for their personal and professional growth.[8]

This diagnosis weakened the potential of the programme to induce institutional reforms (i.e. multicultural curriculums, equality training for educators and school councils) and ironically obscured the pervasive discrimination experienced by Roma pupils in educational settings. Instead, according to local activists, the programme took the shape of supplementary assistance, granted to carefully selected Roma pupils (often those students with higher grades and the strongest commitment to education).[9] Although, the impact of tutorials and after-school activities on individual lives should not be dismissed (Scullion and Brown, 2013), overall the adopted methodology failed to develop tools with which to improve or transform the wider institutional landscape. In short, PROMOCIONA prepared Roma pupils to enter (or stay in) the mainstream education system, which at its core remained unproblematized.

The EU and a wide range of international Roma inclusion stakeholders praised FSG efforts to target funds along the ethnic dimensions of exclusion. Yet such an allocation of money diverged from the 'ethnically neutral' standards embedded in the Spanish SF programming and local inclusion strategies. During an interview held at the Mayor's Office in Seville, the senior public manager insisted that he would rather talk about the general weaknesses of public education, than the 'circumstances of a small ethnic group'.[10] Many mayors and local councillors opposed the funding of 'Roma projects' from their already squeezed public purses, often arguing that the Roma were already well (if not better) supported by the central authorities and the EU itself. They were also reluctant to promote activities targeted at 'unpopular groups' in fear of losing electoral support. As explained by the regional representative of the FSG:

> During our presentations or negotiations with the localities, the same question would resurface, how will the other vulnerable pupils benefit? [...] How will we rationalize the spending priorities to our non-Roma constituencies? In some cases, the local authorities who were willing to provide their support asked us not to publicize their involvement. Nobody wanted to be directly associated with the Roma.[11]

The PROMOCIONA team, while acknowledging these tensions, maintained that some degree of affirmative action is indispensable to improve Roma integration:

> Given the substantial underperformance of Roma pupils in mainstream education compared to the general population, we cannot pretend that extra resources are unnecessary, we simply must convince the localities that tailored assistance is the way to move forward.[12]

Yet, the FSG failed to couple its commitment to affirmative action initiatives with efforts to institutionalize them in the mainstream educational setting. In many ways, the drive to change attitudes towards education among Roma communities and convince the public that Roma pupils, when given extra resources, can perform on an equal footing with everyone else, made institutional change and mainstream equality measures seem redundant.[13] Most of the localities viewed PROMOCIONA as a supplementary activity, delivered outside of the general curriculum by outsourced staff and volunteers. This resulted in what one activist described as the 'ghettoization of educational support'[14] as students taking part in the programme were automatically excluded from other forms of mainstream support (e.g. guidance counselling).

Yet the reluctance to support targeted measures was also strongly linked to the character of partnership developed in the framework of PROMOCIONA. The co-productive partnership forged among the central government, regional authorities, and IB of OP FAD did not extend to the localities (neither the city halls nor the grassroots NGOs and educational institutions). The network of local agents (in fact, the key implementers of the activities) were neither engaged in the design of the programme nor held decision-making capacity over it. Left outside the sphere of influence, they were expected to act as 'passive financiers' and service providers. An interviewed headmaster of a secondary school in Seville complained:

> We are sort of silent partners, we have no say in what's needed and who should benefit, we are not even sure how many of our students are Roma, and we really do not have the staff to take an extra load of work.[15]

The lack of voice generated inimical attitudes towards the programme and more importantly exempted the local authorities from feeling accountable for the programme's results. According to education professionals working for PROMOCIONA in the city of Huelva, the residual and inconsistent involvement of the local authorities meant that Roma education was rarely discussed during council meetings, and was not brought up during wider discussions about the future of Spanish education.[16] In the interviews, the local authorities often maintained that PROMOCIONA is a Roma project run by the Roma people for the Roma people thus insisting that public input or oversight is redundant. As bluntly expressed by a city hall official in Granada:

> This is an NGO initiative, while we might support it financially, we don't feel it is our responsibility to monitor its performance, this is a job for regional authorities and SF managers [...] our priorities lay somewhere else.[17]

The involvement of the families and community leaders, presented as one of the main strengths of the programme, was also weakly institutionalized. While the programme introduced awareness campaigns[18] among Roma communities (in the hope of increasing their active interest in the education of their children) parents had little opportunity to express their interests and exert pressure on educational institutions.[19]

The managers of PROMOCIONA made consistent efforts to synergize the programme's objectives with national and regional priorities (i.e. emphasizing the preventive dimension of the measures and their impact on reducing dropout rates[20]). However, once again the exclusive targeting of the Roma ethnic minority weakened the potential to restructure or transform the existing educational landscape. Moreover, the programme was not aligned with existing Roma integration programmes (i.e. the National Programme for the Development of Roma and Regional Plans for the Roma Community). According to the senior manager working on these domestic initiatives, this omission severely hindered inter-organizational communication and resource sharing, contributing to duplication of activities and the full isolation of PROMOCIONA from wider integration schemes.[21]

Overall, while ethnic targeting helped individual students, it did little to transform systemic inequalities. More importantly, it reinforced the pervasive view that low educational attainments are driven by cultural norms guiding Roma communities. The residual attention to the structural dimensions of social exclusion not only hindered the realization of key aims but also jeopardized wider political support. The exclusion of the local authorities from decision-making processes strengthened an unwillingness to commit necessary co-financing and endorse the programme on local political agendas. These dynamics combined with the feeble synchronization of PROMOCIONA with the existing integration programmes and projects threatened the sustainability of funding and legitimacy of 'add-on' activities. Despite the limited impact, the programme is now part of the newly established OP Social Inclusion and Social Economy. However, it appears that the FSG has fully abandoned the equal opportunity dimension in favour of 'mentorship' measures focused solely on labour insertion and vocational training.

The Granada Employment Programme

Another initiative which fell short on its promises was the GranadaEmpleo (Granada Employment Programme) introduced in 2008 by the Provincial Department of Culture, Youth and Local Development in Granada. The initiative was an answer to the alarming unemployment rates, which in 2010 reached 27.7%, and the recognition that provincial resources were underutilized in the fight against social exclusion (Pérez and Sánchez, 2013). Financed by the multi-regional OP E&A with co-financing provided by the Andalusian government, the programme aimed to tackle barriers to meaningful employment and facilitate activation and insertion of the long-term unemployed and disadvantaged groups. The espoused objectives called for a removal of barriers to equal and sustainable employment, fighting discrimination in the labour market, and promoting gender equality. The initiative was developed through intensive collaboration among public and social entities including: socio-economic organizations, trade unions, public departments of Andalusian government, Province of Granada, and organizations standing for various disadvantaged groups. The total budget of €8,402,254 (2008–2011) supported 166 municipalities (Delegación de Empleo y Desarrollo Sostenible).

The Granada Employment Programme was composed of two main measures, managed and coordinated by the provincial authorities:

1 Territorial Employment Pacts (TEPs) in municipalities across Granada Province.
2 Integrated Itineraries (IIs) for socio-labour insertion of disadvantaged groups.

The first measure had a territorial dimension, aimed at the creation of local strategies for revitalization of the labour market in the most disadvantaged areas. It brought together more than 2,000 public, private, and social agencies under a common employment strategy which aligned local priorities with wider developmental needs. The second measure served as a complementary component to the territorial approach, providing additional support to groups at risk of social exclusion (including the members of Roma communities).

The 2011 evaluation report assessed the performance of the project positively, both in terms of its outreach and participation rates. The development and implementation of the integrated itinerary inside employment initiatives benefited close to 1,000 people at risk of exclusion – equipping them with marketable skills and helping them secure long-term employment contracts (i.e. in the municipality of Granada alone 188 persons received professional training and more than 60% gained full-time employment). The programme realized over 5,000 workshops, conferences, and lectures, and according to the stakeholders, these activities enhanced the knowledge (among the bureaucrats and NGO workers) about employment insertion schemes, equality safeguards, and macro-level economic developments.[22]

Notwithstanding the positive assessment, the programme was burdened by the extensive delays and discontinuities of the delivered measures. Critics attributed these shortcomings to micro-level mismanagement and inadequate planning. Pérez and Sánchez (2013), for example, argued that extremely vague cost analysis and an underestimation of the actual costs involved in the running of TEP's ambitious initiatives resulted in smaller municipalities withdrawing their support. However, the delays and underfinancing were strongly linked to the overarching design, which failed to provide coordinative mechanisms and secure programmatic synergies. As expressed by NGO manager from Granada:

> We failed to interconnect our efforts with wider employment schemes, we lacked coordination and local inputs […] in the end the common employment strategy began to resemble a tokenistic endeavour, too ambitious in scope to be effectively realized and sustained by the ill-equipped municipalities.[23]

Strengths and challenges

From the start, the vision of the Granada Employment Programme strongly reflected the employment priorities delineated by SF programming. The strategic design brought into focus the dramatic discrimination in the labour market and overly bureaucratized unemployment schemes (which placed an excessive administrative burden on the clients). The diagnosis of wider structural inequalities strengthened the consensus on the need to streamline insertion procedures and run employment agencies in line with the equality principle. As noted by public manager representing Granada Province:

> If we are to have any impact on the rampant unemployment in the marginalized areas, we need to think in terms of institutional change, we first need to make sure that all neighbourhoods have access to equitable services.[24]

To secure these aims, the programme introduced equality conditionality, which required TEPs and IIs to incorporate anti-discrimination measures and elaborate additional incentives for marginalized neighbourhoods. The conditionality, however, did not call for ethnic (Roma) targeting, instead endorsing the term 'all vulnerable and excluded groups'. In an interview, the key project stakeholder insisted that targeting along the lines of ethnicity would be harmful to the solidarity component of the programme:

> Our aim is to facilitate the creation of local employment strategies, fitted to each individual context but reflective of macro-level factors. If some localities feel that they need to target an ethnic group, it is, by all means, a legitimate course of action, but we believe it would be unfair to make it a prerequisite or a focal point of this initiative. We want to focus much more on institutional improvements [...] we believe that in a long-term this will benefit all the excluded groups, including the Roma.[25]

Perhaps the greatest strength of the Granada Employment Programme was its commitment to co-productive partnership, based on a clear designation of responsibilities and consensual decision-making among the local authorities and social actors. This tactic not only allowed for the alignment of the goals and priorities of various institutions, it also secured a great level of accountability for the programme's performance. While countless meetings and debates proved extremely costly, all the participants felt they were the 'real owners' of the delivered measures. Nonetheless, partnership was not accessible to all those wanting to take part, instead, the provincial authorities chose to work with a small set of neighbourhood NGOs with a record of service delivery. As explained by the project manager:

> Reaching consensus takes time and it is often very frustrating, but it is the only way to engage all the stakeholders, and not as passive recipients or beneficiaries but accountable agents. We opted for engaging a smaller number of actors but with extensive experience dealing with labour inclusion. This helped us to create a well-informed strategy and in the end, everybody felt that they contribute to its realization.[26]

The critics maintained that the programme was yet another top-down initiative, with little if any scope for the empowerment of the communities. As exclaimed by a leader of a human rights organization: 'another bureaucratic scheme to fight convoluted bureaucracy, I don't buy it, again we have almost no voice, just another service'.[27] However, the majority of interviewed stakeholders and independent evaluators[28] insisted that partnership arrangements were the stronghold of the programme, with unprecedented authority ceded to the local NGOs.

While the focus on structural barriers and co-productivity enhanced the legitimacy of the programme, it struggled to secure the sustainable financing and deliver effective and far-reaching measures. These shortcomings can be directly linked to the missed opportunities to create programmatic synergy. Despite plans to bring local priorities under one comprehensive strategy reflective of the wider regional needs, the Granada Employment Programme remained fully disconnected from existing labour policies (e.g. The Agreement on Employment Policy and Economic Development for Andalusia). Moreover, local ambitions to develop truly innovative employment inclusion schemes, meant that the programme redirected SF from existing practices, thus abating the 'added value' and additionality principle:

> It is time to scrap the traditional ways of dealing with unemployment and try something new, something inherently reflective of indigenous needs; the bureaucratic approaches need to become more flexible and give way to communal initiatives, which at their core promote solidarity. We cannot keep on spending money on things that do not work.[29]

The determination to replace allegedly dysfunctional regional bureaucracy counterpoised the traditional commitment to use SF as a buttress for existing practices. This conflict explains the difficulties in obtaining a consensus between lower and higher tiers of government regarding the programme's purpose. As explained by a project stakeholder:

> The municipalities have been less involved in the allocation of SF and are more open to innovation, whereas the regional bodies tend to be more conservative. They have always played a decisive role in exploiting the European resources, making sure that they support existing policies and political priorities [...] Although, the word innovation is often used, the regime sees it as a way to continue its services, with minor improvements. The full replacement of existing approaches is never considered. They are not eager to experiment especially when larger sums of money are at stake.[30]

In effect, the Andalusian government fearful of losing its grasp on employment policies was reluctant to commit to co-financing which would exceed the mandatory 15%. It was also reluctant to earmark an additional budget for public servants (mainly social workers and employment officers), whose role in the programme was limited as the NGO workers assumed control over Integrated Itineraries (which in fact were created outside the regional employment schemes). Waning regional financial support, in turn, made localities uneasy about putting forward their own co-financing, as confirmed by a local mayor: 'what if we go all the way, commit everything and the co-financing doesn't arrive, we will be doomed'.[31] Moreover, the critics insisted that by disconnecting the TEPs and the Integrated Itineraries from standard employment services, the programme generated procedural congestion and duplication of efforts, thus threatening the impact of the entire programme (Pérez and Sánchez, 2013). In fact, the regional bureaucratic cadre began to view the Granada Employment Programme as a 'problematic' scheme, more interested in exerting political control over localities than in generating a positive solution. The position of 'an outsider' further delegitimized the programmes' efforts in the eyes of the regional stakeholders. As observed by the programme's manager:

> No matter how well we perform, we can't convince them [regional government] to support our efforts. This just shows you how hypocritical the innovative

discourse is. They want something new, but really they want to load off their work onto to us [local authorities], who are expected to play by their rules.[32]

In short, while strategic design and strong partnership secured accountability for the delivered services, the weak programmatic synergy jeopardized the sustainability of the programme. The case of the Granada Employment Programme clearly illustrates the conflict between 'added value' and innovation inherent to the overall functioning of SF programming. The genuine drive to anchor the input of marginalized neighbourhoods inside the programme, and generate new modes of dealing with local unemployment, faced strong resistance from SF managers (at a regional tier) committed to using SF to buttress existing interventions. While some commentators insisted that regional preoccupation with securing the 'added value' of SF stemmed from a commitment to efficiency and the aggregation of resources, sceptics called it a bureaucratic inertia and a simple dismissal of initiatives coming from those affected by poverty and marginalization: 'it really seems like money is mostly used to reinforce schemes that simply do not work, without SF they would likely waste away, but hey as long as there is money they thrive'.[33]

In the end, the Granada Employment Programme officially concluded on September 2015 with the President of the Granada Authorities, José Entrena assuring that the province would continue to support *similar* employment insertion and generation programmes (Europa Press, 2015). Yet, there is little evidence that the measures worked out in the framework of the programmes will continue throughout the current period. Unfortunately, while the GranadaEmpleo benefited over 600 people, it failed to jump-start or sustain any transformative (and innovative) reforms.

Transition to Employment in the South Industrial Park, Seville

The Transition to Employment Project was one of the first initiatives financed through the ESF that directly targeted one of the most deprived and marginalized neighbourhoods in the City of Seville, the South Industrial Park (Polígono Sur) (Ojeda, 2009). In 2007, the Andalusian Department of Employment invested €14.6 million in active employment measures undertaken in the framework of The Comprehensive Employment Plan for South Industrial Park of Seville. The plan was developed by the government of Andalusia, Seville City Council, and the Commissioner for the South Industrial Park as a joint intervention to promote social inclusion and employment in the neighbourhood. A local employment centre (Centro de Orientación y Dinamización para el Empleo) (CODE) operating in the area since 2006 became a focal point for the implementation of the planned inclusion strategies. In the 2007–2013 funding period, CODE received co-financing from OP ESF Andalusia, as part of the Collaboration Protocol signed on March 18 2009, between the Government of Andalusia, the City Seville, and the Commissioner for the South Industrial Park.

The work of CODE received positive evaluation and many of the projects implemented by the centre were coined as examples of good practice (RETOS, 2011). Mid-term evaluations praised the role of CODE in generating an enabling environment, which provided relevant training and labour insertion opportunities to people at risk of exclusion. Since 2007, CODE's in-house initiatives have assisted more than 10,000 unemployed people, while the educational interventions and awareness raising activities have reached more than 15,000. CODE was also successful in securing 12,714 employment contracts in the construction industry, mostly benefiting youths at risk of exclusion and the long-term unemployed. Upon a visit to CODE headquarters in 2010, the employment minister Manuel Recio stated that CODE's work is:

> An example to follow in terms of coordination and joint effort of the government to boost the labour market in the territories, to promote the formation and integration of the neighbourhoods. He added that it provided a pathway for the transformation of the labour market needs and creation of a just and viable socio-economic model.
>
> (Europa Press 2010)

Although the overall performance of CODE was hailed as a success, the centre struggled to implement all pre-planned activities and faced considerable difficulties in cooperating with the authorities. One initiative that stands out is the EDEM, a 12-month pre-employment intervention introduced in 2011 for improving the 'employability' of youths with no professional qualifications or work experience, and whose socio-economic status negatively affected their employment prospects. Initiated by the Economy and Employment department in the City of Seville, the project was endowed with close to 500,000 Euros. While highly publicized, its implementation was delayed and a number of measures outlined in the initial design were discontinued. Critics point out that 'the losses of the project', particularly the abandonment of community work and labour placement itineraries, were a direct result of a political conflict between the Andalusian government and the local authorities of Seville (Andalucía Información Agencias, 2015a). The Trade Union representatives insisted that a lack of common vision and community input drastically reduced the potential of the project, which over time became little more than 'a charity scheme'. Commentators affiliated with the socialist party pointed towards the inadequate leadership of the local council and the omnipresence of austerity measures, which put a tremendous strain on all local services.[34] Yet, the ongoing spending cuts did not directly affect CODE's operation or the earmarked budgets. A closer look thoroughly exposes that the ineffectiveness of the employment projects stemmed from problematic partnership arrangements and weak programmatic synergies.

Who should promote systemic changes?

The initial success of CODE and its in-house projects could be attributed to a clear strategic design and the acknowledgement that 'institutional transformations' are indispensable for stimulating economic growth and generating equal employment opportunities. The focus on structural inequalities received an enthusiastic welcome from the neighbourhood perversely stigmatized in the media and political discourse. One of the local activists stressed that:

> For far too long citizens of this part of town were treated as troublemakers, nobody even proposed to address wider inequalities, perhaps this is the first step, timid but still, you need to keep your faith.[35]

The framing of exclusion in terms of wider inequalities did generate an array of structural adjustments albeit limited to employment centres and contractual agreements with the private sector. Hitherto, all interventions were in line with the equality principle and anti-discrimination legislation, and CODE put extensive resources into awareness raising activities (including workshops, training sessions, conferences, and audio-visual material) and the support of local social enterprises (run by the residents of the neighbourhood). As explained by the manager from CODE:

> We work on three fronts. First our team reviews existing regulations for setting up social enterprises and developing labour placement initiatives, we identify barriers and negotiate them with local authorities. Second, we develop an outreach community programme to disseminate information about our initiatives but also to gather opinions from the potential beneficiaries. Finally, on the basis of the collected data, we develop a series of training initiatives in close cooperation with private entities.[36]

While CODE did not explicitly target any ethnic group, its territorial dimension (targeting the most impoverished sections of the neighbourhood) meant that more than 45% of participants were of Roma origin. However, the CODE team considered targeted action unnecessary and even counterproductive:

> Our projects are for all disenfranchised youth and adults residing in the neighbourhood. The idea is to become a community contact point, where everybody can feel welcomed and can expect to receive assistance and help. We strongly believe that targeting our projects at one group, is likely to provoke tensions, which are already quite strong in this area.[37]

What undermined CODE's operation, eventually leading to the implementation failure of EDEM and closing of CODE in 2015, was the partnership design, imposed on the organization by the local authorities. The Delegation of Economy and Employment as an initiator of the project had planned to involve a wide range of community stakeholders, allegedly with the aim of securing a 'participatory' dimension to the project.[38] Although the department conducted an ex-ante evaluation of the situation in the targeted districts, it did not consult with the main local stakeholders, and with that excluded their input from the overall project design. As stated by a stakeholder in EDEM:

> The project idea was solid, but the department has neither consulted us, nor other organizations working in the area [i.e. the FSG]. As a result, a lot of

objectives appeared rather ambitious and disconnected from our reality. The department lacked strong links to the community hence it has not really accounted for the potential risks, for example, it assumed that everybody in the community will be excited to participate, failing to understand a great level of mistrust the residents hold towards public employment interventions.[39]

The authorities recruited partners in an ad-hoc manner, with an array of formal and informal meetings undertaken mostly behind closed doors. Lack of vision regarding the scope and scale of participation resulted in a trivial exchange of ideas and opinions with no commitment made or common interests established. Moreover, selected partners had little decision-making discretion, which weakened accountability and commitment. For example, CODE was treated as a 'location where trainings will take place' without having any substantive say regarding the progress of the project. Subsequently, CODE's employees did not consider EDEM as their main priority:

> Our human resources are stretched as it is, thus if the department wants to simply use our facilities, and pay for them, we are fine with that, but at the same time, nobody should expect that we will go out of our way to make sure that project is running well. Either we are on board or not.[40]

The partnership with schools was also not consolidated, although talks with management were undertaken to identify potential beneficiaries, the exact degree and scope of cooperation was never outlined. In fact, according to CODE's education specialist, schools were expected to provide assistance (disseminate information, counsel students on programme benefits) without receiving funding or templates of action:

> You could argue that schools should put students' well-being over financial or power issues, but it is difficult to commit to the project that does not really treat you as one of its vital components, gaining the trust of these youth is extremely difficult. Why would you advertise to them a project of which you know nothing about?[41]

Finally, the project simply bypassed a number of important community stakeholders, including the Trade Union Confederation of Workers and large NGOs present in the community (FSG, Asociación Tierras del Sur[42]). This not only curtailed the opportunity to engage local expertise and aggregate resources but also unleashed antagonistic attitudes towards the local authorities. The comments of a socialist councillor in the City of Seville, Juan Manuel Flores, that 'the apathy and the disinterest of the government of Juan Ignacio Zoido can run any programme to the ground', echoed general sentiments in the area (Andalucía Información Agencias, 2015b).

The future of CODE was further jeopardized by weak programmatic synergies, which left EDEM (and CODE) outside of regional development strategies.

While CODE's objectives and priorities were aligned with Andalusian employment strategies, particularly the Programme of Solidarity for Andalusia (Decree 400/1990; Decree 2/1999) and the equal opportunity principle (Law 43/2006 of 29 December; Royal Decree 395/2007; Law 3/2007 of 22 March), the municipal authorities lacked the coordinating tools for linking grassroots efforts with regional policies. As explained by former CODE manager:

> The municipality does not care about this neighbourhood, unless it can build a shopping mall here, if we are not connected to wider schemes and public budgets we are a drop in the ocean, we will be swept aside under any pretext, this is happening now, after all, who will object if one dysfunctional centre in dysfunctional area closes down?[43]

The case of CODE and EDEM demonstrates that while focus on the structural aspects of exclusion can generate vital interventions, they are likely to fail if partnership and coordination are poorly executed or their importance downplayed. The reluctance of the municipality to nurture co-productive arrangements with local experts destabilized undertaken efforts and antagonized important local stakeholders. A lack of programmatic synergies made the project more vulnerable to public cuts and budgetary amendments, in 2013 measures delivered by CODE were discontinued one by one, leading to the closure of the entire centre in April 2014. Despite commitments to re-open, it remained closed until 2017.

Slovakia: success stories

The failure of Slovak SF programming to elevate the dramatic socio-economic exclusion of the Slovak Roma population has often been commentated on by the critics of European integration strategies (ERRC, 2013). While critical commentators insist that the low impact is driven by lack of political will to address Roma issues, the empirical analysis shows a more complex and nuanced picture. With the overall diversion of funding away from official Roma inclusion objectives, the fragmentation and low sustainability of SF projects were contingent on the lack of recognition of wider structural discrimination, superficial partnership arrangements, and full the disconnection of SF programming from domestic social policies and development strategies. In many ways, the endorsement of an EU-backed targeted approach not only 'ethnicized exclusion', thus isolating Roma issues from the mainstream agenda, but also contributed to further stigmatization of local Roma communities and individuals.

However, on a micro-level, the expectation of failure has not appeared that straightforward, with some projects generating positive results. Commentators often attribute these isolated successes to the determination of a few idealistic individuals and grassroots organizations (Brenner, 2012; Mušinka and Kolesárová, 2012). The empirical analysis, however, shows that these positive outputs were shaped by more systemic factors. The three scrutinized projects – Field Social Work in the Communities, From Benefits to Paid Work, and Integrated Education were all based on a design that paid heed to systemic discrimination, established a co-productive partnership, and linked their goals to broader national or regional development schemes. More importantly, all the initiatives moved away from the prevailing reliance on targeted approaches, instead of using the ESF to promote 'ethnically neutral' initiatives directed at institutional improvements. In many senses, the implementation and management of these projects resembled tactics developed in the context of Spanish SF programming and contrasted the general *modus operandi* governing the allocation of EU funding in Slovakia.

National project: Field Social Work

Since the 1990s, Field Social Work (FSW) has been a key element of the Slovak social policy agenda delivered in the form of various pilot projects and programmes. Between 1998 and 2001, FSW was realized in the framework of EU accession, and in PHARE projects in three short stages (each in about ten localities) by the Office of the Government section for Human Rights and Minorities. In 2004, the government started a programme of support for developing community social work in municipalities, which ran in 198 municipalities and trained 600 social field workers. In the 2007–2013 funding period, the government allocated the ESF (under Measure 2.1[44]) to further develop demand-driven field social work in the localities. The leading idea was to provide 'additional' financial support to municipal authorities, to advance their capacities for addressing endogenous needs and developing tailored approaches to social assistance. The SF experts and policymakers were in consensus regarding the importance of FSW and considered the undertaken initiatives of great value (Hrustič, 2009). Between 2009 and 2010, 346 field social workers and 397 assistants were active in 229 community projects. The task of field social workers was to help people in marginalized situations, among whom many were Roma people, to find solutions to their problems directly in their own environments. Their work was based on regular consultations with the clients, mediation between the communities and the local authorities, and assistance in accessing public services. Although the ongoing activities provided acutely needed assistance, particularly in the most impoverished municipalities, they were prone to discontinuity, fragmentation, and overlaps (see Hrustič, 2009).

As a response to these shortcomings, in 2009 the agency of the Social Development Fund (SDF) took over the implementation of the programmes from the Office of the Government section for Human Rights and Minorities, to ensure a certain level of uniformity of FSW provision through enhanced supervision and monitoring. In 2011, the SDF launched a national project, Field Social Work in the Communities, a three-year initiative to reinforce and systematize the ongoing efforts. The project was endowed with a €30 million budget designated for 250 municipalities, where 860 social workers and assistants would be employed. The goal of the national project was to change the financing of FSW, improve its quality and effectiveness by strengthening the role of the central coordination agency. The SDF made considerable efforts to stabilize field social work activities by anchoring the programme's financing for three years, abolishing the co-financing conditions for the localities (and NGOs) and introducing quality assurance schemes. More importantly, the SDF developed a common methodology with a clearly articulated conditionality (i.e. anti-discrimination clause), regional coordination standards, and the supervision of field social workers and performance indicators. In just two years, these efforts resulted in a more efficient use of public resources (since previous administrative costs had been reduced from 20% to 3%) and a 4% increase in beneficiaries (Csomor and Csillag, 2015).

Structural approach

The success of the programme grew out of its overall design, which presented the situation of marginalized communities as a structural issue, in need of long-term, comprehensive, and mutually reinforcing measures. The key aim was to enforce changes in the methodological approaches to social work from individual counselling to community-based services in line with principles of non-discrimination. The change stipulated measures to strengthen institutional resources of social service agencies (via stable national co-financing and procedural streamlining). As told by an SDF manager:

> Any project that deals with social exclusion needs to focus on the performance of institutions that deliver relevant services. We aim to provide social workers with clear performance guidelines and the proper understanding of legislation and procedures. Their expertise and experience working with the excluded communities is of great value. Hence, there is a need to develop and consolidate comprehensive regulatory frameworks and feedback mechanisms. Only then this knowledge can inform the general workings of the Slovak social and integration policies.[45]

FSW in the Communities was one of a few nationwide programmes co-financed with SF that did not endorse the individualized framing of social exclusion. Instead, the diagnosis identified structural inequalities (including the negative effects of spatial segregation, and low demand for low-skilled labour) and brought attention to a deeply entrenched discrimination among service providers, often compounded by a dramatic lack of resources and supervision (Oravec and Bošelová, 2006; Sirovátka, 2008). According to one of the programme managers, this diagnosis brought attention to the shortage of supervision and administrative burdens placed on individual beneficiaries. More importantly, it moved social work practice towards a community-oriented approach based on the principles of partnership and voluntary cooperation. The principle of partnership made FSW fundamentally different from regular social work practice which represents a coercive state activity, with the power to sanction clients in cases of non-compliance (Csomor and Csillag, 2015). As the MC explained: 'by acknowledging that individuals are not always the biggest problem the programme gained greater legitimacy'.[46]

Moreover, the SDF presented the programme as a tool for modernizing public services, thus challenging a widely held perception that FSW is an initiative designed only for the benefit of 'problematic' Roma neighbourhoods and settlements. According to the designers this reframing helped to secure additional SF allocations under the OP Social Inclusion and Employment, Objective 4.3.6.: *the modernization of public administration.* The state took over the 5% co-financing responsibility from municipalities, consequently easing their administrative burden as they did not have to devote as many financial and human resources to implementation. While the SDF admitted that a focus on discrimination remained limited, the introduction of an anti-discrimination conditionality was successful in curbing explicit racism among local authorities:

> The interested localities had to clearly demonstrate their integration strategies and efforts made to stop discrimination. Of course, they said one thing and did another, but faced with a real threat of losing valuable support, they were at least trying to cooperate. Moreover, we introduced a complex system of professional training, which proved very effective in spreading knowledge about equality legislation.[47]

The co-productive approach to partnership endorsed by the programme further strengthened its effectiveness and the legitimacy of its outputs. Instead of following the standardized practice of 'off-loading' the responsibility for project implementation onto the local authorities or the NGOs, the SDF, acting as an IB for OP E&SI. It assumed the managerial responsibility and, as mentioned above, the steady co-financing (in addition to decreasing non-direct costs related to project management from 20% to 3%). Centralized management, and the introduction of regional coordinators, streamlined administrative regulation, offered methodological guidance and ensured conformity with FSW standards. More importantly, the SDF institutionalized contractual agreements between field social workers and the local authorities. While the OSF criticized this top-down approach for being overly 'constraining',[48] the designers argued that it allowed for the standardization of monitoring and evaluation without impinging on the flexibility and discretion of the service deliverers. This, in turn, reinforced compliance and accountability for the performance of the project:

> For years, interaction between the social field workers and the local public servants has not followed any common standards or protocols, leading to various conflicts [...] the introduction of performance guidelines and incentives literally in just a few months have fixed these issues. Before the assistants to social workers were treated almost as volunteers, a lack of supervision meant that nobody was truly accountable for their performance but at the same time their hands were tied by procedures and local fraternities. Not surprisingly the turnover was extremely high and the social workers tended to lose their motivation rather quickly.[49]

The introduction of supervisory and coordinative agents also allowed for the channelling of local knowledge into policymaking. As expressed by a supervisor working in Sobrance:

> The social field workers are now able to give feedback about their experience into the policymaking apparatus, while more work is still needed to exploit these inputs, a system of regular reporting and meetings helps us to identify barriers and challenges and learn from them.[50]

The partnership design allowed for the alignment of fragmented goals and objectives. This, in turn, strengthened coordination efforts and allowed for the consolidation of synergies between the project and local development programmes. While the SDF introduced numerous procedural changes and institutionalized performance reviews, the form of social services delivered was not substantially altered, allegedly to fit the methods endorsed by the local social services departments. Although the programme was criticized for buttressing 'outdated methods',[51] the choice to support and sustain efforts already implemented on the ground proved very effective. According to the evaluation report, duplication was largely avoided and resources (financial, human, and cognitive) were brought together. Moreover, according to the project stakeholders, the central authorities began to see the project as an effective reinforcement of the Slovak Job Activation and education policies, which generated a greater commitment to supporting it. The importance of continuing efforts rather than promoting the constant introduction of new initiatives became a staple of the project. As expressed by a local mayor:

> There is a predisposition to think that Roma projects need to be innovative, different or unique since nothing worked thus far. This is not necessarily true, there are numerous positive examples of successful projects, the problem is that they are often discontinued due to the lack of support from the government.[52]

The consolidation of programmatic synergy also changed the way SF assistance was viewed by the local mayors. According to the SDF, the FSW was no longer seen as an add-on assistance package, but a way to strengthen the overall workings of the local institutions.[53] While the wages of the social workers were financed strictly from the SF, an increasing number of localities planned their expenditures around the project's activities. The elimination of the competition-based allocations of SF only reinforced planning efforts. It allowed the poorer and more isolated localities to benefit from SF without engaging their scarce resources in costly application procedures.

The design of the national FSW programme, its approach to partnership and coordination, diverged from the model endorsed by SF programming. This brings forward questions regarding a pending need for rethinking the *modus operandi* of the Slovak SF programming. However, it is doubtful that these questions will be addressed by the ruling authorities. The achievements of the project were severely jeopardized as changes in government resulted in the abandonment of the structural focus and synergies championed by the SDF. The widespread request to finance social field work using the state budget continues to be ignored by the new political elites. The majority of the field social work directed at the MRC continues to be financed strictly from the ESF, running the risk of reinforcing the pervasive and ineffective practice of financing Roma inclusion initiatives strictly from European funds.

From benefits to the paid work

Another project which delivered positive results was realized by the municipality of Banská Bystrica, located in one of the most impoverished regions in Slovakia (OECD, 2014). In 2012, the municipality, the Regional Development Agency, the Office of Labour, Social Affairs and Family, and the Education Centre for Non-Profit Organisations came together to find local solutions to long-term unemployment and a way to effectively exploit existing local resources. The partnership succeeded in securing a €313,000 grant (ESF contribution: €266,000) under the framework of OP E&SI, to realize a pilot project, From Benefits to the Paid Work, aimed at tackling long-term unemployment. Although small in scope (40 final beneficiaries), the project tested innovative job insertion methodologies and managed to establish institutional links between social and employment services. Upon its completion, 100% of participants completed their training, 27.5% gained stable employment, and 11% updated their skills. At the same time, the procedural cooperation between social and employment services was consolidated and the working methods informed the future development of the nationwide programme and potential legislative amendments.[54]

The most important achievement of the project was the institutionalization of the intermediate labour market (ILM), a model of waged work in specially created temporary jobs that contributed to neighbourhood regeneration (e.g. gardening, street cleaning, and maintenance work). According to the stakeholders, it provided a more sustained progression of individuals from welfare to work than the traditional activation policy practised in Slovakia:

> Compared with other labour market initiatives targeted at the long-term unemployed, our project offered better value for money, after the adjustments were made for the value of the services provided. It also generated a higher job placement, higher incomes and longer retention of employment. We believe that slow progression into employment is more effective than the punitive measures advocated by the state [withdrawing of welfare support from those not actively seeking employment]. The long-term unemployed need steady assistance, the will to work is there, the problem is that demand for low-skilled untrained workers is low.[55]

This approach was endorsed by the municipality, seeking to formulate innovative approaches to long-term unemployment. Critics maintained that the initiative was a simple continuation of aggressive active employment policies, and an omnipresent perception that the long-term unemployed are unwilling to seek a 'better life'. However, on closer inspection, the proposed initiative endorsed a much stronger focus on structural inequalities than the majority of other employment insertion programmes in the region and the rest of the country.

Tackling systemic barriers

The design of the project framed social exclusion in terms of structural inequalities, mainly through low demand for unskilled labour in the region and discrimination in accessing employment services and employment opportunities. This diagnostic (based on a comprehensive evaluation of the local labour conditions) triggered objectives and measures directed more at institutional (legislative) change than behavioural adjustment. Although the project did emphasize the need for 'personal adaptation' and stressed the importance of 'revitalizing working habits', the very creation of ILM introduced a major shift in the way long-term unemployment had been addressed by the state. The objectives emphasized the need to devise (or simplify) procedures for labour insertion, create financial incentives for trainees, and change the role of employment officers from that of strict 'regulators' to 'supporters'. The project's diagnostics emphasized that cutting social support does not, in fact, serve as an incentive for finding employment, arguing that what is needed instead is ongoing financial support, internships linking training to employment opportunities, and the utilization of anti-discrimination measures (Filipová, 2013). The project partner explained:

> It is irrational to think that reducing social support will motivate people to find employment, such an approach is blind to existing barriers preventing people from entering or re-entering the labour market […] our comprehensive package acts on two fronts – it tackles structural barriers and provides individualized support that is the key to success.[56]

Interestingly, the project did not directly target the Roma minority. Instead, the eligibility criteria pertained to 'the period of unemployment, registration in the employment office, and welfare provision status' (Filipová, 2013). In the interviews, the project manager noted that presenting the project as one geared towards long-term unemployment and not a specific community gained stronger support among city officials and, more importantly, avoided the further stigmatization of Roma people. Nevertheless, the focus on the 'most excluded sectors of the population' meant that close to 50% of participants were of Roma origin. The head of the economic department of Banská Bystrica Town Hall insisted that:

> We can't ignore the fact that a large number of long-term unemployed are Roma people, however, we also cannot pretend that non-Roma do not struggle with the same issues. This is why we need projects that are open to all, and are delivered in an equitable and non-discriminatory manner.[57]

In an unprecedented fashion, the pilot project adopted a co-productive partner-ship arrangement with selected expert NGOs and relevant public agencies. All the recruited partners who contributed to the initial design of the project agreed in a form of consensus (albeit with the municipality playing the role of a strong arbiter) and gained responsibility for the implementation and management of con-crete measures, thus increasing accountability and complementarity. The clear designation of responsibilities and transparent communication channels facili-tated the formulation of common goals and the mediation of different interests. The management team insisted that agreeing on common goals was the key to success: 'it wasn't easy but we did manage to form consensus on what it is that we are trying to do, when everybody is assured of their roles it is much easier to work side by side'.[58]

Bringing on board qualified NGOs with experience of working with marginal-ized communities allowed local knowledge to be tapped into. According to the 2012 evaluation report, the input of local community experts enthused the sim-plification of administrative procedures, including statutory guidelines on labour placement and compensation payments (Filipová, 2013). Overall, gaining the support of the leading body (City Office of Banská Bystrica) and relying on the appointment of high-quality managers (with assistance from the Education Centre for Non-Profit Organisations) ensured a solid delivery infrastructure:

> Only through strategic partnership, can the ILM deliver effective outputs […]. Sole training of individuals by one organization is futile without regula-tory concessions provided by the local decision-makers and earmarking of the local resources. Only if these efforts are synchronized something can be achieved. We are not accustomed to working like this in this country, where everybody wants to do their own thing.[59]

Finally, the pilot project tried to complement (or add to) ongoing local labour insertion initiatives. Although geared towards the testing of novel approaches, emphasis rested on coordinating individual measures with existing employment and social services (for example, all project participants had to first register with the employment office). The creation of temporary employment adhered to legis-lative provisions for contracting and wage rates, with the local authorities conduct-ing mid-term reviews and taking part in monitoring schemes. The key element of the project, the 'job search support', was coordinated with activities delivered by the employment office, and subsidized through the public budget. Although the majority of interviewed project partners held negative opinions about the design and impact of the active labour measures, there was a strong consensus that From Benefits to Paid Work should improve rather than fully replace existing initia-tives. As explained by the project's manager:

> We recognize that basic infrastructure for labour insertion is in place, it is not about cancelling it and creating something new, but rather about thinking how the provided services could be improved.[60]

This stance brought about criticisms, as commentators argued that such measures are nothing more than a reinforcement of neoliberal politics and the pervasive individualization of social problems. Many activists also raised concerns about the co-optation of local innovative initiatives by public bureaucrats who use EU funds to mask cuts in welfare provisions.[61] Nevertheless, the endorsement of complementarity opened the door for a meaningful dialogue between the local partnership and national authorities (a fairly rare dynamic in a centralized setting), and strengthened the position of the employment insertion model as a viable policy alternative:

> We are dependent on the central government and their funding, if we alienate them we will be left with no resources after the SF run out, it is all about compromise and incremental changes [...] we provided a good service and our methods could serve as a springboard for needed reforms.[62]

The promotion of incremental changes (rather than ground-breaking reforms) appealed to the central authorities, heavily invested in labour activation measures. Towards the end of the project, Bratislava held an array of consultation meetings to discuss the potential scaling up of the initiative and showed interest in ILM.[63] Moreover, as explained by a project stakeholder:

> There is a shift in thinking about long-term unemployment; it is no longer viewed solely as an individual matter, a product of some sort of pathology. The civil servants are beginning to realize that some sort of supportive infrastructure is needed. The unemployed need to find the motivation to work but pathways to employment need to be improved and sustained.[64]

The focus on the structural dimension of exclusion almost automatically induced a commitment, at the local level, to shared responsibility over the improvements of employment services and sustainable economic growth. It encouraged the local authorities to affirm that institutional adaptations are indeed necessary and should become one of the government's key priorities. The experience of Banská Bystrica also showed that Roma communities can benefit from SF projects without being identified as the main target group:

> This project is small, so it is probably not very representative of the entire country, but I really believe that moving away from the ethnic targeting of SF projects can end the deadlock and reluctance of the local authorities to sponsor inclusion programmes. After all, the long-term unemployed Roma are not that different from the long-term unemployed non-Roma, in fact, there is evidence that both groups struggle with similar barriers and problems.[65]

Overall, the project's success stems from its insubordination to the norms underlying SF programming, further proving that the Slovak SF programming is ineffective and in need of serious revisions. At the same time, it shows that Slovak project managers were more capable of challenging the overarching policy design, than their counterparts in Spain. This leeway raises important questions about the capacity (or willingness) of the state and the MAs to maintain the status quo and the role of SF in prompting experimentation and innovation. Unfortunately, with the progressive institutionalization of strict activation policies and re-emphasis of ethnic targeting in the new funding period, innovations created in Banská Bystrica were left behind, with project components being manipulated to fit overarching frames.

Spišský Hrhov: integrated education

Over the last ten years, a small municipality, Spišský Hrhov in Eastern Slovakia, has become a euphemism for successful integration and commitment to Roma inclusion. Located in the Levoča district with 1,355 inhabitants, 300 of which are Roma, the municipality and its local projects have received numerous awards and became a poster child for the wise and consistent use of SF and innovative approaches to social exclusion. A closer scrutiny shows that the successes of this tiny locality are not exaggerated. Since 2000, the local Mayor's Office has introduced an array of effective integration programmes in the area of employment and housing. The locality created its own company, with the aim of creating jobs. The first product was pavement tiles for sidewalks. Its success led to the creation of a construction company for local infrastructure projects and to help local residents with home building. Later, the village began to produce its own cheese, jams, and sausages. As asserted by the local mayor, Vladimir Ledecky: 'we grew so fast and started making a profit, so we kept expanding'.[66]

However, in the context of SF programming, the initiatives that delivered the most promising results were realized in the field of education. According to the Council of Europe's 'good practice' catalogue, the work undertaken by the local elementary school provided a 'positive example of problem-free coexistence, cooperation and removal of minority tensions and barriers'. The public countryside school with nine grades, operating in accordance with international standards for classification of education (ISCED), offered a primary education for approximately 270 pupils and a pre-primary education for 60 pupils. Educational activities were provided by 20 fully qualified teachers and professional employees (including three Roma assistants). From the total number of pupils, a little more than half (51%) were of Roma origin, a scenario that significantly influenced the character of the school's educational programme. The elements of inclusion and a multicultural dimension were strongly supported and the school cooperated with numerous NGOs (e.g. People in Need) to develop community-based educational programmes. The cooperation resulted in numerous in-house projects and joint initiatives, which promoted desegregation and intercultural dialogue.[67] Although a high dropout rate continued to be an issue (especially among girls) second chance initiatives were offered, together with socio-economical support, which provided means, as well as motivation, for continuing education. In 2017, close to 90% of pupils completed their compulsory education, an extraordinary achievement given that the national average stands at 59% (EC, 2014a).

For the period 2007–2013, the school received, via the Ministry of Education, grants from the ESF amounting to €227,050, for a 24-month project, Social Inclusion of Students through Improved Education. The initiative was targeted at 131 school pupils and 11 educators. The project was linked to the OP Education under the objective: *securing long-term competitiveness of the Slovak Republic by adapting the education system to a knowledge society*. It also espoused the internal aims of the school, including;

- Facilitating access to formal education and the acquisition of skills needed in the labour market, and
- The use of innovative forms and methods of teaching, and development of competencies among the educators.

At the end of 2013, the school had undergone extensive modernization, championing innovative educational methodologies, which combined 'scenario-based instructions' and communication technology with leisure and motivational activities. In the region it has earned the reputation as a modern, rapidly developing institution, where school-pupil-parent relations are an elementary element in the process of management and communication (Čupka, 2012). In 2016, Spišský Hrhov received the European Spirit Award for tackling Roma exclusion through education, and for championing intercultural coexistence in the region.

Strategic planning

This case demonstrates that the effective outputs of education initiatives were greatly influenced by the adopted strategic design. First and foremost, the design moved away from associating patterns of social exclusion with individual or group adaptability. The endorsed integration action plans emphasize the structural dimension of social exclusion, identifying discrimination, weakly institutionalized social support systems, and the low quality of education as the main causes of marginalization:

> We consistently lack resources to develop a high-quality education for all, but without strong systemic support, the vulnerable communities simply have no chance to get out of the poverty trap. It is easy to blame the poor but it is much harder to accept that our institutions are weak, under-resourced and unprepared to face modern day problems.[68]

This stance was reflected in the objectives of the project, which called for the development and modernization of the school's management, teaching methods, and outreach programmes. The measures were geared towards cognitive developments, the innovation of teaching methodologies (adequate to pupils' needs and skills), the utilization of information and communication technology (ICT) in the education process, and the training of pedagogues. The school budget was earmarked for the acquisition of equipment, assessment exercises, and training sessions. Within the scope of the project, one extra Roma teacher assistant was employed to work with the students on an individual basis. Although there were some criticisms concerning residual attention to desegregation, the school convincingly argued:

> Modernization of teaching methodology is the key, we need to train teachers first so they can be able to provide pupils with the best instruction, we need technology which would allow for setting in motion innovative education processes. It is not the best idea to focus only on securing quota of Roma and non-Roma children in each classroom, especially if they will not get the best possible attention they need.[69]

While the motivation of individual pupils was often stressed as a factor influencing a high dropout rate and academic underperformance, socio-economic factors were strongly acknowledged within the design. This legitimized the provision of economic support to vulnerable students and their families. Moreover, instructors were to consider the 'immediate environment of the children and their problems stemming from everyday life'[70] in order to provide individual guidance when necessary. The teachers and teacher's assistants received systematic training and were encouraged to develop tailored courses reflecting the needs and interests of children (i.e. Roma culture, leadership training, and early childhood education programmes).

The conviction that educational integration required rethinking the standard methodologies and procedures, motivated the management of the school to seek expert opinions and international assistance. The management formed extensive networks with various organizations, but most importantly, it motivated the local authorities and private firms to take an active part in the school and its activities. The reliance on working through partnership facilitated the aggregation of resources and allowed for expanding the scope and sustainability of the introduced measures. Well-designed management structures,[71] with a clear designation of responsibilities, improved the operational efficiency, but more importantly, it gave rise to community interest and a demand for high-quality education. As explained by a school employee:

> The collaboration was crucial in nurturing the notion that everybody is in some form responsible for the education of children, Roma and non-Roma. The community has begun to see the empowering potential of education. Changing of attitudes is a key, without respect and commitment to quality education; no amount of money will be really effective.[72]

Finally, the measures were designed to ensure communication with the local employers (i.e. companies in Prešov, as well as local social enterprises) in an effort to provide internships and part-time employment opportunities for pupils who completed their compulsory education.[73]

The school also took steps to coordinate its activities with existing legislative provisions (e.g. teacher's assistants and zero-grade curriculums). The school's management board delegated a person to communicate directly with the local authorities and keep close contact with the relevant departments of the Ministry of Education. Moreover, the school's management underwent training on the use and management of SF and maintained communication with the MAs of the OP Education and OP E&SI. While SF were used to prompt modernization and the development of innovative curriculums and pedagogical approaches, efforts were also made to adhere to regional and national educational reforms and development plans:

> Sometimes it is extremely difficult to promote innovation while adhering to legislative regulations, as we are constrained by bureaucratic tenets; however, with the right planning and support of the local authorities, we can push our agenda forward.[74]

The integration objectives were also reflective of the Strategy of the Slovak Republic for Roma Integration, up to 2020. In line with the principles and recommendations of the strategy, the school developed material about Roma history and culture and added it to the main curriculum. The aim was to positively portray the contribution of the Roma ethnic group to the national heritage.

Once again, this case demonstrated that attention to the structural dimensions of exclusion is indispensable for effective SF outputs. It also showed that using SF as a means to improve institutional approaches is best realized through partnership, which serves to inform the proposed measures and facilitate their efficient implementation. In this particular case, the school's efforts to coordinate its plans and activities with general education legislation and integration strategies, not only impinged on innovation and modernization but also opened the doors for policy learning and the potential scaling up of localized practices. At the same time, it is important to note that the strategies developed in Spišský Hrhov have never been properly scaled up or used as a springboard for dramatically needed reforms. In fact, the new SF programming, fully focused on ethnic targeting, is more likely to disadvantage localities and educational institutions interested in mainstreaming intercultural education. The stubborn focus on individual adaptability and individual assistance (or insertion) is now buttressed with conditionality (competing projects must show that they will aim to insert Roma students into mainstream education) and is unlikely to induce institutional changes.

Concluding remarks

This chapter has demonstrated empirically that outputs of SF programming are determined by the presence and interaction of three structuring factors – policy design, partnership arrangement, and programmatic synergies. The Slovak cases show that success is very much based on recognition of the institutional dimension of social exclusion (framing which moves away from ethnic targeting), a close-knit co-productive partnership supported by enabling resources and decision-making authority granted to local experts, and programmatic synergies emphasizing the 'added value' of SF. In turn, non-conformity with any of these normative dimensions weakens efforts to secure effective, legitimate, and sustainable outputs, as was clearly demonstrated by the Spanish projects.

The analysis of each case study also confirmed that the policy design not only influences allocation and absorption rates but also shapes partnership arrangements and coordination processes. This proves that cohesion policy as a whole operates in a top-down manner, and while social and local actors can provide considerable input into overarching strategies and can, in fact, derail implementation goals, they are bound by procedural norms and protocols, with a limited leeway for autonomous decision-making. Although Slovak project managers appeared to challenge the status quo and depart from standards embedded in SF programming, more so than their Spanish counterparts, their successes remained isolated from general practice and have not managed to induce changes to the way SF programming conceptualizes *exclusion, partnership*, or *'added value'* at a general level. This somewhat pessimistically demonstrates the residual influence the local initiatives have on the shape and aim of cohesion policy.

The in-depth examination of on-the-ground dynamics further confirmed that community empowerment (and ownership) has not been championed in either of these two countries, a fact that problematizes the very notion of success championed by the EU and national authorities. Moreover, while synergies underscore successful initiatives, they tend to curtail opportunities for innovation and risk granting financial support to practices that are not necessarily optimal or in line with a range of local needs. Sadly, this analysis clearly shows that the omnipresent discourse of innovation propagated by the EU is little more than a popular simple slogan, difficult to realize, but more importantly, often resisted by MAs and national states.

Notes

1 Within the general budget, the Spanish Integration Fund forms the bulk of spending, much of which is disbursed to municipalities and regions often as the co-financing of ESF initiatives. The funding given to ACs reached a plateau of €200 million in 2009 (Parella and Petroff, 2014). However, in February 2009, the Spanish government cut this fund by half, from €200 million to €100 million. In 2011, the budget dropped to €70 million. In 2012, the Ministry of Employment and Social Security eliminated the fund's entire resources in the general budget. This suppression has been seen as one of the hardest cuts delivered to public policies for integration in recent years.

2 The examined interventions have many components, as they provide various measures in different localities and for different target groups. The 'good practice' evaluation conducted by the Council of Europe and EURoma has generally focused on a 'grand design' of the programme without comprehensive intake on the outputs delivered by its various components. Moreover, the emphasis was placed on the absorption and allocation capacity while little scrutiny was given to the way the 'allocated funds' had been utilized.

3 The yearly costs of running the programme account for close to €500,000.

 4 FSG research shows that 64% of Roma students aged between 16 and 24 years did not complete compulsory education compared to 13% of the whole student group (FSG, 2011).
 5 These included: 'get to know them before judging them', 'your prejudices are other people's voices', 'when I grow up I want to be…'
 6 Interview #26, 28 February 2013 (Zagreb).
 7 Interview #26, 28 February 2013 (Zagreb).
 8 Interview #25, 20 June 2011 (Seville).
 9 Interview #75, 3 October 2014 (Seville).
10 Interview #16, 8 October 2013 (Seville).
11 Interview #25, 20 June 2011 (Seville).
12 Interview#26, 28 February 2013 (Zagreb).
13 More so, any failure of individual students partaking in PROMOCIONA's activities reinforced the biased perception that Roma people cannot adapt to a well-functioning and all-inclusive educational system.
14 Interview #16, 8 October 2013 (Seville).
15 Interview #82, 3 October 2014 (Seville).
16 Interview #27, 5 March 2013 (Huelva).
17 Interview #17, 18 June 2011 (Granada).
18 See 'when I grow up I want to be…', www.gitanos.org/campannas/de_mayor_quier o_ser.html.en.
19 An exception is an effort to encourage Roma parents to become members of parents' associations, an initiative undertaken in some participating localities (e.g. Seville).
20 One of the measures of PROMOCIONA, the support classes, resemble the model of '*aulas de acogid a*' (insertion classes), a national/regional strategy directed at what Spanish policymakers call: 'normalization policy'. The aims of PROMOCIONA have also been aligned with the Constitutional Law for the Quality of Education of 2002, which prescribes equal rights of education for foreigners, as well as the norms of coexistence in the educative centres and the need to develop language assistance.
21 Interview #11, 22 June 2011 (Seville).
22 Interview #34, 6 March 2013 (Huétor-Tájar).
23 Interview #80, 2 October 2014 (Granada).
24 Interview #17, 18 June 2011 (Granada).
25 Interview #34, 6 March 2013 (Huétor-Tájar).
26 Interview #35, 6 March 2013 (Guadix).
27 Interview #74, 1 October 2014 (Granada).
28 Interview #83, 1 October 2014 (Granada).
29 Interview #35, 6 March 2013 (Guadix).
30 Interview #34, 6 March 2013 (Huétor-Tájar).
31 Interview #84, 1 October 2014 (Granada).
32 Interview #80, 2 October 2014 (Granada).
33 Interview #74, 1 October 2014 (Granada).
34 Interview #79, 3 February 2015 (Skype).
35 Interview #75, 3 October 2014 (Seville).
36 Interview #31, 1 October 2013 (Seville).
37 Interview #31, 1 October 2013 (Seville).
38 An informant from Seville City Hall commented that this strategy mirrored the political aspirations of single members of the department, who wanted to present themselves as community leaders, 'close to the people', in a time of growing frustration with the authorities. Interview #16, 08/10/2013 (Seville).
39 Interview #32, 27 March 2013 (Seville).
40 Interview #31, 1 October 2013 (Seville).
41 Interview #31, 1 October 2013 (Seville).

42 Both the FSG and Asociación Tierras del Sur have been running employment initiatives with a similar methodology and positive results. Both confirmed that they were not contacted or consulted by the authorities, despite close contact and previous involvement with CODE.

43 Interview #31, 1 October 2013 (Seville).

44 Support for social inclusion through the development of social services, with a focus on MRC.

45 Interview #50, 26 July 2011 (Bratislava).

46 Interview #58, 3 March 2011 (Bratislava).

47 Interview #50, 26 July 2011 (Bratislava).

48 Interview #63, 23 July 2011 (Bratislava).

49 Interview #71, 23 May 2011 (Bratislava).

50 Interview #57, 28 July 2011 (Kosice).

51 Interview #63, 23 July 2011 (Bratislava).

52 Mayors for Roma Inclusion Forum Meeting, Skalica, Slovakia 2011.

53 Interview #50, 26 July 2011 (Bratislava).

54 The partners involved in the project have been lobbying the central government for amendments to the employment legislation, in particular the introduction of the terms, 'employer of an interim worker' and 'social public procurement' (Páleník, 2013). However, by 2017 the reforms had not been realized.

55 Interview #64, 13 June 2013 (Banská Bystrica).

56 Interview #66, 18 June 2013 (Banská Bystrica).

57 Interview #85, 13 June 2013 (Banská Bystrica).

58 Interview #64, 13 June 2013 (Banská Bystrica).

59 Interview #65, 13 June 2013 (Banská Bystrica).

60 Interview #66, 18 June 2013 (Banská Bystrica).

61 Conference *From Pilots to Outcomes*, Brussels, Belgium 2013.

62 Interview #65, 13 June 2013 (Banská Bystrica).

63 While in the 2014–2020 funding period, OPs adopted a few methods worked out in Banská Bystrica, the scaling efforts proved disappointing, as the newly elected government pushed for stricter labour activation measures and a withdrawal of welfare support from the most marginalized individuals (Gill, 2015).

64 Interview #64, 13 June 2013 (Banská Bystrica).

65 Interview #65, 13 June 2013 (Banská Bystrica).

66 Interview #86, 14/03/ March 2016 (Ljubljana).

67 A description of the project can be found at: www.skolahrhov.sk/sk/o-skole/ and http://goodpracticeroma.ppa.coe.int/en/pdf/127.

68 Interview #67, 1 February 2011 (Skype).

69 Interview #67, 1 February 2011 (Skype).

70 See www.skolahrhov.sk/data/projekty/projekt.pdf

71 External assessment by the European Council Thematic Team extensively praised the well-designed and executed management, based on clear objectives, performance indicators, feedback mechanisms, and transparent communication (European Council, 2012).

72 Interview #67, 1 February 2011 (Skype).

73 The creation of links between education and employment was envisioned as a 'motivation tool' for pupils as well as parents, but also allowed for an assessment of employment needs and how they could be met through education methodologies.

74 Interview #67, 1 February 2011 (Skype).

8   Concluding remarks

We have seen in *Financing Roma Inclusion with European Structural Funds* that the zealous promotion of SF as highly suitable instruments for addressing the systemic causes of inequality and social exclusion has not delivered the expected results. The multimillion-Euro investment and heightened political attention to the deeply entrenched disenfranchisement of Roma people has in fact corresponded with the deteriorating socio-economic conditions of the already deeply marginalized Roma communities. Endemic problems were compounded by the impact of the economic crisis on welfare provisions, employment opportunities, and equality measures. This situation contributed to the exacerbating segregation and negative perceptions of Roma people and to increasing populism and extremism (Andor, 2018). Not surprisingly, a growing number of commentators proclaim that EU-funded inclusion schemes are a blunt policy failure. However, there is empirical evidence that the exploitation of SF has been far from uniform, and some countries are indeed more effective in using EU financial transfers to address the social exclusion of ethnic minorities. *Financing Roma Inclusion with European Structural Funds* suggests that this divergence is related to the way a 'grand' design of national SF strategies *structures* the implementation process. In other words, to explain what drives policy success or failure, the analysis must venture beyond political commitments and shed light on the intricate relationships unravelling across the complex and multi-layered implementation process. The book set out to empirically scrutinize the interplay of ideas, structures, and agency in order to understand whether and how European cohesion objectives have translated into legitimate and equitable interventions, ones which actually correspond to the needs and expectation of SF final beneficiaries – the Roma communities.

Over the years, major stakeholders have eagerly blamed the negligent performance of SF on the lack of strong political leadership and the insufficient local capacities to access and manage sophisticated and overly complex funding schemes. Yet, the majority of these claims have been either anecdotal or based on 'report literature', underpinned by the ideological convictions cultivated by the EC. The bureaucratization of Roma issues and vested international interest in 'solving the Roma problem' effectively stultified the potential for a far-reaching critical analysis of the status quo. The prerogative of policy-driven research has been to provide fast, efficient, and cost-effective assessments, capable of generating simple recommendations to address complex problems and maintain the continuity of practice. This effectively meant that accumulated knowledge has complemented and reinforced the dominant political discourses, offering limited critical input. Rather than focusing on wider normative claims and power asymmetries embedded in the design of EU funding schemes, policy reports have probed the performance of individual Roma inclusion projects, often publicizing the more spectacular forms of managerial ineptitudes and pervasive ethnic discrimination at the local level. This has left us with overly deterministic, expert-driven portrayals of policy performance that tend to obscure the ideational dimensions of policymaking and its conservative underlining.

The theoretical accounts of cohesion policy, while more critical of EU templates for action, continue to place Roma issues as the backwater of wider Europeanization scholarship, and have so far failed to account for the complexity of inclusion initiatives. The 'added value' of SF in the social inclusion domain remains empirically both under-theorized and under-researched. The traditional focus on *compliance* suggests incentives and coercive mechanisms have a vital role in facilitating the transposition of EU directives and recommendations (Moravcsik, 1998; Majone, 2000; Pollack, 2003; Tallberg, 2003; Börzel et al., 2007). However, the methodological approaches pose national legislation as a dependent variable, rarely accounting for the dynamics taking place after statutory adjustments. Thus the scholarship largely glosses over the nuances of implementation processes. This leaves the false impression that the scrupulous incorporation of EU rules and recommendations automatically generates desired and equitable policy outputs. Once again, the ineffective realization of stipulated goals is pinned onto the implementers under a mistaken presumption that policy success is a product of the programme's adaptability in the field rather than its underlying strategy. The omnipresent belief that financial incentives alone can generate far-reaching changes on the ground, diminishes interest in conducting empirically informed research on how cohesion policy is actually realized in practice. While some scholars argue that the meritocracy-based and competitive EU funding mechanisms tend to disadvantage deprived and marginalized regions and communities, their key recommendations rarely go beyond technocratic postulates related to capacity building and rules simplification. In turn, the unshaken faith of sociological accounts that with time policymakers will become 'experts' in the European 'ways of doing things', silences real concerns about the legitimacy of overarching aims and norms endorsed by cohesion policy architects. Depoliticization of SF transfers obscures power asymmetries and administrative imbroglios which, as shown in this book, often generate and sustain suboptimal and ethnically bias SF interventions.

Financing Roma Inclusion with European Structural Funds set out to mend these explanatory gaps by undertaking a long-overdue empirical analysis of the implementation process in two countries with highly divergent SF outputs. From the beginning, the intention of this work was to capture the precise workings of the funding schemes in a complex and highly politicized area. The analysis was placed in a context of changes in public administration towards the decentralization, devolution of responsibilities, and restructuring of accountability relationships in service delivery. As a result of such transformation, public policies are increasingly being implemented in concert with non-state actors in cooperative or collaborative partnership arrangements. These new inter-organizational partnerships are not merely a passing fancy but are likely to be a permanent fixture on the landscape of policy implementation. To account for such complexity, the book developed an expansive analytical framework to understand how government organizations interact with their external environment in the delivery of SF. Given that inclusion policies are not value-free, but laden with social ideals, norms, and practices, the analysis focused on the prevailing moral convictions and power dynamics underpinning the design of cohesion policy. The key thesis of this book is that the SF programmes have built into them a particular representation of what the problem is, and it is these representations that determine the type of decisions, measures, and tools, that are employed to realize political goals. Therefore, the book scrutinizes the constellations of ideas, interests, and administrative procedures that often spill over institutional boundaries. Such a multi-focused perspective not only identified key factors driving policy success and failure, but also allowed for the development of a strong argument on how financial incentive schemes could, in fact, deepen social exclusion and marginalization.

While the book focuses on a specific ethnic group, the expansive framework captures dynamics that are not unique to Roma policies but have to do with how categories of deservingness are built and sustained within the European anti-poverty and anti-discrimination agenda. This focus not only challenges normative convictions about the purpose and benefits of EU funding schemes but also confronts 'common truths' lodged inside scholarship on implementation and governance. By scrutinizing the implementation of SF in Spain and Slovakia, we learn that the championed approaches to distribution of SF – ethnic targeting, all-inclusive partnerships, and an additionality principle – are not necessarily conducive to successful policy outputs. In fact, the empirical findings confirm that adherence to such methods results in an ethnicization of poverty, and the derision of measures directed at progressive institutional change.

Losing faith in targeting

Financing Roma Inclusion with European Structural Funds directly challenges a widely held conviction that the targeting of SF at specific ethnic groups or communities constitutes an effective and transformative policy practice. Directing EU funding to those 'who need it the most' has become so embedded in common sense as to be taken for granted and not open to question. As an organizing principle of cohesion policy, targeting sits comfortably with a wider EC ambition to address deprivation as experienced by individuals and disadvantaged groups (EC, 2003). Champions of the targeted approach vow that it not only prevents the pervasive redirection of money from 'ostracized communities' (to priorities more popular with the broader electorate) but also generates demand-driven and cost-efficient interventions. The rationale for targeting has been strongly conditioned by fiscal deflects and the rise of a neoliberal ideology, which expects the state to guarantee efficient and cost-effective responses to popular unrest. Prevailing faith that an inflow of money to marginalized communities will induce immediate and suitable responses to public problems has successfully silenced those advocating alternative approaches. In fact, the EU continues to orate that the marginalization of Roma communities persists mainly because the available money is misused (by incompetent, ill-informed managers) or never reaches the communities. Interestingly, confidence in the targeting approach did not incite the EC or any member states to introduce overt affirmative action schemes. Instead, the EC endorsed an ambiguous concept of *explicit but not exclusive targeting* as an organizing principle for SF allocations. So far, few have questioned the striking choice to conflate (and dilute) positive discrimination with universal or mainstream approaches.

The majority of policy experts invested in Roma inclusion strategies promote targeted schemes, even though there are few empirical studies confirming their unequivocal benefits. Currently, *all* policy reports, toolkits, and situational assessments recommend targeting as the optimal measure for improving the impact of SF in Roma communities. It can be questioned whether these convictions are a product of superficial analysis or serve as a distraction from graver problems pervading EU funding schemes. The calls for enhanced targeting, not only pay residual attention to the methodological difficulty in defining a 'Roma community', but, more importantly, fall silent on the potential risks targeting caries. As shown in Chapter 4, targeting articulated in cohesion policy inscribes difference in the patterns of exclusion as experienced by the Roma minority (and other 'minority' groups, including women, migrants, and disabled people). This not only makes social differences seem natural and permanent but also divides societies into 'givers' and 'receivers'. The analysis clearly showed that such divisions lead to stigmatization and the reluctance to use valued EU financial resources for the advancement of the 'deviant' sector of the population. Slovakia, complying with EU recommendations, endorsed the targeting of ethnic categories under the assumption that the circumstances of Roma exclusion differed from the disadvantages experienced by mainstream society and thus required tailored policy interventions. The difference, however, was not conceived as a result of discrimination and negative stereotypes, but as an unequal socio-economic position, which was pinned on group inadaptability and pathological behaviours. As such, targeted interventions aspired to change the behaviour of a group labelled as 'problematic', leaving structural inequalities intact. These dynamics not only unveiled the hidden risks of targeted actions but also showed that the way policymakers 'frame' social exclusion has far-reaching implications for policy outputs.

By framing Roma poverty in terms of a cultural facet driven by an individual rejection of common norms, accepted standards, and responsibilities, SF were automatically redirected away from interventions aimed at deeper institutional change. The notorious neglect of institutionalized discrimination and racism render projects of little practical value. As expressed by a local Roma activist: 'we are now better trained, so what? We are still treated less than human, the only change is that the majority now thinks that we have piles of Euros under

our beds'.[1] Moreover, allocating funds towards a delineated ethnic group reinforced the isolation of Roma measures, decoupling them from regional and local
development strategies. Overall, the objectives stressing the need for institutional
modernization fell silent on issues of discrimination, while the Roma inclusion initiatives were confined to measures lacking any structural component.
As confirmed by the majority of Roma inclusion stakeholders in Slovakia (see
Chapters 4, 5, and 6), the opportunity for systemic transformation was effectively
lost, as Roma communities gained access to short-lived training and consulting
activities, not linked in any way to national public services or poverty reduction
programmes. Numerous stakeholders argued that the adherence to the targeted
approach, in fact, only deepened the exclusion and stigmatization of the Roma
population. As commented by an activist: 'targeted projects simply inflamed the
'us against them' talk, and strengthened the perception that Roma get a lot of
money from the EU, but refuse to integrate anyway'.[2]

Of course, as shown in Chapter 4, part of the problem was also related to the
lack of planning, dispersal of funding, superficial articulation of key priorities, and
lack of clear indicators or conditionality (all stemming from the individualization
of social exclusion). However, even if these issues were addressed, it is doubtful
that targeting would deliver more effective or equitable outputs. As SF come from
outside the nation-state, as a fixed social inclusion allocation, and are disbursed
by autonomous specialized agencies, the tendency is to conduct the discussion
on exclusion in a non-political or technocratic way. Thus, SF programming does
not deal with the relationship between targeting and the political economy of
domestic resource mobilization. It pays even less attention to the empowerment of
impoverished people. Effective empowerment demands the politicization of both
poverty itself and the means to combat it. In the words of David Mosse: '[m]aking
poverty a public, moral, and political issue is often the basis upon which the poor
gain leverage by making power work to their advantage through enrolling elite
interests, through pro-poor coalitions, and from competition between elite groups'
(2004, p. 61). By defining social exclusion in terms of individual inadaptability,
the Slovak approach paid little attention to the rights, freedom, status, and dignity
of the Roma population. Instead, SF programming endorsed forms of targeted
assistance that were explicitly disempowering and even humiliating. While the
EC would like us to believe that such 'interpretations' of SF aims stems solely
from the political leadership of individual member states, the truth is that cohesion policy at the EU level lacks principles or mechanisms for promoting social
justice, equality, and minority rights. Despite ongoing reforms, ESF objectives
still individualize social exclusion and advocate for personal advancement rather
than systemic change.

The Spanish case further destabilizes the conviction that targeting is a cure for
all evils. Implementation of SF by the Spanish state did not succumb to targeting
logic, despite increasing pressure from the EU and international Roma advocacy
bodies. Instead, the design of SF programming leaned towards mainstreaming and a more universalistic approach to financial allocations. The concept of
mainstreaming at its core calls for public interventions to place critical focus on

structural power arrangements and strive to remodel the institutional order, which is plagued by biases that disenfranchise certain groups and individuals, who for a variety of reasons do not 'fit' with accepted standards (Reese, 1998; Verloo, 2001; Woodward, 2003). While mainstreaming adopted in Spain is not without its faults, it did bring political attention to persistent institutional barriers to socio-economic activity. Political acknowledgement that social exclusion is reinforced by systemic inadequacies, including a lack of integrationist strategies and institutional discrimination, prompted policymakers to devise action plans geared towards institutional change. This meant that SF interventions did not target a particular ethnic groups or social category, instead of being used to develop and modernize the equality and non-discrimination infrastructure. The negligent attention paid to the specificity of Roma exclusion generated counterintuitive results, as the expected redirection of SF away from Roma communities did not take place. In fact, this 'ethnically neutral' approach directed greater political attention towards structural patterns of social exclusion and reinforced inter-group solidarity, most visible in an enhanced cooperation between mainstream NGOs and Roma-led organizations and associations. In many ways, the SF contributed to the institutionalization of an array of anti-discrimination measures beneficial to all those deemed at risk of social exclusion. However, the Spanish success needs to be treated with caution. The residual endorsement of exclusion, expressed solely in terms of access to the labour market, meant that SF were allocated exclusively to interventions tackling unemployment. While this strategy strengthened the overall managerial efficiency and aggregation of funding (increasing the scale, reach, and sustainability of interventions), it ignored the multidimensional aspect of exclusion (including access to health services and housing). In many ways, the Spanish social inclusion framework moved away from the socialization of risk associated with the welfare state, towards a commodified and individualized system whereby the individual's pursuit of employment (through upgraded skills, stronger anti-discrimination measures in the labour market, and lifelong learning) is seen as a way to greater social cohesion.

Nevertheless, the Spanish case highlights the merits of the universal approach, which is systematically side-lined by the engineers of cohesion policy. Social inclusion involves not only decreasing disparities in material well-being, but also in citizenship, sense of belonging, voice, autonomy, and power relations. While Spain's residual definition of inclusion severely diminished the potential to deliver social justice, the universalist underpinning of SF programming enhanced the legitimacy of rights-based claims, which members of society could call upon on equal terms. Having non-ethnic categories to determine eligibility prevented the potential stigma attached to the poverty-targeted funding. Hence by placing Roma people on equal ground, rather than emphasizing difference, the universalistic approach to SF allocation reinforces social solidarity and de-legitimized (at least on paper) systemic discrimination. In short, as the universal approach strives to ensure broad support and resource allocation, poor and marginalized people have better chances to access the resourced and higher-quality programmes serving the rest of society. Above all, universalist ambitions reinforced consistency between overarching objectives and on-the-ground needs, thus conditioning the overall effectiveness of SF interventions. It is, however, the case that the current design of cohesion policy does not privilege these forms of interventions.

Gathering experts

Another important finding concerns the multi-level character of cohesion policy and the impacts of the partnership principle on legitimate and equitable policy outputs. The multi-level, participatory character of cohesion policy is now presented as axiomatic with few, if any, researchers proposing a different interpretation of modern governance. Partnership, as a core governing principle of the SF, is viewed as an imperative engine for engaging a wide range of stakeholders (including Roma representatives) in the planning and implementation of cohesion policy. The involvement of Roma in all aspects of policymaking has been presented not only as a litmus test of 'good governance', but also as an imperative tactic for addressing rampant discrimination, and an accountability deficit. While scholarship on Roma inclusion is now more critical of the concept of *Roma representation* (bringing attention to substantive and descriptive forms of representation), at a policy level its normative dimension remains ambiguous. Who should participate, how, and to what effects is rarely discussed in detail by those in charge of vital decisions over cohesion policy. More importantly, public policy analysis pays only limited attention to the actual impact partnership with Roma representatives (and more broadly with local stakeholders and civil society) has on policy outputs. Restructuring of power relations permits the re-drawing of knowledge. However, this has yet to be empirically verified. Moreover, few studies analyze how the empowerment of sub-national actors takes place, thus obscuring the potential impact such dynamics have on effective, equitable, and legitimate policy outputs. In this light, the findings appear crucial, as they challenge a widely held assumption that national governments seek partnership with non-state actors, and that existing partnerships contribute to more informed and equitable SF interventions.

The findings first contest the participatory nature of SF programming, particularly the devolution of decision-making processes related to the design and implementation of cohesion goals. Close scrutiny of the implementation processes (taking place after SF have been parcelled out among member states and eligible regions) demonstrated that EU funding is planned and delivered in a top-down manner. Major decisions still take place at the central level, which places substantial restraints on the sub-national social inclusion stakeholders. While the principal implementation agencies maintain a considerable discretion over allocations, they work through the state and adhere to predetermined rules and expectations. More importantly, they fully rely on the tools supplied by the centre (or regional authorities in a federalist setting) and, as in the case of Slovakia, are financially dependent on national budgets. While contestation certainly takes place, blunt non-compliance with the stipulations of SF programming has been uncommon and often penalized with the rechannelling of funds (see Chapter 7). The findings clearly show that within SF programming local participation takes place in the 'shadow of hierarchy', and remains outside the locus of power. Despite the endorsement of partnership by the two countries under study, the vertical chain of command remained much more pronounced than many cohesion scholars would like to admit.

The analysis of the partnership principle, in terms of who participates, how, and to what effect (Chapter 5) demonstrated that in both countries, the central and regional authorities continue to dictate partnership opportunities, acting as gatekeepers and selection agents. While interests that are more powerful are in a position to lobby for policy influence, the disenfranchised and less resourced groups remain on the peripheries of decision-making processes. More often than not, they are expected to deliver pre-packaged strategies designed in places far removed from the communities affected by poverty and exclusion. At the same time, the failure to implement measures designed by national experts is blamed on local agencies, often with little regard for the actual capabilities and needs of the localities. More importantly, the empowerment of marginalized communities through partnership remains weak. In both countries, the conceptualization of *empowerment* is residual and in the case of Spain, viewed as unnecessary under the presumption that expert-driven top-down inclusion programmes will eventually build the organizational capacities of marginalized groups. These findings alone clearly demonstrate that EU commitments to empowerment are symbolic, cynically endorsed by SF architects, who fail to provide the basic enabling instruments to marginalized groups.

At the same time, the absence of community voices at the crucial stages of implementation processes was not necessarily detrimental to SF outputs (as one would expect). In fact, the research clearly showed that successful outputs were contingent on a rather constrained and expert-driven partnership model (Spain), while aims to pluralize partnership resulted in blunt policy failure (Slovakia). Spain, for example, has institutionalized a corporatist partnership model, opening participatory opportunities to a limited number of preselected organizations and interests. While not without criticisms from grassroots organizations and activists, corporatist partnership has not delegitimized the delivered interventions or diverted funding from marginalized communities. However, an important aspect of the Spanish approach to partnership was that selected actors (many of whom were representatives of civil society) received substantial technical support from the national/regional budget. These enabling subsidies improved the participatory capacities of social agents allowing them to act as equal partners for the MAs and regional and central authorities. Moreover, partnerships were based on consensus making (rather than consultations) with the designation of responsibility clearly allocated. The SF stakeholders confirmed that 'safety in numbers' contributed to the efficient and effective management of SF and the streamlining of priorities and objectives. While critics highlighted the pervasive co-option of civil society, it is difficult to deny that this strategy has contributed to the overall success of Spanish inclusion strategies. In many ways national NGOs established themselves as 'buffer zones' between the state and the communities, using their status and acquired resources, to channel local knowledge into public bureaucracy, thus contributing to more informed programmes and projects. Many grassroots Roma associations admitted that working with 'bureaucratically savvy' organizations opened access to funding opportunities which otherwise would be out of their reach.

In contrast, the Slovak endorsement of an all-inclusive recruitment of partners was not reinforced with the needed technical assistance and the designation of decision-making responsibilities. The aim to gain input from a wide array of miscellaneous actors was presented by the government as a way to deliver more informed and legitimate action plans. However, this commitment proved tokenistic, as the partnership design failed to incorporate enabling tools and negotiation mechanisms. This not only impinged the possibility of forming a common stance and articulate common demands but also excluded Roma interests from wider debates. As explained by the interviewed stakeholders, partnership took the form of strict consultations, stripping the new partners of influence over final policy decisions. This meant that input was filtered by the authorities, who continued to promote their own priorities while holding a pretence of equal collaboration. Moreover, the lack of strong Roma lobby groups meant that Roma representatives were often selected by the authorities, with little regard given to their status within the community or experience working with social exclusion issues. Often the only prerequisite for participation was an ethnic background and self-identification. These tactics were combined with the notorious practice of off-loading the responsibility of programme delivery onto ill-equipped Roma representatives and communities. While ideationally this was supposed to engage Roma people in shaping the measures according to their local needs, in practice it led to non-absorption or redirection of funding. This, in turn, reinforced the misconception that Roma people do not wish to integrate and disregard (or misappropriate) available assistance.

Overall, the empirical research showed that while giving voice to disenfranchised groups is promoted as indispensable for cohesive, just, and equitable development, the very structure of SF programming prevents equitable engagement of marginalized communities in policymaking processes. In the overly complex, bureaucratic setting, it is the policy experts and corporatist partnerships that play a key role in devising and implementing SF measures. The existing cohesion regulations continue to favour powerful interests, a dynamic already well documented by various cohesion scholars. Partnerships with Roma stakeholders are not only deficient in democratic terms but also lack the power and capacity to exercise serious influence within the SF apparatus. Particularly in Slovakia, Roma representatives are burdened by the weight of great expectations and large power constraints. An insidious side-effect of partnership is that it converts NGOs and grassroots activists into dependent clients of EU funding (or agents of the state), a co-opting that effectively mutes critical voices and weakens the accountability of partners to constituencies. Not only are such partnerships deficient in democratic terms, they also lack the power and capacity to exercise serious influence within the state apparatus. This, of course, does not mean that the mobilization of Roma interests or resistance to co-optation do not take place; rather that the very design of cohesion policy and its national adaptations rescind popular demands in favour of expert-driven postulates. The top-down approach is virtually incompatible with grassroots mobilization unless the former aligns its goals with those of the state. Unfortunately, within the cohesion policy framework, Roma people (and other marginalized social categories) are not recognized as fully-fledged citizens and capable contributors to the development of society. Instead, they are stubbornly presented as passive recipients (final beneficiaries) of generous financial support.

Resisting change

The book's analytical focus on the ideational and participatory aspects of cohesion policy was complemented with an in-depth examination of administrative dynamics, particularly the coordination of SF objectives and measures with domestic policies, budgetary plans, and regulations. As an external tool, the SF programming must comply with a grander European vision associated with multi-annual strategic planning and a systematic and structured approach to programme management procedures and inclusiveness. Chapter 6 demonstrated that such alignment, or synergy, generates an array of coordinative challenges, as governance structures multiply and intersect. Hence, the way member states conceive and manage SF programmes, which transcend organizational boundaries and entail additional administrative input, strongly affects implementation processes. The cohesion literature argues that the close alignment of European objectives with domestic goals tends to generate effective and sustainable interventions while meeting the growing demands of accountability, vis-à-vis the budgetary authorities, and thereby European taxpayers, on the use of SF. The findings of this book validate this hypothesis empirically. However, once again, scrutiny of the implementation process identified causal dynamics largely circumvented by macro-level analysis and single case studies. What emerged was a crucial trade-off between effective SF outputs and policy innovation. While the creation of synergies increased the overall efficiency and effectiveness of SF allocations, it circumscribed innovative thinking about social inclusion. Bureaucratic path-dependencies, reinforced by cognitive and moral maps orienting the routines of SF administrators, authorized use of the findings to preserve the status quo. In other words, the 'added value' of SF was exploited to reinforce existing practices, even without solid evidence that they generated positive impacts. As such, the potential of SF to induce progressive change was dramatically curtailed, and more often than not SF extended the lifespan of suboptimal practices (which without the steady supply of external funding would most likely terminate). In cases where administrators were keen to use SF as a springboard for innovation and modernization (as in the case of Slovakia), the implementation took place in isolation, without any links to domestic policies and programmes. This resulted in a consolidation of a 'double-tier system' in which SF programming and its social inclusion priorities were decoupled from domestic reform plans. This dynamic proved particularly detrimental for Roma inclusion initiatives, already side-lined from public budgets and mainstream socio-economic policies. The targeted inclusion programmes became fully dependent on European funding, were characterized by a short lifespan (reflective of a five-year funding cycle), and had limited potential to generate legislative reforms or amendments. It meant that complex issues related to poverty, discrimination, and violation of human rights, were addressed by miscellaneous 'pilot projects' and ad-hoc initiatives not reflected in mainstream governance. As exclaimed by a Roma activist: 'this is the real Gypsy-industry, countless EU projects that benefit project managers and administrative cadre, no impact on the community, no impact on the politics of this country, business as usual'.[3]

These gloomy findings confirm that any analysis of cohesion policy needs to pay attention to bureaucratic protocol and coordinative capacities of the state. More importantly, it shows that the design of cohesion policy lacks progressive breadth and tends to favour the continuation of conventional approaches (or at best incremental adjustments) over transformative change. In this context, it appears implausible that SF can inspire the creation of far-reaching inclusion strategies, especially when member states have not developed their own equality infrastructure. Similarly, in a climate of austerity, dilution of equality measures, and ongoing cuts to welfare provisions, SF often take the form of 'charity schemes' which fill areas neglected by national and regional development plans. The developments in Spain and Slovakia reflect these perturbing dynamics.

Spain more than Slovakia shows how risk-averse SF programming really is. The reluctance to finance policy experimentation stemmed from political motivations and a consolidation of a domestic equality infrastructure, which took place somewhat independently of EU pressure.

It might be an exaggeration to argue that EU pressure did not play a significant role in shaping Spanish equality reforms. However, available research confirms that accession negotiations and membership played a fairly insignificant role in modelling the treatment of minorities and disenfranchised populations. Hence, from the start, the national and regional authorities used SF to buttress existing social inclusion schemes, which were developed with domestic budgets. This focus was as much dictated by 'political motivations' as by the ability of the public administration to steer and coordinate a complex system of governance. The nurturing of inter-organizational communication (not without a certain level of resistance from bureaucratic cadre) allowed for a considerable knowledge exchange and an alignment of fragmented organizational goals. This resulted in the emergence of the complementary *modus operandi*, which strengthened the efficiency of allocation processes (by eliminating duplications and contradictions). However, this well-executed alignment dwarfed the pursuit of innovative solutions. As demonstrated in the case study analysis (Chapter 7), initiatives that proposed original methodologies and challenged the status quo (e.g. prioritization of employment schemes) were sidelined and discredited. As explained by a local activist: 'they treat us like some kind of radicals, if the bureaucrats say it cannot be done, nobody will support you, so we keep doing the same things'.[4] The analysis clearly shows that the quick allocation and aggregation of funding was prioritized and took precedence over reflection regarding the impact and transformative potential of social inclusion schemes.

A different scenario took place in Slovakia where EU transfers were seen as a critical instrument for developing social exclusion schemes. This motivation should not be attributed to progressive politics, but rather to the fact that upon accession to the EU Slovakia lacked inclusion policies and equality legislation. Slovakia appeared quite eager to comply with cohesion objectives and was willing to induce innovative thinking into its public administration. Therefore, from the very beginning, Slovakia made insipid efforts to create synergies and align the organizational goals of an inherently compartmentalized public administration. This resulted in the creation of a double-tier system, driven by conflicting objectives, incompatible priorities, and dramatically different administrative procedures. The overtly bureaucratized system of SF programming was not easily accessible to the non-involved public departments and agencies, which prevented reciprocity, and in fact, only further consolidated the practice of working in silos.

Paradoxically, the double-tier dynamic severely dwarfed ambitions to develop innovative social inclusion schemes, as isolated SF interventions were unable to induce wider administrative changes or even minor alterations. The very design of SF interventions often required distinctive administrative procedures not used in the overall system of governance. This generated resistance from the domestic public servants who did not possess the proper knowledge or skills to manage and monitor SF projects. The fact that Slovakia lacked domestic social inclusion strategies (particularly at a local level) only reinforced the channelling of funding to isolated and short-lived interventions, which were rarely scaled up or disseminated. Even as some of the projects generated positive impacts, they were not used as templates for further action. This, in turn, exaggerated the perception that nothing works and the Roma quandary cannot be 'fixed'.

In sum, the findings showed that administrative coordination is a crucial factor for exploiting the 'added value' of SF programming. The ability to compound different priorities, administrative protocols and intrinsic departmental values secured a more efficient management and sustainability of SF interventions. However, it is crucial to understand that coordinative traditions within a country, as well as the presence of endogenous social inclusion action plans, are indispensable for achieving some degree of synchronization between SF programming and domestic development plans. This observation provides a rather pessimistic outlook on the potential of cohesion policy to facilitate innovative policy-thinking and generate policy convergence. Instead, the SF tends to reinforce existing domestic practices even if these do not deliver effective interventions. In this light, the success of Spain is more reflective of the domestic attention to social exclusion than of European vision. It is also a fragile success, increasingly affected by austerity measures and the dismembering of the equality infrastructure. As Spain introduces draconian cuts to social provisions, SF are used as a residual substitute for welfare programmes, in many ways mimicking the practices adopted in Slovakia. Once again, the design of cohesion policy disappoints, as it appears more concerned with efficient governance than with social justice, equity, and socio-economic progress.

What the future holds

In 2012–2013, the draft regulations for the 2014–2020 period of cohesion policy provided a framework – with reference to country-specific recommendations, thematic concentration, and ex-ante conditionalities – to embed provisions favouring an improved use of the funds also for Roma inclusion. From the 2014–2020 SF budget, the 28 member states altogether allocated €98 billion for human capital, including €32 billion to education, €34 billion to employment, and €32 billion to social inclusion.[5] At the time of writing, it is still difficult to predict how much money will be allocated to Roma specific measures, with commentators pointing out that earmarking will not exceed 5% of the ESF budget (Kullmann, 2015). This is surprising given that in the negotiations with the member states on the OPs, the Commission aimed to ensure that Roma inclusion was a key investment area. In 2012, communication from the EC stated that most member states have failed to allocate sufficient budgetary resources for Roma inclusion and to develop effective interventions. Unfortunately, the situation has not changed much since then.

SF are still peddled as the best tool for addressing the multidimensional aspects of Roma exclusion. However, as the 2014–2020 period is slowly coming to the end, various EU institutions have yet to agree on how the new provisions should work. What remains unopposed is the devotion to the targeted approach, now espoused by the EU Framework for National Roma Integration Strategies, community-led local development strategies (CLLD), and various commitments adopted by the EP, European Ombudsman, and the ESF Learning Network on Roma Inclusion (launched in spring 2013). While targeting is unleashed with even more force, the commitment of the general population regarding financial support explicitly for Roma inclusion is deteriorating. The latest policy survey, TARKI (2018), shows that the perception of the general population is that the Roma receive more social aid than any other beneficiary group (pensioners, disabled people, unemployed people) and that such support should be eliminated (or curtailed). It is not difficult to imagine that such attitudes could be detrimental to the implementation of Roma specific financial support, as the resistance of the people involved would be high. Yet international stakeholders continue to ignore this hostile environment, stubbornly insisting that ethnic targeting will eventually succeed. Few voices call for more universal approaches, and even Spain is now leaning more towards explicit ethnic targeting, despite its dubious results (ERIO, 2018). The dilution of mainstreaming strategies is again puzzling as there is empirical evidence that the strong resistance of the general population is only against financial support explicitly for Roma inclusion, not against investment in the improvement of access to and quality of mainstream education, employment, and healthcare services (Kallmann, 2015). While commentators insist: 'progress was made in terms of better linking Roma integration and the Europe 2020 Strategy' (Andor, 2018), this optimism is not reflected on the ground.

In terms of Roma participation, the future looks bleak as few member states employ 'enabling' strategies based on the principle of social justice and equality. Recruitment of partners is still controlled by the state, unwilling to cede power over major funding decisions. The endorsement of CLLD mirrors the Local Strategies of Comprehensive Approach introduced in Slovakia, with all their shortcomings – lack of strategic focus and clearly stipulated objectives. The technocratic nature of these interventions (which have yet to be evaluated) once again depoliticizes Roma representation, curtailing grassroots mobilization and obscuring accountability. More importantly, SF stakeholders still frame Roma communities as a 'social problem', in need of 'fixing' by expert-driven initiatives (albeit now more informed by local needs). Although policy experts maintain that community-led initiatives can help to mobilize and involve local communities in promoting integration, how this is to be achieved with SF remains an enigma.

Regrettably, the ongoing commitment to Roma exclusion remains in the realm of symbolic policies. Apart from minor changes to allocation procedures, cohesion policy is business as usual, legitimized not by its impacts, but by the good intentions of its architects. While talks about equality and social justice are now more pronounced, the design of SF programmes continues to frame exclusion in terms of individual inadaptability. It seems that the zealous targeting of the most impoverished people reflects a broader trend of welfare state retrenchment and rebranding of poverty as a personal failure. European financial instruments could be a very attractive tool. However, *Financing Roma Inclusion with European Structural Funds* unequivocally showed that in order to reinforce their potential to generate equitable, legitimate, and lasting interventions, a conceptual, political, and instrumental change is critically needed.

Notes

1 Interview #73, 14 May 2011 (Skalica).
2 Interview #73, 14 May 2011 (Skalica).
3 Interview #74, 1 October 2014 (Granada).
4 Interview #75, 3 October 2014 (Sevilla).
5 See https://cohesiondata.ec.europa.eu/.

References

Abrahamson, P. (1996). Social Exclusion in Europe: Old Wine in New Bottles. *Druzboslovane rozprave* XI (19–20):119–136.

Adams, N., Cotella, G., and Nunes, R., eds., (2011). *Territorial Development, Cohesion and Spatial Planning: Knowledge and Policy in an Enlarged EU.* New York: Routledge.

Alonso, A. and Verge, T. (2014). Territorial Dynamics and Gender Equality in Spain. *Fédéralisme Régionalisme* 14, ISSN 1374–3864.

Andalucía Información Agencias (2015a). CCOO Valora el Inicio del EDEM en Polígono Sur, 'Tres Años Después', Pero Alerta de 'Mermas' en su Desarrollo, [online]. Available at: http://andaluciainformacion.es/m/?a=533002&friendly_url=sevilla&t=CCOO%20 valora%20el%20inicio%20del%20EDEM%20en%20Pol%C3%ADgono%20 Sur,%20"tres%20a%C3%B1os%20despu%C3%A9s",%20pero%20alerta%20de%20 "mermas"%20en%20su%20desarrollo [Accessed 7 Dec. 2017].

Andalucía Información Agencias (2015b). El PSOE Critica la 'Apatia' del Gobierno de Zoido con el Polígono Sur Exige la Reapertura del Centro de Empleo, [online]. Available at: http://andaluciainformacion.es/m/?a=493316&friendly_url=sevilla&t=el-psoe-critica-la-apatia-del-gobierno-de-zoido-con-el-poligono-sur-y-exige-la-reapertura-del-centro-de-empleo [Accessed 7 Dec. 2017].

Andor, L. (2018). EU Policy and Roma Integration (2010–2014). *Journal of Poverty and Social Justice* 26(1):113–126.

Arriba, A. and Moreno, L. (2005). Spain: Poverty, Social Exclusion and 'Safety Nets'. In: M. Ferrera, ed., *Welfare State Reform in Southern Europe: Fighting Poverty and Social Exclusion in Italy, Spain, Portugal and Greece.* London, New York: Routledge.

Atkinson, R. and Davoudi, S. (2000). The Concept of Social Exclusion in the European Union: Context, Development and Possibilities. *JCMS* 38(3):427–448.

Bacchi, C.L. (1999). *Women, Policy and Politics: The Construction of Policy Problems.* London: Sage Publications Incorporated.

Bacchi, C. (2004). Policy and Discourse: Challenging the Construction of Affirmative Action as Preferential Treatment. *Journal of European Public Policy* 11(1):128–146.

Bache, I. (2008). *Europeanization and Multilevel Governance Cohesion Policy in the European Union and Britain.* Lenham: Rowman & Littlefield.

Bache, I. (2010). Partnership as an EU Policy Instrument: A Political History. *West European Politics* 33(1):58–74.

Bache, I. and Chapman, R. (2008). Democracy Through Multilevel Governance? The Implementation of the Structural Funds in South Yorkshire. *Governance* 21(3):397–418.

Bache, I. and Olsson, J. (2001). Legitimacy through Partnership? EU Policy Diffusion in Britain and Sweden. *Scandinavian Political Studies* 24(3):215–236.

Bachtler, J. and Taylor, S. (2003). The Added Value of the Structural Funds: A Regional Perspective. IQ-Net Report on the Reform of the Structural Funds. European Policies Research Centre. Glasgow: University of Strathclyde.

Bachtler, J. and Mendez, C. (2007). Who Governs EU Cohesion Policy? Deconstructing the Reforms of the Structural Funds. *JCMS* 45(3):535–564.

Bachtler, J., Mendez, C. and Oraže, H. (2013). From Conditionality to Europeanization in Central and Eastern Europe: Administrative Performance and Capacity in Cohesion Policy. *European Planning Studies* 22(4):735–757.

Bachtler, J., Berkowitz, P., Hardy, S., and Muravska, T., eds., (2016). EU Cohesion Policy: Reassessing Performance and Direction. Abingdon: Regions and Cities.

Bachtler, J., Martins, J.O., Wostner, P. and Zuber, P. (2017). Towards Cohesion Policy 4.0. Structural Transformation and Inclusive Growth. Brussels: Regional Studies Association Europe.

Backhouse, P. (1996). Social Constructionism and its Relevance to Health Policy. *Annual Review of Health Social Sciences* 6:173–202.

Bafoil, F. and Hibou, B. (2003). Les Administrations Publiques et les Modes de Gouvernement à l'épreuve de l'européanisation : Une Comparaison Europe du Sud, Europe de l'Est. *Les Etudes du CERI 102.*

Bailey, D. and De Propris, L. (2002). The 1988 Reform of the European Structural Funds: Entitlement or Empowerment? *Journal of European Public Policy* 9(3):408–428.

Bailey, N. (2003). Local Strategic Partnerships in England: The continuing search for collaborative advantage, leadership and strategy in urban governance. *Planning Theory and Practice* 4(4):443–57.

Bancroft, A. (2005). *Roma and Gypsy-Travelers in Europe.* Aldershot: Ashgate Publishing.

Barany, Z. (2002). *The East European Gypsies: Regime Change, Marginality, and Ethnopolitics.* Cambridge: Cambridge University Press.

Barca, F. (2009). An Agenda for a Reformed Cohesion Policy: A Place-Based Approach to Meeting European Union Challenges and Expectations. Brussels: Economics and Econometrics Research Institute.

Bassa, Z. (2007). New Modes of Governance and EU Structural and Cohesion Policy in the Czech Republic and Slovakia. In: K. Dezséri, ed., *New Modes of Governance and the EU Structural and Cohesion Policy in the New Member States.* Budapest: Akadémiai Kiadó.

Batory, A. and Cartwright, A. (2011). Re-visiting the Partnership Principle in Cohesion Policy: The Role of Civil Society Organizations in Structural Funds Monitoring. *JCMS* 49(4):697–717.

Bauer, M. (2002). The EU 'Partnership Principle': Still a Sustainable Governance Device across Multiple Administrative Arenas? *Public Administration* 80(4):769–789.

Begg, I. (2009). The Future of Cohesion Policy in Richer Regions. Working Papers, No. 3. [online]. Brussels: EU Regional Policy. Available at: http://ec.europa.eu/regional_policy/sources/docgener/work/2009_03_richer.pdf [Accessed 5 Dec. 2017].

Bekkers, V., Geske, D., Edwards, A., and Fenger, M., eds., (2007). *Governance and Democratic Deficit. Assessing the Democratic Legitimacy of Governance Practices.* London: Routledge, Taylor & Francis Group.

Béland, D. (2005). Ideas and Social Policy: An Institutionalist Perspective. *Social Policy and Administration* 39(1):1–18.

Bell, S. and Park, A. (2006). The Problematic Metagovernance of Networks: Water Reform in New South Wales. *Journal of Public Policy* 26(1):63–83.

Benítez, O.S. (2016). The Fragility of Gender Equality Policies in Spain. *Social Sciences* 5(2):1–17.

Bereményi, B.A. and Mırga, A. (2012). Lust in Action? Evaluating the 6 years of the Comprehensive Plan for the Gitano Population in Catalonia. The Federation of Roma Associations in Catalonia and the EMIGRA Group, Barcelona: Universitat Autònoma de Barcelona.

Berghman, J. (1995). Social Exclusion in Europe: Policy Context and Analytical Framework. In: G. Room, ed., *Beyond the Threshold*. Bristol: Policy Press.

Berman, P. (1978). The Study of Macro- and Micro-Implementation. *Public Policy* 26(2):157–84.

Berman, P. (1980). Thinking about Programmed and Adaptive Implementation: Matching Strategies to Situations. In: H. Ingram and D. Mann, eds., *Why Policies Succeed or Fail*, Beverly Hills: Sage.

Beyers, J. (2004). Voice and Access: Political Practices of European Interest Associations. *European Union Politics* 5(2):211–240.

Beyers, J. and Kerremans, B. (2007). Critical Resource Dependencies and the Europeanization of Domestic Interest Groups. *Journal of European Public Policy* 14(3):460–481.

Bleich, E. (2002). Integrating Ideas into Policy-Making Analysis – Frames and Race Policies in Britain and France. *Comparative Political Studies* 35(9):1054–1076.

Blunkett, D. (2003). Towards a Civil Society. Speech at the IPPR Fringe Event 'Are We Nearly There Yet'. Bournemouth: IPPR.

Bodenstein, T. and Kemmerling, A. (2011). Ripples in a Rising Tide: Why Some EU Regions Receive More Structural Funds than Others. *European Integration Online Papers* 16(1):1–20.

Bogason, P. (2000). *Public Policy and Local Governance: Institutions in Postmodern Society*. Northampton: Edward Elgar Publishing Limited.

Börzel, T.A. (2005). Mind the Gap! European Integration between Level and Scope. *Journal of European Public Policy* 12(2):1–20.

Börzel, T.A., Dudziak, M., Hofman, T., Panke, D., and Sprungk, C. (2007). Recalcitrance, Inefficiency, and Support for European Integration: Why Member States Do (Not) Comply with European Law. CES Working Paper. Harvard: Harvard University.

Börzel, T.A. and Knoll, M. (2012). Quantifying Non-compliance in the EU. A Database on EU Infringement Proceedings. Berlin Working Paper on European Integration No. 15. Berlin: Freie Universität.

Bouvet, F. and Dall'Erba, S. (2010). European Regional Structural Funds: How Large is the Influence of Politics on the Allocation Process? *JCMS* 48(3):501–528.

Bowring, F. (2000). Social Exclusion: Limitations of the Debate. *Critical Social Policy* 20(3):307–330.

Brenner, K. (2012). EU Structural Funds. In: ERIO's Seminar: EU Structural Funds and Advocacy for Roma Inclusion. Brussels: ERIO. Available at: http://cloud2.snappages.com/ecc3fa83da15cf423fe3aaa342f545fa355b24f3/Report%20Seminar_130712.pdf [Accessed 3 Nov. 2017].

Brinkerhoff, J.M. (2002). Government-Non-profit Partnership: A Defining Framework. *Public Administration and Development* 22(1):19–30.

Brock, R. and Owings, S. (2003). Lobbying for Intergovernmental Grants. *Regional Science and Urban Economics* 33(2):139–156.

Bromley, D.B. (1986). *The Case-Study Method in Psychology and Related Disciplines*. New York: Wiley.

Bulmer, S. (2005). Multi-level Governance. *JCMS* 43(2):418–419.

Bustelo, M. (2009). Intersectionality Faces the Strong Gender Norm. *International Feminist Journal of Politics* 11(4):530–546.

Cala, A. (2010). Spain's Tolerance of Gypsies: A Model for Europe? *Time* [online]. Available at: http://content.time.com/time/world/article/0,8599,2019316,00.html [Accessed 3 Nov. 2017].

Caluser, M. (2008). Minority Participation at Local and National Levels in Romania. In: F. Bieber, ed., *Political Parties and Minority Participation*. Skopje: Friedrich Ebert Stiftung.

Campbell, J.L. (2002). Ideas, Politics and Public Policy. *Annual Review of Sociology* 28: 21–38.

Cameron, C. (2006). Geographies of Welfare and Exclusion: Social Inclusion and Exception. *Progress in Human Geography* 30(3):396–404.

Carey, G. and Dickinson, H. (2017). A Longitudinal Study of the Implementation Experiences of the Australian National Disability Insurance Scheme: Investigating Transformative Policy Change. *BMC Health Services Research* 17: 570.

Charron, N. (2016). Quality of Government, Regional Autonomy, and Cohesion Policy Allocations to EU Regions. In: S. Piattoni and L. Polverari, ed., *Cohesion Policy and Europeanization*. Cheltenham: Edward Elgar Publishing, pp. 79–99.

Centre for Strategy and Evaluation Services (2011a). Evaluation of ESF Support for Enhancing Access to the Labour Market and the Social Inclusion of Migrants and Ethnic Minorities. Final Report, VT: 2009/058. Oxford: CSES.

Centre for Strategy and Evaluation Services (2011b). Evaluation of ESF Support for Enhancing Access to the Labour Market and the Social Inclusion of Migrants and Ethnic Minorities, Roma Thematic Report. Oxford: CSES.

Clarke, M., and Stewart, J. (1997). Handling the Wicked Issues: A Challenge for Government. Birmingham: University of Birmingham, Institute of Local Government Studies.

Coaffee, J. and Healey, P. (2003). My Voice: My Place: Tracking Transformations in Urban Governance. *Urban Studies* 40(10):1979–1999.

Cohen, S., Fuhr, C. and Bock, J. (2018). *Austerity, Community Action, and the Future of Citizenship in Europe*. Bristol: Policy Press.

Commission of the European Communities (1992). Towards a Europe of Solidarity: Intensifying the Fight Against Social Exclusion, Fostering Integration. COM (92) 542.

Conway, M. (1999). Partnerships, Participation, Investment, Innovation: Meeting the Challenge of Distressed Urban Areas. Dublin: European Foundation.

Cornwall, A. (2004). Introduction: New Democratic Spaces? The Politics and Dynamics of Institutionalized Participation. *IDS Bulletin* 35(2):1–10.

Council of Europe: Database of Policies and Good Practices [online]. Available at: http://goodpracticeroma.ppa.coe.int/en [Accessed 7 Dec. 2017].

Crescenzi, R. and Giua, M. (2016). The EU Cohesion Policy in Context: Does a Bottom-up Approach Work in All Regions? *Environment and Planning A* 48(11):2340–2357.

Csomor, G. and Csillag, M. (2015). Field Social Work in Slovakia. Budapest: Budapest Institute.

Čupka, M. (2012). Začleňovanie Rómov má aj Svoje Biele Vrany. *Spravy.Pravda.SK* [online]. Available at: http://spravy.pravda.sk/regiony/clanok/253608-zaclenovanie-romov-ma-aj-svoje-biele-vrany/ [Accessed 7 Dec. 2017].

Dąbrowski, M. (2011). Institutional Change, Partnership and Regional Networks: Civic Engagement and the Implementation of the Structural Funds in Poland. In: N. Adams,

G. Cotella, and R. Nunes, eds., *Territorial Development, Cohesion and Spatial Planning Knowledge and Policy Development in an Enlarged EU.* London: Routledge.

Dąbrowski, M. (2013). EU Cohesion Policy, Horizontal Partnership and the Patterns of Sub-National Governance: Insights from Central and Eastern Europe. *European Urban and Regional Studies* 21(4):364–383.

Dąbrowski, M. and Graziano, P.R. (2016). Cohesion Policy and Europeanization. In: S. Piattoni and L. Polverari, eds., *Handbook on Cohesion Policy in the EU.* Cheltenham: Edward Elgar Publishing, pp. 79–99.

Dall'Erba, S., Guillain, R., and Le Gallo, J. (2009). Impact of Structural Funds on Regional Growth: How to Reconsider a 9 Year-Old Black Box. *Regional Development* 30:77–100.

Daley, S. and Minder, R. (2010). In Spain, Gypsies Find Easier Path to Integration. *The New York Times* [online]. Available at: www.nytimes.com/2010/12/06/world/europe/06gypsy.html [Accessed 3 Nov. 2017].

Daly, M. (2006). Social Exclusion as Concept and Policy Template in the European Union. Working Paper Series No. 135, Florida:Centre for European Studies.

Davey, P. and Gábor, P. (2008). Taxes, Transfers and Transition – Adjusting Local Finances to New Structures and Institutions: The Experience of Czech Republic, Hungary and Slovakia. In: A. Coulson and A. Campbell, eds., *Local Government in Central and Eastern Europe: The Rebirth of Local Democracy.* Abingdon: Routledge.

Dellmuth, L.M. (2011). The Cash Divide: The Allocation of European Union Regional Grants. *Journal of European Public Policy* 18(7):1016–1033.

Derkzen, P. and Bock, B. (2009). Partnership and Role Perception, Three Case Studies on the Meaning of Being a Representative in Rural Partnerships. *Environment and Planning C: Government and Policy* 27(1):75–89.

De Rynck, S. and McAleavey, P. (2001). The Cohesion Deficit in Structural Fund Policy. *Journal of European Public Policy* 8(4):541–557.

Dimock, M. (1958). *A Philosophy of Administration.* New York: Harper.

Dingeldey, I., Assmann, M., and Steinberg, L. (2017). The Strengths and Weaknesses of Policy Coordination and Policy Outcomes in a System of Multi-Level Governance: A Comparative Analysis. Negotiate Working Paper No. 8.3. Germany: Universität Bremen.

Dobbs, L. and Moore, C. (2002). Engaging Communities in Area-based Regeneration: The Role of Participatory Evaluation. *Policy Studies* 23 (3–4):151–71.

Dotti, N.F. (ed.) (2016). Learning from Implementation and Evaluation of the EU Cohesion Policy. Lessons from a Research-Policy Dialogue. RSA Research Network on Cohesion Policy. Brussels: Regional Studies Association.

Drál, P. (2008). Symbolic Processes of Social Exclusion of Roma in Slovak Public Policy Discourse. *Ethnicity Studies*, ISSN 1822-1041.

Drysek, J. (1990). *Discursive Democracy: Politics, Policy and Political Science.* Cambridge: Cambridge University Press.

Dudek, M. C. (2003). Creation of a Bureaucratic Style: Spanish Regions and EU Structural Funds. In: J. Bukowski, S. Piattoni, and M. Smyrl, eds., *Between Global Economy and Local Society: Political Actors and Territorial Governance.* Lanham: Rowman and Littlefield.

Dudek, M.C. (2014). The History and Challenges of Cohesion Policies. *The Jean Monnet/ Robert Schuman Paper Series* 14(2):3–18.

Dudley, J. and Vidovich, L. (1995). The Politics of Education: Commonwealth School Policy 1973–1995. *Australian Education Review* 36.

Dye, T.R. (1976). *What Governments Do, Why They Do It, and What Difference It Makes.* Tuscaloosa: University of Alabama Press.

Eckey, H.F. and Türck, M. (2006). Convergence of EU-Regions. A Literature Report. Institut für Volkswirtschaftslehre, Universität Kassel Nr. 80/06.

Edelman, M. (1985). *Symbolic Uses of Politics.* Champaign: Illinois University Press.

ERIO (2018). Spain Falls Behind in the Implementation of its Roma Integration Strategy. Press Release. Brussels: ERIO.

Europa Press (2010). El Plan Integral de Empleo del Polígono Sur ha Generado 536 Puestos de Trabajo y 33 Empresas [online]. Available at: http://www.europapress. es/andalucia/sevilla-00357/noticia-plan-integral-empleo-poligono-sur-generado-536-puestos-trabajo-33-empresas-20101129152032.html [Accessed 7 Dec. 2017].

Europa Press (2015). El Proyecto de la Diputación 'Granada Empleo II' Logra la Inserción Laboral de 600 Personas en la Provincia [online]. Available at: http://www. ahoragranada.com/noticia/el-proyecto-de-la-diputacion-granada-empleo-ii-logra-la-insercion-laboral-de-600-personas/ [Accessed 7 Dec. 2017].

European Commission (1992). Towards a Europe of Solidarity: Intensifying the Fight Against Social Exclusion, Fostering Integration. COM (92) 542.

European Commission (1993). European Social Policy. Options for the Union. Green Paper. Luxembourg: OOPEC.

European Commission (1998). Regular Report from the Commission on Slovakia's Progress towards Accession [online]. Available at: https://ec.europa.eu/neighbourhood-enlargement/sites/near/files/archives/pdf/key_documents/1998/slovakia_en.pdf [Accessed 7 Dec. 2017].

European Commission (2000). Structural Indicators. COM (2000) 594 final.

European Commission (2003). Strengthening the Social Dimension of the Lisbon Strategy: Streamlining Open Co-ordination in the Field of Social Protection. COM (2003) 261.

European Commission (2003a). Comprehensive Monitoring Report on Slovakia's Preparations for Membership [online]. Available at: https://ec.europa.eu/neighbourhood-enlargement/sites/near/files/archives/pdf/key_documents/2003/cmr_sk_final_en.pdf [Accessed 7 Dec. 2017].

European Commission (2004). *The Situation of Roma in and Enlarged European Union.* Luxembourg: Publications Office of the European Union.

European Commission (2006). Indicative Guidelines on Evaluation Methods: Monitoring and Evaluation Indicators. Working Document No. 2 [online]. Available at: http://ec.europa.eu/regional_policy/en/information/publications/cocof-guidance-documents/2006/indicative-guidelines-on-evaluation-methods-monitoring-and-evaluation-indicators_0 [Accessed 3 Nov. 2017].

European Commission (2008). Community Instruments and Policies for Roma Inclusion. COM (2008) 420 final.

European Commission (2010). The European Platform against Poverty and Social Exclusion: A European Framework for Social and Territorial Cohesion. COM (2010) 758 final.

European Commission (2010a). Europe 2020: the European Union Strategy for Growth and Employment. COM (2010) 2020 final.

European Commission (2010b). Strategic Report 2010 on The Implementation of the Programmes 2007–2013. SEC (2010) 360. COM (2010) 0110 final.

European Commission (2010c). The Social and Economic Integration of the Roma in Europe. COM (2010)133 final.

European Commission (2011). An EU Framework for National Roma Integration Strategies up to 2020. COM (2011) 173 final.

European Commission (2012). *What Works for Roma Inclusion in the EU. Policies and Model Approaches*. Luxembourg: Publications Office of the European Union.

European Commission (2013). Cohesion policy: Strategic Report 2013 on Programme Implementation 2007-2013. COM (2013) 210 final.

European Commission (2013b). Empowering Local Authorities in Partner Countries for Enhanced Governance and More Effective Development Outcomes. COM (2013) 280 final.

European Commission (2014). Investment for Jobs and Growth – Promoting Development and Good Governance in EU Regions and Cities: Sixth Report on Economic, Social and Territorial Cohesion. Brussels: Directorate-General for Regional and Urban Policy Publication Office.

European Commission (2014a). Report on Discrimination of Roma Children in Education. Thematic Report [online]. Available at: http://ec.europa.eu/justice/discrimination/files/roma_childdiscrimination_en.pdf [Accessed 19 Dec. 2017].

European Commission (2016). Country Report Spain – Work Package 1 Ex Post Evaluation of Cohesion Policy Programmes 2007–2013, Focusing on the European Regional Development Fund (ERDF) and the Cohesion Fund (CF). Brussels: Regional Policy, InfoRegio.

European Commission (2017). Midterm Review of the EU Framework for National Roma Integration Strategies. COM (2017) 458 final.

European Commission Roma Task Force (2010). Roma Integration: First Findings of the Roma Task Force and Report on Social Inclusion. MEMO/10/701.

European Court of Auditors (2016a). EU Policy Initiatives and Financial Support for Roma Integration: Significant Progress Made over the Last Decade, but Additional Efforts Needed on the Ground. Special Report. Luxembourg: Publications Office of the European Union.

European Court of Auditors (2016b). Roma Integration: Significant Progress, but Obstacles and Dilemmas Remain, Say EU Auditors. Press Release, Luxembourg, 28 June.

European Economic and Social Committee (2017). EU-funded Roma Programmes Lack Political Support and Need to Reflect Local Needs Better [online]. Available at: www.eesc.europa.eu/en/news-media/news/eu-funded-roma-programmes-lack-political-support-and-need-reflect-local-needs-better [Accessed 19 Dec. 2017].

European Parliament (2010). Parliamentary Questions [online]. Available at: www.europarl.europa.eu/plenary/en/parliamentary-questions.html [Accessed 26 March. 2018].

European Parliament (2011). Measures to Promote the Situation of Roma EU Citizens in the EU. Brussels: Citizens' Rights and Constitutional Affairs.

European Roma Rights Centre (2013). Slovakia, Country Profile 2011–2012 [online]. Available at: www.errc.org/cms/upload/file/slovakia-country-profile-2011-2012.pdf [Accessed 7 Dec. 2017].

EURoma (2010). Structural Funds: Investing in Roma. Madrid: Fundación Secretariado Gitano.

EURoma (2011). The potential contribution of the Structural Funds to National Roma Integration Strategies. EURoma Position Paper [online]. Available at: http://www.euromanet.eu/resource_center/archive/105922.html [Accessed 3 Nov. 2017].

EURoma (2016). Promoting the Use of ESI Funds for Roma Inclusion. A Glance at EURoma's Eight Years of Work and How Roma Inclusion is Considered in the 2014–2020 Programming Period [online]. Available at: http://www.gitanos.org/publications/Euroma.Final.Report.2007_2013.Programming.Period.pdf [Accessed 9 Dec. 2017].

Evaluation of the Impact of the Multi-Regional Operational Programme Fight against Discrimination (2013). El Empleo de las Personas Vulnerables: Una Inversión Social Rentable. Madrid: RegioPlus Consulting.

Evaluation of the Operation Programme of Andalusia 2007–2013 (2010). Contribution to the Spanish Reforms. Madrid: RegioPlus Consulting.

Ezcurra, R., Pascual, P., and Rapún, M. (2007). Spatial Disparities in the European Union: An Analysis of Regional Polarization. *The Annuals of Regional Science* 41(2):401–429.

Falkner, G., Treib, O., and Holzleithner, E. (2008). *Compliance in the Enlarged European Union: Living Rights or Dead Letters?* Burlington: Ashgate Publishing Company.

Farole, T., Rodriguez-Pose, A., and Storper, M. (2011). Cohesion Policy in the European Union: Growth, Geography, Institutions. *JCMS* 49(5):1089–1111.

Fernandes, T. (2012). Civil Society after Dictatorship: A Comparison of Portugal and Spain 1970s–1990s. Working Paper No. 384, Notre Dame: The Helen Kellogg Institute for International Studies.

Ferry, M. and McMaster, I. (2005). Implementing Structural Funds in Polish and Czech Regions: Convergence, Variation, Empowerment? *Regional and Federal Studies* 15(1):19–39.

Filipová, M. (2013). Od Dávok k Platnej Práci. Banská Bystrica: City Office [online]. Available at: www.ef.umb.sk/dsr_2013/pdf/Filipov%C3%A1.pdf [Accessed 7 Dec. 2017].

Finn, D. (2000). Welfare to Work: The Local Dimension. *Journal of European Social Policy* 10(1):43–57.

Fischer, F. (1990). *Technocracy and the Politics of Expertise.* Newbury Park: Sage.

FRA and UNDP (2012). The Situation of Roma in 11 EU Member States. Survey Results at a Glance. Luxembourg: Publications Office of the European Union.

Frank, K. (2011). Expert Evaluation Network, Delivering Policy Analysis on the Performance of Cohesion Policy 2007–2013. Task 2: Country Report on Achievements of Cohesion Policy, Slovakia. Bratislava: Institute of Economic Research – Slovak Academy of Science.

Fraser, N. (1997). *Justice Interrupts: Critical Reflections on the 'Post-socialist' Conditions.* London: Routledge.

Froy, F. and Giguère (2010). Putting in Place Jobs that Last: A Guide to Re-building Quality Employment at Local Level. Paris: OECD Programme on Local Economic and Employment Development, ISSN 2079–4797.

Fundación Secretariado Gitano (2009). PROMOCIONA [online] Available at: www.gitanos.org/que-hacemos/areas/educacion/promociona.html [Accessed 7 Dec. 2017]

Fundación Secretariado Gitano (2011). Roma Students in Secondary Education in Spain. A Comparative Study. Madrid: FSG.

Fundación Secretariado Gitano (2013). Annual Review for the Year 2012 [online]. Available at: www.gitanos.org/centro_documentacion/publicaciones/informes_anuales.html.en [Accessed 7 Dec. 2017].

Fundación Secretariado Gitano (2016). FSG Annual Report 2015 [online]. Available at: www.gitanos.org/centro_documentacion/publicaciones/fichas/117213.html.en [Accessed 4 Nov. 2017].

Fung, A. (2004). *Empowered Participation: Reinventing Urban Democracy.* Princeton, NJ: Princeton University Press.

Fung, A. (2006). Varieties of Participation in Complex Governance. *Public Administration Review* 66(1):66–75.

Geddes, M. (2006). Partnership and the Limits to Local Governance in England: Institutionalist Analysis and Neoliberalism. *International Journal of Urban and Regional Research* 30(1):76–79.

Gheorghe, N. (1997). The Social Construction of Romani Identity. In: T. Acton, ed., *Gypsy Politics and Traveller Identity*. Hatfield: University of Hertfordshire Press.

Gittell, J. (2001). Supervisory Span, Relational Coordination, and Flight Departure Performance: A Reassessment of Post-Bureaucracy Theory. *Organization Science* 12 (4):467–482.

Goetz, A.M. (2009). Governing Women: Will New Public Space for Some Women Make a Difference for All Women? In: A.M. Goetz, ed., *Governing Women: Women's Political Effectiveness in Contexts of Democratization and Governance Reform*. New York: Routledge.

Goffman, E. (1974). *Frame Analysis: An Essay on the Organization of Experience*. New York: Harper & Row.

Goodwin, N. (1996). Governmentality in the Queensland Department of Education: Policies and the Management of Schools. *Discourse: Studies in the Cultural Politics of Education* 17(1):65–74.

Grambličková, M. (2010). Efektívnosť Využívania Fondov EÚ na Podporu Rómskych Komunít [Effectiveness of the EU funds in supporting Roma Communities]. Košice: Priatelia Zeme-CEPA.

Grau, I. and Creus, M. (2000). Spain: The Incomplete Federalism. In: U. Wachendorfer-Schmidt, ed., *Federalism and Political Performance*. London: Routledge.

Gusfield, J.R. (1989). Constructing the Ownership of Social Problems: Fun and Profit in the Welfare State. *Social Problems* 36(5):431–41.

Guy, W. (2009). EU Initiatives on Roma: Limitations and Ways Forward. In: N. Sigona and N. Trehan, eds., *Romani Politics in Contemporary Europe. Poverty, Ethnic Mobilization, and the Neoliberal Order*. Basingstoke: Palgrave Macmillan

Guy, W. (2011). Roma Inclusion at the Crossroads: Can the Lessons from PHARE be Learned. *Roma Rights Journal 2011: Funding Roma Rights: Challenges and Prospects* [online]. Available at: www.errc.org/article/roma-rights-2011-funding-roma-rights-challenges-and-prospects/4062/1 [Accessed 3 Nov. 2017].

Guy, W., ed., (2013). *From Victimhood to Citizenship. The Path of Roma Integration*. Budapest: Kossuth Publishing Corporation.

Guy, W., Liebich, A., and Marushiakova, E. (2010). Improving the Tools for the Social Inclusion and Non-Discrimination of Roma in the EU Report. Luxembourg: Publications Office of the European Union.

Hagemann, C. (2017). How Politics Matter for EU Funds' Absorption Problems – A Fuzzy-Set Analysis. *Journal of European Public Policy*, DOI: 10.1080/13501763.2017. 1398774.

Hall, P. A. (1993). Policy Paradigms, Social Learning and the State. *Comparative Politics* 25(3):275–296.

Harlow, C. and Rawling, R. (2014). *Process and Procedure in EU Administration*. Oxford: HART Publishing.

Harvey, B. (2008). Making the Most of EU Funds: A Compendium of Good Practice of EU Funded Projects for Roma. Budapest: Open Society Institute.

Heil, P., Hojsik, M., and Kostka, J. (2012). Study on Roma Phare Programmes in Bulgaria, Hungary and the Slovak Republic. Budapest: Open Society Institute.

Hill, M. (1997). Implementation Theory: Yesterday's Issue? *Policy and Politics* 25(4):375–385.

Hill, M. and Hupe, P. (2014). *Implementing Public Policy: An Introduction to the Study of Operational Governance.* Third Edition. London: Sage Publications.

Hjern, B. (1982). Implementation Research – The Link Gone Missing. *Journal of Public Policy* 2(3):301–8.

Hjern, B. and Hull, C. (1982). Implementation Research as Empirical Constitutionalism. *European Journal of Political Research* 10(2):105–17.

Hjern, B. and Hull, C. (1985). Small Firm Employment Creation: An Assistance Structure Explanation. In: K. Hanf and T. Toonen, eds., *Policy Implementation in Federal and Unitary Systems.* Dordrecht: Marinus Mijhoff.

Hjern, B. and Hull, C. (1987). *Helping Small Firms Grow: An Implementation Approach.* Beckenham, Kent: Croom Helm.

Holstein, J.A. and Miller, G., eds., (1993). *Reconsidering Social Constructionism: Debates in Social Problem Theory.* New York: Aldine de Gruyter.

Hooghe, L. (1998). EU Cohesion Policy and Competing Models of European Capitalism. *JCMS* 36(4):457–477.

Hooghe, L. and Marks, G. (2001). Types of Multi-Level Governance. *European Integration Online Papers* 5(11):1–24.

Hoerner, J. and Stephenson, P. (2012). Theoretical Perspectives on Approaches to Policy Evaluation in the EU: The Case of Cohesion Policy. *Public Administration* 90(3):699–715.

Hrustič, T. (2009). Výkon Terénnej Sociálnej Práce v Marginalizovaných Rómskych Komunitách. Bratislava: The Institute of Ethnology of the Slovak Academy of Science.

Hurrle, J., Ivanov, A., Grill, J., Kling, J., and Škobla, D. (2012). Uncertain Impact: Have the Roma in Slovakia Benefited from ESF? Findings from an Analysis of ESF Employment and Social Inclusion Projects in the 2007–2013 Programming Period. Roma Inclusion Working Papers. Bratislava: UNDP Europe and the CIS, Bratislava Regional Centre.

Jordana, J., Mota, F. And Noferini, A. (2012). The Role of Social Capital Within Policy Networks: Evidence from EU Cohesion Policy in Spain. *International Review of Administrative Sciences* 78(4):642–664.

Jacquot, S. (2010). The Paradox of Gender Mainstreaming: Unanticipated Effects of New Modes of Governance in the Gender Equality Domain. *West European Politics* 33(1):118–135.

Jessop, B. (2004). Hollowing out the 'Nation State' and Multi-level Governance. In: P. Kennett, ed., *A Handbook of Comparative Social Policy.* Cheltenham: Edward Elgar.

Jones, P. (2003). Urban Regeneration's Poisoned Chalice: Is There an Impasse in (Community) Participation-Based Policy? *Urban Studies* 40(3):581–601.

Jönsson, C. and Tallberg, J. (1998). Compliance and Post-Agreement Bargaining. *European Journal of International Relations* 4 (4):371–408.

Jovanović, Ž. (2013). Values, Leadership, Power. In: W. Guy, ed., *From Victimhood to Citizenship: The Path of Roma Integration.* Budapest: Kossuth Kiadó.

Kahanec, M. and Sedláková, M. (2016). The Social and Employment Situation in Slovakia and Outlook on the Slovak EU Presidency 2016. Brussels: European Parliament.

Karamessini, M. and Rubery, J., ed., (2014). *Women and Austerity. The Economic Crisis and the Future for Gender Equality.* London and New York: Routledge.

Kaul, I. (2005). Private Provision and Global Public Goods: Do the Two Go Together? *Global Social Policy* 5(2):137–140.

Kaul, I., Conceicao, P., Le Goulven, K., and Mendoza, R. U., eds., (2003). *Providing Global Public Goods; Managing Globalization.* New York: Oxford University Press.

Kawczynski, R. (1997). The Politics of Romani Politics. *Transitions* 4(4):no pagination.

Keating, M.J. and Wilson, A.B. (2009). Renegotiating the State of Autonomies: Statute Reform and Multi-level Politics in Spain. *West European Politics* 32(3):536–558.

Kelton, S. (2015). The Failure of Austerity: Rethinking Fiscal Policy. *The Political Quarterly* 86(S1):28–46.

Kendea, A., Hadaricsa, M., and Lášticováb, B. (2017). Anti-Roma Attitudes as Expressions of Dominant Social Norms in Eastern Europe. *International Journal of Intercultural Relations* 60:12–27.

Keohane, R.O. (1984). *After Hegemony: Cooperation and Discord in the World Political Economy*. Princeton, NJ: Princeton University Press.

Kingdon, J. (1984). *Agendas, Alternatives, and Public Policies*. Boston: Little Brown and Company.

Klímová-Alexander, I. (2004). Development and Institutionalisation of Romani Representation and Administration. Part I. *Nationalities Papers* 32(3):599–630.

Kóczé, A. and Trehan, N. (2009). Racism, (Neo-)Colonialism and Social Justice: The Struggle for the Soul of the Romani Movement in Post-Socialist Europe. In: G. Huggan and I. Law, eds., *Racism Postcolonialism Europe*. Liverpool: Liverpool University Press.

Kóczé, A., Kullmann, A., Scharle, A., Szendrey, O., Teller, N., and Zentai, V. (2014). Toolkit on Programming the Structural Funds for Roma Inclusion in 2010–2020. Making the Most of EU Funds for Roma program, Open Society Foundation [online]. Available at: file:// lancs/homes/45/koskta/Downloads/Roma_inclusion_toolkit_20140403.pdf [Accessed 3 Nov. 2017].

Kohler-Koch, B. (2002). European Networks and Ideas: Changing National Policies? *European Integration Online Papers* 6(6):1–14.

Kooiman, J., ed., (1993). *Modern Governance. New Government-Society Interactions*. London: Sage.

Kooiman, J. (2003). *Governing as Governance*. New York: Sage Publications.

Kovats, M. (2002). The European Roma Question. Briefing Paper New Series No. 31, London: The Royal Institute of International Affairs.

Kovats, M. (2012). The EU's Roma Role. *Open Democracy* [online]. Available at: https:// www.opendemocracy.net/martin-kovats/eus-roma-role [Accessed 3 Nov. 2017].

KPMG (2016). EU Funds in Central and Eastern Europe. Progress Report 2007–2015 [online]. Available at: https://assets.kpmg.com/content/dam/kpmg/pdf/2016/06/ EU-Funds-in-Central-and-Eastern-Europe.pdf [Accessed 4 Nov. 2017].

Kröger, S. (2008). Nothing but Consultations: The Place of Organized Civil Society in EU Policymaking across Policies. European Governance Papers (EUROGOV) No. C-08-03 https://www.ceses.cuni.cz/CESES-136-version1-7B_NMG_civil_society_nothing_ but_consultation_kroger.pdf.

Krugman, P. (2013). *End this Depression Now*. New York: Norton and Company.

Kullmann, A. (2015). Litmus Test of Effective Use of Structural Funds: Supporting Structural Reforms of Basic Public Services to Promote Roma Inclusion. *European Structural and Investment Funds Journal* 3(4):231–238.

Kurzydlowski, D.H. (2013). Programming EU Funds in Bulgaria: Challenges, Opportunities and the Role of Civil Society. *Studies of Transition States and Societies* 5(1):22–35.

Kusá, Z. (2011). Slovak Republic Promoting the Social Inclusion of Roma: A Study of National Policies. Bratislava: The Institute for Sociology of the Slovak Academy of Science.

Kusá, Z. and Gerbery, D. (2007). Europeanization of Slovak Social Policy, Social Policy in Europe: Changing Paradigms in an Enlarged Europe. Vienna: ESPAnet Conference.

Ladeur, K.H., ed., (2004). *Public Governance in the Age of Globalization.* Aldershot: Ashgate.

Ladrech, R. (2010). *Europeanization and National Politics.* Hampshire: Palgrave Macmillan.

Laparra, M., Fernández Díez, C. Hernéndez Enríquez, M., Salinas Catalá, J., and Tsolakis, A. (2013). Civil Society Monitoring Report on the Implementation of the National Roma Integration Strategy and Decade Action Plan in 2012 in Spain. Budapest: Decade of Roma Inclusion Secretariat Foundation.

Lascoumes, P. and Le Gale`s, P. (2007). Introduction: Understanding Public Policy through its Instruments – From the Nature of Instruments to the Sociology of Public Policy Instrumentation. *Governance* 20(1):1–21.

Law, I. and Kovats. M. (2018). *Rethinking Roma Identities, Politicisation and New Agenda.* Basingstoke: Palgrave Macmillan.

Leech, N.L. and Onwuegbuzie, A.J. (2007). An Array of Qualitative Data Analysis Tools: A Call for Data Analysis Triangulation. *School Psychology Quarterly* 22(4):557–584.

Lekhi, R. (2007). Public Service Innovation. A Research Report for the Work Foundation's Knowledge Economy Programme, Manchester: Research Republic LLP.

Leonardi, R. and Nanetti, R.Y. (2011). Multi-level Governance in the EU: Contrasting Structures and Contrasting Results in Cohesion Policy. Vienna: RSA Research Network on Effectiveness, Added Value and Future of EU Cohesion Policy.

Levitas, R. (1996). The Concept of Social Exclusion and the New Durkheimian Hegemony. *Critical Social Policy* 16(1):5–20.

Liegeois, J.P. and Gheorghe, N. (1995). Roma/Gypsies: European Minority. *Minority Rights Group International Report* 95/4.

Lindblom, C.E. (1980). *The Policymaking Process*, Second Edition. Englewoods Cliffs: Prentice-Hall.

Linder, S.H and Peters, B.G. (1987). A Design Perspective on Policy Implementation: The Fallacies of Misplaced Prescription. *Policy Studies Review* 6(3):459–75.

Lindsay, C., McQuaid, R. W., and Dutton, M. (2008). New Approaches to Employability in the UK: Combining 'Human Capital Development' and 'Work First' Strategies? *Journal of Social Policy* 36 (4):539–60.

Ling, T. (2002). Delivering Joined-up Government in the UK: Dimensions, Issues and Problems. *Public Administration* 80(4):615–642.

Lipsky, M. (1978). Standing the Study of Policy Implementation on its Head. In: W.D. Burnham and M. Weinberg, eds., *American Politics and Public Policy*. Cambridge: MIT Press.

Lombardo, E. (2005). Integrating or Setting the Agenda? Gender Mainstreaming in the European Constitution – Making Process. *Social Politics* 12(3):412–432.

Lowndes, V. And Sullivan, H. (2004). Like a Horse and Carriage or a Fish on a Bicycle: How Well Do Local Partnerships and Public Participation Go Together? *Local Government Studies* 30(1):51–73.

Macrae, H. (2006). Rescaling Gender Relations: The Influence of European Directives on the German Gender Regime. *Social Politics* 13(4):522–550.

Magazzini, T. (2016). Cultural Institutions as a Combat Sport. Reflections on the European Roma Institute. *The Age of Human Rights Journal* 7: 50–76, ISSN:2340-9592.

Maggetti, M. and Gilardi, F. (2014). Network Governance and the Domestic Adoption of Soft Rules. *Journal of European Public Policy* 20(9):1293–1310.

Mairate, A. (2006). The 'Added-Value' of European Union Cohesion Policy. *Regional Studies* 40(2):167–177.

Majone, G. (2000). The Credibility Crisis of Community Regulations. *JCMS* 38(2):273–302.

March, J.G. and Simon, H.A. (1958). *Organizations*. New York: Wiley.

Marcinčin, A. and Marcinčinová, L. (2009). Straty z Vylúčenia Rómov, Kľúčom k Integrácii je Rešpektovanie Inakosti [online] Available at: www.iz.sk/download-files/sk/osf-straty-z-vylucenia-romov.pdf [Accessed 5 Dec. 2017].

Marks, G. (1993). Structural Policy and Multi-Level Governance in the EC. In: A. Cafruny and G. Rosenthal, eds., *The State of the European Community: The Maastricht Debates and Beyond*. Boulder: Lynne Rienner.

Marks, G. and Hooghe, L. (2004). Contrasting Visions of Multi-Level Governance. In: I. Bache and M. Flinders, eds., *Multi-Level Governance*. Oxford: Oxford University Press, pp. 15–31.

Marks, G. and McAdam, D. (1996). Social Movements and the Changing Structure of Political Opportunity in the EU. *West European Politics* 19(2):249–278.

Marušák, M. and Singer, L. (2009). Social Unrest in Slovakia 2004: Romani Reaction to Neoliberal 'Reforms'. In: N. Sigona, and N. Trehaneds., eds., *Romani Politics in Contemporary Europe: Poverty, Ethnic Mobilization, and the Neoliberal Order*. New York: Palgrave Macmillan, pp. 186–208.

Marushiakova, E. and Popov, V. (2015). European Policies for Social Inclusion of Roma: Catch 22? *Social Inclusion* 3(5):19–31.

Matland, R.E. (1995). Synthesizing the Implementation Literature: The Ambiguity-Conflict Model of Policy Implementation. *Journal of Public Administration Research and Theory* 5(2):145–174.

May, P.J. (2003). Policy Design and Implementation. In: B.G. Peter and J. Pierre, eds., *Handbook of Public Administration*. London: Sage Publications.

Mayall, D. (2004). *Gypsy Identities 1500–2000: From Egyptians and Moon-Men to the Ethnic Romany*. London: Routledge.

Maynard-Moody, S., Musheno, M., and Palumbo, D. (1990). Street-Wise Social Policy: Resolving the Dilemma of Street-Level Influence and Successful Implementation. *Western Political Quarterly* 43(4):833–48.

McGarry, A. (2010). Who Speaks for Roma? London: Bloomsbury Publishing.

McGarry, A. (2017). *Romaphobia, The Last Acceptable Form of Racism*. Chicago: Zed Books.

McGarry, A. and Agarin, T. (2014). Unpacking the Roma Participation Puzzle: Presence, Voice and Influence. *Journal of Ethnic and Migration Studies* 40(12):1972–1990.

McGinnis, M. D., ed., (1999). *Polycentricity and Local Public Economies: Readings from the Workshop in Political Theory and Policy Analysis*. Michigan: University of Michigan Press.

McLaughlin, K., Osborne, S., and Ferlie, E., eds., (2002). *New Public Management: Current Trends and Future Prospects*. London: Routledge, Taylor and Francis Group.

McQuaid, R. W. (1999). The Role of Partnerships in Urban Economic Regeneration. *International Journal of Public–Private Partnerships* 2(1):3–28.

McQuaid, R.W. (2010). Theory of Organizational Partnerships: Partnership Advantages, Disadvantages and Success Factors. In: S.P. Osborne, ed., *The New Public Governance? Emerging Perspectives on the Theory and Practices of Public Governance*, London and New York: Routledge.

Méndez, C., Wishlade, F., and Yuill, D. (2007). Made to Measure? Europeanization, 'Goodness of Fit' and Adaptation Pressures in EU Competition Policy and Regions. *European Policy Research Paper No. 61*. Glasgow: European Policy Research Centre.

Meyer-Shaling, J. and Veen, T. (2012). Governing the Post-Communist State: Government Alternation and Senior Civil Service Politicisation in Central and Eastern Europe. *East European Politics* 28(1):4–22.

Mazmanian, P.A. and Sabatier, P., eds., (1989). *Implementation and Public Policy.* Washington DC: University Press of America.

Michels, A. and De Graaf, L. (2010). Examining Citizen Participation: Local Participatory Policy Making and Democracy. *Local Government Studies* 36(4):477–491.

Mirga-Kruszelnicka, A. (2017). Revisiting the EU Roma Framework: Assessing the European Dimension for the Post-2020 Future. Brussels: Open Society European Policy Institute.

Moore, M. (1995). *Creating Public Value.* Cambridge: Harvard University Press.

Morata, F. and Popartan, L. (2008). Cohesion Policy in Spain. In: M. Baun and D. Marek, eds., *EU Cohesion Policy after Enlargement.* Groundhills: Palgrave.

Moravcsik, A. (1998). *The Choice for Europe: Social Purpose and State Power from Messina to Maastricht.* London: UCL Press.

Mosse, D. (2004). Power Relations and Poverty Reduction. In: R. Alsop, ed., *Power, Rights, and Poverty: Concepts and Connections.* Washington DC: World Bank.

Mörth, U. (2004). *Soft Law in Governance and Regulation.* Cheltenham: Edward Elgar.

Mueleman, L. (2008). *Public Management and the Metagovernance of Hierarchies, Networks and Markets.* Heidelberg: Physica.

Mulgan, G. (2000). Accountability: An Ever-expanding Concept, *Public Administration* 78(3):555–73.

Mulgan, G (2005). Reshaping the State and its Relationship with Citizens: The Short, Medium and Long-term Potential of ICT. In: M. Castells and G. Cardoso, eds., *The Network Society from Knowledge to Policy.* Washington, DC: Johns Hopkins Centre for Transatlantic Relations.

Mulgan, G. (2007). Ready or not? Taking Innovation in the Public Sector Seriously. London: NESTA.

Müller, W. C. and Wright, V. (1994). Reshaping the State in Western Europe: The Limits to Retreat. *West European Politics*, 17(3):1–11.

Mušinka, A. and Kolesárová, J. (2012). Situation of the Roma in Slovakia and their Situation in the Contemporary Slovak Society – Brief Outline of the Roma Situation and of Associated Problems. Debrecen, Hungary: Central European Regional Policy and Human Geography, Article No. 2012-7.

Nakamura, R.T. and Smallwood, F. (1980). *Politics of Policy Implementation.* London: Palgrave Macmillan.

Nelson, J. and Zadek, S. (2000). Partnership Alchemy: New Social Partnerships in Europe. Copenhagen: Copenhagen Centre.

Newman, J. (2001). *Modernising Governance. New Labour, Policy and Society.* London: Sage.

Nicolae, V. (2012). Systemic Reform is Urgently Needed for Roma. *Open Democracy* [online]. Available at: https://www.opendemocracy.net/valeriu-nicolae/systemic-reform-is-urgently-needed-for-roma [Accessed 3 Nov. 2017].

National Strategic Reference Framework (NSRF). (2007–2013). Spain, Ministry of Economy and Finance, available at: www.dgfc.sgpg.meh.es

Oates, W.E. (1999). An Essay on Fiscal Federalism. *Journal of Economic Literature* 37(8):1120–1149.

OECD (2009). Breaking Out of Silos: Joining Up Policy Locally. Paris: OECD Publishing.

OECD (2014). OECD Economic Surveys. Slovak Republic [online]. Available at: www.oecd.org/economy/surveys/Overview_Slovak%20Republic_2014.pdf [Accessed 7 Dec. 2017].

Ojeda, D.G. (2009). El Plan Concertado de Vivienda y Suelo 2008 2012. Rehabilitación del Polígono Sur de Sevilla.

O'Nions, H. (2007). *Minority Rights Protection in International Law: The Roma of Europe.* Burlington: Ashgate Publishing Company.

Operational Programme Employment and Adaptability. (2007–2013). Spain, Ministry of Labour and Immigration, available at: http://www.mtin.es/uafse

Open Society Institute (2010). Decade Watch Report: Results of the 2009 Survey. Budapest: Open Society Institute.

Olsson, J. (2003). Democracy Paradoxes in Multi-level Governance. *Journal of European Public Policy* 10(2):283–300.

Oravec, L. and Bošelová, Z (2006). Activation Policy in Slovakia: Another Failing Experiment? *Roma Rights Journal* 1.

Osborne, S.P. (2001). *Public – Private Partnerships: Theory and Practice in International Perspective.* New York: Routledge.

Osborne S.P. ed., (2010). *The New Public Governance? Emerging Perspectives on the Theory and Practices of Public Governance.* London and New York: Routledge.

Osborne, D. and Gaebler, T. (1992). *Reinventing Government: How the Entrepreneurial Spirit is Transforming the Public Sector.* New York: Addison-Wesley Publishing.

O'Toole, L.J. and Mountjoy, R.S. (1984). Interorganizational Policy Implements: A Theoretical Perspective. *Public Administration Review* 44(6):491–503.

Páleník, M. (2013). Medzitrh Práce. Institute of Employment, Banská Bystrica [online]. PowerPoint presentation delivered during the Conference on the project From Benefits Paid Work, 26 November 2013, Banská Bystrica. Available at: www.iz.sk/download-files/sk/inkluzivny/prezentacia-mesto-bb-2013-nov.pdf [Accessed 7 Dec. 2017].

Paleo, N. and Alonso, A. (2015). ¿Es sólo una cuestión de austeridad? Crisis económica y políticas de género en España'. *Revista de Investigaciones Feministas* 5:36–68.

Palumbo, D.J., Maynard-Moody, S., and Wright, P. (1984). Measuring Degrees of Successful Implementation. *Evaluation Review* 8(1):45–74.

Parella, S. and Petroff, A. (2014). Migración de Retorno en España: Salidas de Immigrantes y Programas de Retorno en un Contexto de Crisi. In J. Arango, D. Moya, and J. Oliver, eds., *Inmigración y Emigración: Mitos y Realidades.* Barcelona: CIDOB.

Parker, C. and Clements, L. (2012). The European Union Structural Funds and the Right to Community Living. *The Equal Rights Review* 9: 95–116.

Patton, M.Q. (1990). *Qualitative Evaluation and Research Methods.* Newbury Park, London: SAGE.

Per, L. Sarapuu, K. Rykkja, L.H., and Randma-Liiv, T. (2014). *Organizing for Coordination in the Public Sector. Practices and Lessons from 12 European Countries.* New York: Macmillan.

Pérez, O.P. and Sánchez, M. (2013). Dynamize Agents as Determinant Actors in the Socio-Laboral Insertion Policy. Paper for the 1st International Conference on Public Policy. ICPP: Grenoble.

Peters, B.G. (2010). Meta-Governance and Public Management. In: S.P. Osborne, ed., *The New Public Governance? Emerging Perspectives on the Theory and Practices of Public Governance.* London and New York: Routledge.

Peters, B.G. and Pierre, J. (2004). Multi-level Governance and Democracy: A Faustian Bargain? In: I. Bache and M. Flinders, eds., *Multi-Level Governance*, Oxford: Oxford University Press.

Peterson, J. and Bomberg, E. (1999). *Decision-making in the European Union.* Basingstoke: Palgrave.

Petrova, V. P. (2007). Civil society in Post-Communist Eastern Europe and Eurasia: A Cross-National Analysis of Micro- and Macro-Factors. *World Development* 35(7):1277–1305.

Piattoni, S. and Polverari, L., eds. (2016). *Handbook on Cohesion Policy in the EU*. Cheltenham: Edward Elgar Publishing.

Pierre, J. and Peters, B.G. (2000). *Governance, Politics, and the State*. Basingstoke: Macmillan.

Pierson, P. (2004). Increasing Returns, Path Dependence, and the Study of Politics. *The American Political Science Review*, 49(2):251–267.

Pi-Sunyer, C.V. (2010). *The Transition to a Decentralized Political System in Spain*. Ottawa: Forum of Federations.

Pollitt, C. (2003). Joined-Up Government: A Survey. *Political Studies Review* 1(1):34–49.

Pollitt, C. and Talbot, C., eds. (2004). *Unbundling Government: A Critical Analysis of the Global Trend to Agencies Quango's and Contractualisation*. New York: Routledge Studies in Public Management.

Pollack, M.A. (2003). *The Engines of European Integration: Delegation, Agency, and Agenda Setting in the EU*. Oxford: Oxford University Press.

Polverari, L. and Michie, R. (2009). New Partnership Dynamics in a Changing Cohesion Policy Context. IQ-Net Thematic Paper No. 25(2). Glasgow: European Policies Research Centre.

Potluka, O., Spacek, M. and Schnurbein, G. (2017). Impact of the EU Structural Funds on Financial Capacities of Non-profit Organizations. *Voluntas* 28:2200–2223.

Powell, C. (2001). International Aspects of Democratization. The Case of Spain. In: L. Whitehead, ed., *The International Dimensions of Democratization. Europe and the Americas*. Oxford: Oxford University Press.

Pressman, J. and Wildavsky A. (1973). Implementation: How Great Expectations in Washington are Dashed in Oakland: Or, why It's Amazing that Federal Programs Work at All, this Being a Saga of the Economic Development Administration as Told by Two Sympathetic Observers who Seek to Build Morals on a Foundation of Ruined Hopes. Berkeley: University of California Press.

Quing (2012). Quality in Gender + Equality Policies, Integrated Project [online]. Available at: http://www.quing.eu/component/option,com_frontpage/Itemid,1/ [Accessed 13 Nov. 2017].

Rahman, K.S. (2016). Democracy against Domination. Oxford: Oxford University Press.

Ram, M.H. (2014). Europeanized Hypocrisy: Roma Inclusion and Exclusion in Central and Eastern Europe. *Journal on Ethnopolitics and Minority Issues in Europe* 13(3):15–44.

Ravallion, M. (2003). Targeted Transfers in Poor Countries: Revisiting the Trade-Offs and Policy Options. Social Protection Discussion Paper Series, No. 0314. Washington DC: The World Bank.

Reese, T. (1998). *Mainstreaming Equality in the European Union: Education, Training and Labour Market Policies*. London and New York: Routledge.

Responsabilidad Social Territorial: Ejemplos y Buenas Prácticas RETOS (2011). Exposición Itinerante de los Proyectos de Formación y Empleo de Polígono Sur, Sevilla [online]. Available at: www.castello.es/web20/archivos/contenidos/84/Sevilla_feria_DUNA.pdf [Acessed 7 Dec. 2017].

Révauger, J.P. (1997). Depoliticizing Inequality: 'Exclusion' and 'Discrimination' in French, British and European Discourses. In: J. Edwards and J.P. Révauger, eds. *Discourse on Inequality in France and Britain*. Ashgate: Aldershot.

Rhodes, R.A.W. (1996). The New Governance: Governing without Government. *Political Studies* XLIV:652–667.

Rhodes, R.A.W. (1997). *Understanding Governance: Policy Networks, Reflexivity and Accountability.* Buckingham: Open University Press.

Rhodes, J., Tyler, P., and Brennan, A. (2003). New Developments in Area-based Initiatives in England: The Experience of the SRB. *Urban Studies* 40(8):1399–1426.

Richardson, S.A. (1965). *Interviewing: Its Forms and Functions.* New York: Basic Books.

Richardson, J. and Ryder, A. (2012). *Gypsies and Travellers: Accommodation, Empowerment and Inclusion in British Society.* Bristol: Policy Press Book

Ringold, D., Orenstein, M.A., and Wilkens, E. (2005). *Roma in an Expanding Europe: Breaking the Poverty Cycle.* Washington, DC: World Bank.

Rigon, A. (2014). Participation of People Living in Poverty in Policymaking. Lessons for Implementation of Post-2015. London: CAFOD.

Rivero, S.S., Serrano, C.G., Rodriguez, M.A.D. and Galleg, V.M. (2013). Evaluation of the impact of the Multiregional Operational Programme Fight against Discrimination. ISBN: 978-84-7899-301-7 Available at: https://www.gitanos.org/upload/44/37/1.3-EMP_El_empleo_de_las_personas_vulnerables.pdf

Robbins, D. (1994). *Observatory on National Policies to Combat Social Exclusion.* Third Annual Report, Lille: A&R.

Robichau, R.W. and Lynn Jr. L.E. (2009). The Implementation of Public Policy: Still the Missing Link, *Policy Studies Journal* 37(1):21–36.

Robson, C. (1993). *Real World Research. A Resource for Social Scientists and Practitioner–Researchers.* Oxford: Blackwell Publishers.

Rodríguez Cabrero, G. (2011). Spain: Promoting Social Inclusion of Roma: A Study of National Policies [online]. Peer Review in Social Protection and Social Inclusion and Assessment in Social Inclusion. Available at: http://ec.europa.eu/social/main.jsp?catId=1025&langId=en&newsId=1407&moreDocuments=yes&tableName=news [Accessed 7 Dec. 2017].

Rodríguez-Pose, A. and Novak, K. (2013). Learning Processes and Economic Returns in European Cohesion Policy. *Investigaciones Regionales* 25:7–26.

Romea.cz (2015). Slovakia Internationally Criticized for Forced Sterilization, Policy Impunity for Brutality against Roma, Position on Refugee Reception and Segregated Education [online]. Available at: www.romea.cz/en/news/world/slovakia-internationally-criticized-for-forced-sterilization-police-impunity-for-brutality-against-roma-position-on-refugee [Accessed 1 Dec. 2017].

Rorke, B. (2014). Roma Integration and 'A Normal Way of Living'. Open Democracy [online]. Available at: www.opendemocracy.net/can-europe-make-it/bernard-rorke/roma-integration-and-normal-way-of-living [Accessed 5 Dec. 2017].

Royo, S. (2007). Lessons from Spain and Portugal in the European Union after 20 Years. *Pole Sud* 1(26):19–45.

Russell, H.A. (2015). Neo Synthesis Approach to Policy Implementation of Social Programs: An Alternative Approach to Policy Implementation. *Journal of Sociology and Social Work* 3(1):17–26.

Sabau-Popa, D. and Mara, R. (2015). Flexibility and Simplification of EU Financial Regulation in the Future Programming Period 2014–2020. *Procedia Economics and Finance* 32:1590–1597.

Sabatier, P.A. (1988). An Advocacy Coalition Framework of Policy Change and the Role of Policy-Oriented Learning Therein. *Policy Sciences* 21(3):129–168.

Salamon, L.M. (2000). The New Governance and the Tools of Public Action: An Introduction. *Fordham Urban Law Journal* 28(5):1611–1674.

Sanz, I. A. (2010). Spanish Decentralization and the Current Autonomous States: A Budgetary Review. Public Budget International Association, ASIP.

Sasse, G. (2005). EU Conditionality and Minority Rights: Translating the Copenhagen Criterion into Policy, EUI Working Paper RSCAS No. 2005/16, Florence: European University Institute.

Sbragia, A. (1992). Thinking about the European Future: The Uses of Comparison. In: A. Sbragia, ed., *Euro-Politics: Institutions and Policymaking in the 'New' European Community*, Washington DC: Brookings Institution.

Scharpf, F.W. (1994). Games Real Actors Could Play: Positive and Negative Coordination in Embedded Negotiations. *Journal of Theoretical Politics* 6(1):27–53.

Schimmelfennig, F. and Sedelmeier, U., eds., (2005). *The Europeanization of Central and Eastern Europe*. London: Cornell University Press.

Schreier, C., ed., (2015). 25 Years After. Mapping Civil Society in the Visegrád Countries. Stuttgart: Lucius and Lucius.

Scott, J. (1998). Law, Legitimacy and EC Governance: Prospects for Partnership. *JCMS* 36(2):175–94.

Scullion, L.C. and Brown, P. (2013). 'What's Working?': Promoting the Inclusion of Roma in and through Education: Transnational Policy Review and Research Report. Manchester: University of Salford.

Sedelmeier, U. (2008). After Conditionality: Post-Accession Compliance with EU Law in East Central Europe. *Journal of European Public Policy* 15(6):806–825.

Shirlow, P. and Murtagh, B. (2004). Capacity-building, Representation and Intercommunity Conflict. *Urban Studies* 41(1):57–70.

Sigona, N. and Trehan, N., eds., (2009). *Romani Politics in Contemporary Europe: Poverty, Ethnic Mobilization, and the Neo-liberal Order*. Basingstoke: Palgrave Macmillan.

Silver, H. (1994). Social Exclusion and Social Solidarity: Three Paradigms. *International Labour Review* 133(5):531–77.

Sirovátka, T. (2008). Activation Policies under Conditions of Weak Governance: Czech and Slovak Cases Compared. *Central European Journal of Public Policy* 2(1):4–29.

Smismans, S. (2008). The European Social Dialogue in the Shadow of Hierarchy. *Journal of Public Policy* 28(1):161–79.

Smith, H.W. (1975). *Strategies of Social Research: The Methodological Imagination*. Englewood Cliffs: Prentice-Hall.

Smith, P. (2011). The Roma in Europe. *Harvard International Review* [online]. Available at: http://hir.harvard.edu/article/?a=2899 [Accessed 3 Nov. 2017].

Sobotka, E. (2002). The Limits of the State: Political Participation and Representation of Roma in the Czech Republic, Hungary, Poland and Slovakia. *Journal on Ethnopolitics and Minority Issues in Europe* Winter 2001/2002: 1–23.

Sorenson, E. (2006). Metagovernance: The Changing Role of Politicians in Processes of Democratic Governance. *The American Review of Public Administration* 36(1):98–124.

Spicker, P. (1997). Exclusion. *JCMS* 35(1):133–43.

Squires, J. (2005). Is Mainstreaming Transformative? Theorizing Mainstreaming in the Context of Diversity and Deliberation. *Social Politics* 12(3):366–388.

Stephenson, P. (2013). Twenty Years of Multi-level Governance: 'Where Does It Come From? What Is It? Where Is It Going?' *Journal of European Public Policy* 20(6):817–837.

Stevens, A., Bur, A.M., and Young, L. (1998). Partial, Unequal and Conflictual: Problems in Using Participation for Social Inclusion in Europe. Social Work in Europe, European Institute of Social Services. Canterbury: University of Kent.

Stoker, G. (1998). Governance as Theory: Five Propositions. *International Social Science Journal* 50(155):17–28.

Stone, D. (2004). Think Tanks beyond Nation States. In: D. Stone and A. Denham, eds., *Think Tank Tradition: Policy Research and the Politics of Ideas*. Manchester: Manchester University Press.

Surdu, M. (2016). *Those Who Count: Expert Practices of Roma Classification*. Budapest: Central European University Press.

Surdu, M. and Kovats, M. (2015). Roma Identity as an Expert-Political Construction. *Social Inclusion* 3(5):2183–2803.

Surubaru, N. (2016). Revisiting the Role of Domestic Politics: Politicisation and European Cohesion Policy Performance in Central and Eastern Europe. *East European Politics* 33(1):106–125.

Swyngedouw, E. (2005). Governance Innovation and the Citizen: The Janus Face of Governance-beyond-the-State. *Urban Studies* 42(11):1991–2006.

Tallberg, J. (2003). The Agenda-Shaping Powers of the EU Council Presidency. *Journal of European Public Policy* 10(1):1–19.

TARKI: Policy Analysis (2018). Social and Economic Research, Surveys, Statistics, Data Mining [Online]. Available at: www.tarki.hu/en/ [Accessed 26 March 2018].

Tarnovschi, D. (ed.) (2012). Roma from Romania, Bulgaria, Italy and Spain between Social Inclusion and Migration. Comparative Study. Bucharest: Soros Foundation Romania.

Taylor, M. (2007). Community Participation in the Real World: Opportunities and Pitfalls. *Urban Studies* 44(2):297–317.

Timmer, A.D. (2010). Constructing the 'Needy Subjects': NGO Discourses of Roma Need. *Political and Legal Anthropology Review* 33(2):264–281.

Torfing, J. and Triantafillou, B., eds., (2011). Interactive Policy Making, Metagovernance and Democracy. Colchester: ECPR Press.

Toshkov, D.D. (2012). The Disaster that Didn't Happen: Compliance with EU Law in Central and Eastern Europe. *L'Europe en formation* 2:91–109.

Trehan, N. (2001). In the Name of the Roma? The Role of Private Foundations and NGOs. In: G. Will, ed., *Between Past and Future: the Roma of Central and Eastern Europe*. Hatfield: University of Hertfordshire Press.

Trehan, N. (2009). The Romani Subaltern within Neoliberal European Civil Society: NGOization of Human Rights and Silent Voices. In: N. Trehan and N. Sigona, eds., *Romani Politics in Contemporary Europe: Poverty, Ethnic Mobilization, and the Neoliberal Order*, Basingstoke: Palgrave Macmillan.

Van Caeneghem, J. (2017). The Necessity and Complexity of Data Collection on the Roma People in Europe. *Berkeley Journal of International Law Blog* [online]. Available at: http://berkeleytravaux.com/necessity-complexity-data-collection-roma-people-europe/ [Accessed 4 Nov. 2017].

Verge, T. (2012). Party Strategies towards Civil Society in New Democracies: The Spanish Case. *Party Politics* 18(1):45–60.

Vermeersch, P. (2006). *The Romani Movement: Minority Politics and Ethnic Mobilization in Contemporary Central Europe*. New York: Berghan Books.

Verloo, M. (2001). Another Velvet Revolution? Gender Mainstreaming and the Politics of Implementation. IWM Working Paper No. 5/2001. Vienna: IWM.

Verloo, M. (2005). Mainstreaming Gender Equality in Europe: A Critical Frame Analysis Approach. *The Greek Review of Social Research* 117(B):11–34.

Villagómez, E., Oteo, E., and Carbonell, D. (2009). Case Study, State Council for the Roma People in Spain, Contract No. VC/2008/0325. Available at: www.stakeholders socialinclusion.eu/site/en [Accessed 5 Dec. 2014].

Villarreal, F. (2001). Spanish Policy and Roma. *Roma Rights Journal* [online]. Available at: www.errc.org/article/spanish-policy-and-roma/1740 [Accessed 30 Nov. 2017].

Villarreal, F. (2013). Acceder: Programme for the Employment of Roma through the Operational Programme Fight against Discrimination under the European Social Fund. Assessment Report [online]. Making the Most of EU Funds for Roma program. Available at: www.fresnoconsulting.es/upload/79/47/2013_assessment_report_acceder_fresno-osi.pdf [Accessed 7 Dec. 2017].

Walker, R. (1995). The Dynamics of Poverty and Social Exclusion. In G. Room, ed., *Beyond the Threshold*. Bristol: Policy Press.

Weatherley, R. and Lipsky, M. (1977). Street-Level Bureaucrats and Institutional Innovation: Implementing Special Education Reform. *Harvard Educational Review* 47:170–96.

Weaver, R.K. (1986). The Politics of Blame Avoidance. *Journal of Public Policy* 6(4):371–98.

Weaver, R.K. (2009). Target Compliance: The Final Frontier of Policy Implementation. *Brookings Institute Issues in Governance Studies* 27.

Whitehead, M. (2000). The Concepts and Principles of Equity and Health. Discussion Paper, Programme on Health Policies and Planning of the WHO Regional Office for Europe.

Wilson, W.J. (2000). Rising Inequality and the Case for Coalition Politics. *Annals of the American Academy of Political and Social Science* 568(1):78–99.

Winter, S. (2005). Implementation Perspectives: Status and Reconsideration. In: B.G. Peters and J. Pierre, eds., *Handbook of Public Administration*. London: Sage Publications.

Woodward, A. (2003). European Gender Mainstreaming: Promises and Pitfalls of Transformative Policy. *Review of Policy Research* 20(1):65–88.

Woodward, A. and Kohli, M. (2001). European Societies: Inclusions/Exclusions? In: A. Woodward and M. Kohli, eds., *Inclusions and Exclusions in European Society*. London: Routledge.

Yıldız, C. and De Genova, N. (2017). Un/Free Mobility: Roma Migrants in the European Union. *Social Identities*, DOI: 10.1080/13504630.2017.1335819

Zadek, S. and Radovich, S. (2006). Governing Collaborative Governance: Enhancing Development Outcomes by Improving Partnership Governance and Accountability. Working Paper No. 23, Cambridge: John F. Kennedy School of Government.

Zielonka, J., ed. (2001). *Democratic Consolidation in Eastern Europe, Vol. 1*, Oxford: Oxford University Press.

Legislation

Spain

Law 2/1999 of 20 April, Andalusian Cooperative Companies.

Law 9/1999 of 18 November, Solidarity in Education of the Junta de Andalucía.

Constitutional Law No. 10/2002, Quality of Education (Law 45/2002).

Royal Decree 891/2005 of 22 July, the State Roma Council.

Royal Decree 102/2005 Roma Advisory Board, establishing the Interdepartmental Commission Comprehensive Plan Advisory Board and Roma.

Law 43/2006 of 29 December, Employment Growth.

Decree 109/2006, Integrated Territorial Plans for Employment (ATIPE), Andalusia.

Royal Decree 395/2007 of 23 March, Vocational Training for Employment.

Organic Act 3/2007, Effective Equality of Men and Women.

Education Law of Andalusia 17/2007 of 10 December.

Royal Decree 1135/2008 of 4 July, Development of the Basic Organic Structure for the Ministry of Equality.

Royal Decree 1044/2009 Council for the Promotion of Equal Treatment and Non-Discrimination due to Race or Ethnicity.

Slovakia

Resolution No. 357/2002 the Priorities of the Government of the Slovak Republic with regard to Roma Communities for the year 2002, the Comprehensive Development Programme for Roma Settlements and the Programme of Social Terrain Workers.

Resolution No. 278/2003, The Government adopted the document Base Postulates of the Government Approach to Integration of Roma Communities

Act No. 45/2004, amending Act No. 195/1998 on Social Assistance.

Resolution No. 498/2004 the Strategy for Integrated Education of Roma Children and Youth including High-School and University Education – Addendum to the National Programme for Education and Upbringing in Slovakia

Act No. 365/2004 Coll., of 20 May, Equal Treatment in Certain Areas and Protection against Discrimination.

Resolution No. 28/2005, National Action Plan for the Decade of Roma Inclusion 2005–2015.

Resolution No. 183/2008, Mid-term Concept of Developing Roma National Minority in the Slovak Republic Solidarity–Integrity–Inclusion 2008–2013.

School Act No. 245/2008, Zero Grade Education.

Act No. 373/2010, amending Act No. 5/2004 of 23 September, Employment Services

Act No. 252/2012, of 10 August 2012 Coll., relating to Social Insurance Legislation (amending Act No. 461/2003)

Strategic Documents

EU

Council Regulation (EC) No 1083/2006 of 11 July 2006, laying down general provisions on the European Regional Development Fund, the European Social Fund and the Cohesion Fund and repealing Regulation (EC) No 1260/1999.

Regulation (EC) No 1081/2006 of the European Parliament and of the Council of 5 July 2006, on the European Social Fund and repealing Regulation (EC) No 1784/199

Slovakia

National Development Plan and the Community Support Framework for Slovak Republic 2004–2006.

National Strategic Reference Framework of the Slovak Republic for 2007–2013 (Approved 17 August 2007).

Operational Programme Employment and Social Inclusion of the Slovak Republic for 2007–2013 (Approved 26 October 2007)

Operational Programme Education of the Slovak Republic for 2007–2013 (Approved 07 November 2007)

Regional Operational Programme of the Slovak Republic for 2007–2013 (Approved 24 September 2007)

National Reform Programme of the Slovak Republic for 2008–2010.

National Strategy on Social Protection and Social Inclusion 2008–2010.

National Regional Development Strategy of Slovak Republic 2008–2012 (Act. No. 539/2008).

Strategy to Support Employment Growth through Reforming the Social Security System and the Labour Market.

National Action Plan of the Slovak Republic Regarding the Decade of Roma Inclusion 2005–2015.

Spain

Community Support Framework for Period 2000–2006 Programming (Approved 18 October 2000).

Operational Programme Technical Assistance 2000–2006 (Approved 2000).

National Strategic Reference Framework of Spain 2007–2013 (Approved 07 May 2007).

Multi-Regional Operational Programme Fight Against Discrimination 2007–2013 (Approved 24 September 2008).

Multi-Regional Operational Programme Employment and Adaptability 2007–2013 (Approved 24 September 2008).

Operational Programme ESF Andalusia 2007–2013 (Approved 12 March 2007).

National Action Plan on Social Inclusion of the Kingdom of Spain 2008–2010.

Spain National Reform Programme – 2009 Progress Report (approved 16 October 2009).

Action Plan for the Development of the Roma Population (Decade of Roma Inclusion) (Approved 09 April 2010).

Comprehensive Plan for the Roma Community of Andalusia (Resolution of the Governing Council 26 December 1996).

Index